Love & Theft

A Memoir of Mental Illness

Content Warning

This book contains sensitive content pertaining to: suicide and suicide ideation, severe mental health issues, eating disorders and body shaming, alcohol abuse, and debt and financial issues; there are some references to sexual assault.

Although this is a true account of the author's experiences, as they remember them, some names and some identifying details have been changed to protect personal privacy.

Several paragraphs from Chapter 16 were first published in the folio Writing Ourselves / Mad (Anomaly Magazine #32), guest-edited by [sarah] Cavar.

ISBN 978-1-7782012-2-6 (hardcover)
ISBN 978-1-7782012-0-2 (paperback)
ISBN 978-1-7782012-1-9 (epub)

Cover art and design by Jeff Moffet
Proofread and formatting by Jennifer Dinsmore

This is an original print edition of *Love & Theft: A Memoir of Mental Illness*.

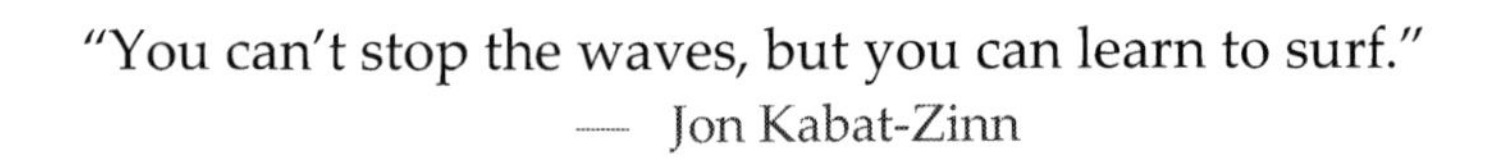
"You can't stop the waves, but you can learn to surf."
— Jon Kabat-Zinn

For those who live in silence, may this book be a comfort.

Contents

Introduction

The breeze was warm. The sky was filled with floating white puffs that could easily change shape: an airplane, a bunny, corkscrew pasta. I walked with my usual unhurriedness, my head in dream mode, where it always seemed to be at the age of 25.

I was right next door to my house when I saw what I would later realize was a catastrophe. There were raccoons everywhere, all over the front lawn, crawling up the elm that hung over my driveway, and high up onto the roof of the house next to mine. And there was a large white van, its back doors open, the floor of the vehicle crawling with yet more animals. And then I saw the men. There were quite a few of them, I'd say five or six, all in various stages of retrieving raccoons and throwing them into the back of the van. I was horrified.

There was one man with long hair, who stood apart from the group, whom I would later understand to be the boss. When he caught me looking at him, he pulled on his cigarette and scowled, a real scowl, a scowl that frightened me down to my toes. I looked away, picking up my pace, my hands shaking as I clutched the keys to my front door.

Once inside the vestibule, I knew what the drill had to be—everything fell into place, though I had never before thought of such a drill and had never planned it out. I locked the door, put my keys in the bowl, my bag on the floor. I moved quickly to the side window overlooking my neighbour's yard. The man was closer now. He was bigger than when I first saw him, with a moustache, a bit of a beard. I couldn't really tell the rest. As I watched him, he suddenly looked directly at me and sneered. I knew at that moment that he would come for me.

Acting quickly, I dropped to the floor and crawled to the centre of the windows and closed the drapes on both sides. Into the dining room next, on all fours, more curtains to close. Shades down in the TV room.

I knew the man was circling the house, trying to get at me, and I had to make my move. I bolted upstairs, closing curtains, closing doors, until I was in my room. It was like the Blitz in London, the blackout curtains securely drawn. I dove under my duvet and lay in my bed, shaking. The man wanted in, and he still might make it, but for now, I had stopped him.

My cat purred in bed beside me; I hoped she wasn't too loud. I lay hidden under my duvet for hours, until all was completely dark. Was he gone now? I still felt his presence, still felt the fear. What did he want from me?

My mother came home later that night, calling out my name. She came to my door, leaned over, turned on the light. I could tell she was scared too.

But not of the man.

***

The other day, my psychiatrist told me that I am one of the funniest people he knows. At the time, my mood was elevated, and my racing thoughts were coming out before they were fully formed in my brain, a jumble. Because they were disjointed, I lost my way and was stranded on an icy island of ideas.

He gradually went through the various skeins of topics that I had tangled over the preceding 20 minutes and led me back to the beginning. He even used his hands like he was corralling my ideas into one spot, a spot with good fences. I thought back to Ireland and the Border Collies that worked so beautifully with hundreds of sheep, herding them to the boats that would take them to uninhabited islands to finish the season out. So, I told my doctor that he was a very good Border Collie. We laughed and joked about Border Collies setting up shop as psychiatrists. The Dog Is In.

And that's a bit of black humour. But in reality, mental illness is not funny. It is not a joke. I am writing this because I am sick with an illness that occupies my mind but affects all of me. Mental illness is messy. For many people, it isn't solved by a simple pill and some therapy. It doesn't sit neatly in its box. Symptoms seep out the sides, dripping over everything, wrecking jobs, relationships, and even lives. Throw alcohol and drugs on the fire, and you have disaster. This is my story, but it is also the story of so many.

I am privileged. I am white, and English is my native language. My family is upper middle class and very supportive. I live in a country with universal health care. I have the absolute best psychiatrists. Everything was set up for me, and yet I nearly failed. At one point in my journey, I almost slipped through the cracks entirely, nearly ended up on the streets due to addiction. I was lucky.

I cannot imagine what it is like for those who don't know how to navigate the system, who are poor, or newly arrived, or whose families are in disarray. The lack of mental health services doesn't help. It takes ages on a waiting list to see a good psychotherapist or psychiatrist. This is true across Canada, from coast to coast to coast.

As I write this, there is a global pandemic, a coronavirus circling the globe, killing many and destroying so many lives. Everything I thought of as my story in the mental health system has now been turned right side over. So many are in need of help now. People who have lost their jobs, their businesses, their livelihoods. People who are experiencing mental health problems like anxiety and depression for the first time. People who are lost. And accessing help? That same waiting list, only now it groans under its weight.

I am adding my voice to the growing movement to tear down the stigma of mental illness. There are so many beautiful books out there that lead us into the lives of people who suffer from depression: *Prozac Nation*; *Darkness Visible*; *The Noonday Demon*. There are fantastic books by people with bipolar disorder: *An Unquiet Mind* and *Haldol and Hyacinths* are two good examples. And I've read a couple of books by people with schizophrenia that were awe-inspiring. *The Center Cannot Hold* comes to mind, and *The Quiet Room*.

Serious mental illness can hit any one of us, and we need these books to record the truth and show the rest of the world what it's like to have your life demolished right in front of you. And then to be able to pick up the pieces and move on.

It is wonderful to hear people talk about their depression and anxiety. I think of the athletes who have done this, and I am amazed by their bravery. There is still stigma surrounding any form of mental illness. Depression, anxiety, post-traumatic stress disorder (PTSD), obsessive-compulsive disorder (OCD), bipolar disorder, eating disorders, personality disorders. . .the list goes on. There are nearly 300 mental disorders listed in the DSM-5, otherwise known as psychiatry's bible (though this number and, quite frankly, the system, is ridiculous). I think, I hope, things will change, and talking about having a mental illness will be a normal thing to do.

At the end of February 2019, I took a large overdose of some very dangerous pills. I was on life support for two days. My mother got a lot of support from her family and friends, and I was grateful for that.

While I was in the ICU, I developed a mild lung infection, which was treated with antibiotics. I'd been back home a couple of days when one of my mother's friends, with whom I was quite friendly, called to chat with my mum. But I answered, and when I told her it was me and not my mother, all she said was, "Oh, so, I hear you had a lung infection."

We chatted for a minute or two, ignoring the real issue at work.

I laughed when I got off the phone, but over the days, something was bugging me about our conversation. How are we ever going to normalize conversations about mental illness if a friend can't even say something as simple as, "So, I hear you've had a rough time"? Talk about sweeping it under the carpet, nice and tidy, out of view from our conversation.

There are some mental illnesses that are so misunderstood people walk right on by or turn away in fear, which only maintains the stigma—like schizophrenia and other illnesses with a psychotic component. Like my diagnosis, which is schizoaffective disorder, bipolar type—basically a melding of my bipolar disorder with a psychotic disorder similar to schizophrenia. I have walked down streets talking to my voices. I see and hear things that are there just for me. I believe things that no one else agrees with. We don't talk about that stuff. Not yet.

Mine is the story of the progression of an illness, what so

many people have faced. From its roots in major depression and then manic depression, to the terror of schizoaffective disorder, my illness grew over the first six or seven years into what it is now. Many of you will recognize that terror, whether it is personally or through the eyes of a family member or friend. We are all touched by mental illness in one way or another.

I am also writing this for all the people who don't go on to be successful entrepreneurs, respected doctors, beautiful stars. I am writing for the people whose drugs are flipped around all the time, yet things seem to stay the same. People who have never found love, never had a wish come true. The people who wait for months to see a psychiatrist or access other supports, while their families or friends, if they are fortunate enough to have them, are terrified of what might happen in the intervening time. I stand with you.

Some people with mental illness prefer to call themselves "psychiatric survivors." Others prefer the term "consumer." Neither term does it for me. Although I am not my illness, it does inform so much of me and my life. I view my life through its lens. I cannot separate myself from it.

And so, at the end of my story, do I ride off into the sunset? You'll see. Or rather, you'll learn just what riding off into the sunset is for me. Maybe, despite the evidence before you, you'll even be happy for me. Sometimes even the craziest stuff will seem normal after a while.

Part One

Chapter 1

It started with a simple shower in early April of 1994, when I was 24. I got out of the tub, wrapped myself in a towel, and started to cry. I didn't know why I was sobbing—a powerful sense of emptiness washed over me, something that I couldn't understand. And then it was gone, and I let it go. It was a stand-alone incident that I tucked away somewhere in my brain and quickly forgot.

That is, until several months later, on a Friday in June. I am sure it was June because I was alone in the backyard, clutching my glass of wine, pretending to admire the peonies. My mother says those thrive only in early summer, so I am certain it was June and weeks after the bathroom incident. I was alone in the yard, unless you count the large screened-in porch that juts out off the back of my childhood home, filled with two dozen members or so of my extended family. Family members who I was trying to avoid. I wasn't feeling chatty or sociable, and found myself pouring glass after glass of white wine to facilitate any conversation I might find myself in.

I'd had a doctor's appointment the day before, and I was still reeling from it. Since the age of 16, I've lived with an unbelievably powerful fear of public speaking, stemming, I think, from the time I messed up a high school play by going completely blank, frozen solid, and forgetting all my lines. I decided to finally deal with my phobia, and my GP referred me to a psychiatrist in the city centre. After explaining how all-encompassing my fear was, and how it prevented me from doing so many things, he sat back and said, "I think you're depressed. Would you like to try some Prozac?"

I was stunned by this change in the script and sat there for what felt like hours, finally replying, "No."

He gave me a prescription for a benzodiazepine, a minor tranquilizer, and instructed me to take some right before Toastmasters, a public speaking support group that I was supposed to join. (I never did join Toastmasters since it terrified me, and to this day I am deathly afraid of public speaking.)

It was around this time that I moved out for the first time to an apartment in the trendy Ottawa neighbourhood known as the Glebe, with my best friend, Ruby Tuesday. I think moving out was a really big deal in my brain, a real catalyst for what was to come. People assume my first major episode of depression at the age of 24 was because of my dad's death several years before, or the more recent death of my grandfather. While I'm sure those events played a role, I really do think leaving home was the kicker.

I took the front bedroom overlooking the street, and Ruby took the back. We decorated the flat nicely, and with my cat Mickey we settled in for a season on the gorgeous back porch. But already I was beginning to feel a change.

I was working at a kitchen store in Ottawa's ByWard Market, where I oversaw the cookbook section. I was beginning to lose my focus there. I spent most of my time straightening cookbooks and pacing. Regulars would come in to chat about the newest titles, but I couldn't get excited about my lovely books anymore. I was in charge of ordering and reordering them, but I just wasn't interested. Sales reps would come, take me to lunch, and I could hardly hold myself together. Surely, the reps knew something was going on.

My birthday passed as it became August, and I turned 25. As summer ripened, I found my mood getting shakier. I would wake early in the morning and stare out my window at the grey street below. I didn't relax until after work, when I walked back in the apartment, usually with a liquor store bag in my hand.

"How are you?" I would ask Ruby, opening a new bottle. "Do you want some wine?" Often, she would say no thanks to this, and I would be relieved. More for me—the whole bottle in fact. That was just the start of the night.

"What did you do at work today?" Ruby would ask me. "Any interesting new cookbooks?" We would sit on our back porch, with Mickey winding her way around us, settling on the table, stretched out on the paisley table cloth.

I would have to focus really hard on what she was asking me, what she was saying to me. My mind would shift so easily—I could describe the best recipe I had seen in a while, the whole time my brain running through the line, "I am going to kill myself," or, "I want to die." It was just a flirtation with these suicidal thoughts, a practice run, even. I think going through them in my mind was a form of release, it calmed me. Nothing could get much worse if I had suicide in my back pocket.

The drinking increased, and with it, my mood went lower. By September, I was drinking more than a bottle of wine a night, waiting for Ruby to go to bed. Then I would get into the hard stuff, usually scotch mixed with Dubonnet. Sometimes, I'd lie on the floor in the living room, the TV on low, *M*A*S*H* reruns on the screen, the cat circling me with concern. Mornings brought Pepto-Bismol, lots of Tylenol, and dried pink crusts at the corners of my mouth.

And I smelled. My long hair was a greasy mess, washed maybe once every two weeks. I wore the same clothes over and over, about three outfits in rotation. They were dirty, unkempt. I had the coat of a sick dog. My face was ashen, my eyes dull. There was dirt under my nails and my breath stank; brushing my teeth was something I did only now and then.

I didn't see myself as having a mental illness. In no way did I think in those terms. I was meant to be down in the dirt, feeling completely empty. It was my punishment for being the horrible person I thought I was.

Conversations were a challenge, and my ability to read had all but disappeared, except for one category: psychology. For some reason, I was attracted to stories of people who seemed to feel and behave like me. Was I on the right track? I probably was, but even these shared stories didn't feel right. I knew I wasn't really sick; I was just drinking too much, and remained overly focused on me, me, me.

People were becoming concerned. My mum was at her wit's end. She was watching her daughter become zombie-like, lost in her own world. I agreed to talk to a professional. My GP referred me to a Dr. L, an old-school psychoanalyst treating patients not too far from me. Old-school as in Freud and a couch to lie on, while you talk about how your mother fucked you up.

I don't remember much about my two appointments with Dr. L. After he berated me for having seen a psychiatrist who mentioned drugs, I got the sense that maybe I shouldn't mention my intensely suicidal feelings to him. I didn't want to know what he would make of them.

He asked me if, while growing up, I had found my mother to be cold because she was German. At the end of our second appointment, Dr. L told me that I clearly wasn't into therapy, that I was not a good candidate, and to come back only when I was ready to lie on his couch and open up my mind a little more.

It was November, and I pulled my coat around me, walking back home in a bad wind. People on the sidewalk were moving shadows, the traffic lights blurry rings that hurt my eyes. I knew what Dr. L had said was true. It was obvious to me that there was nothing wrong with me, that I simply wasn't able to put in the effort needed to feel better. I felt empty, betrayed even, though by whom I wasn't sure. I felt rejected. When I arrived home, I poured myself a drink.

Christmas of 1994 wasn't that great. At a celebration, I sat quietly in my spot, feigning laughter. When it was time to eat, I didn't move. An aunt came to me, and, putting her hand on my knee, said softly, "You are so quiet and lost. Are you okay?"

I worked up a smile and said I was tired, just tired, that's all.

But things with me were getting serious. I was out of control, quickly sloshing about in dangerous puddles. I wouldn't say that I was sad. I had gone beyond sad a long time ago. Now, it was a deep and dark emptiness. Thoughts of suicide were my constant companion. My mum would come and take me outside for short, gentle walks along the canal. Her brother, who was a family doctor at the time, called the head of psychiatry at the Ottawa Civic Hospital and got the name of a doctor who had just set up a private practice.

I was at the back of the store, straightening cookbooks for

the seventh time, when the call came through. It was a psychiatrist, Dr. G. He said, "I hear you are having some trouble with your mood. Why don't we get together and chat?" An electric bolt went through me—a sudden surge of hope mixed with terror. We agreed to meet several days later, in the middle of February 1995.

I felt I had to prepare for the meeting. So, I thought about what I was going to say and what I was going to leave out. Although it appeared that Dr. G used other approaches to the pure psychoanalytic process (as reassured to me by my uncle when I questioned him about it, not wanting a repeat of November), he could still reject me. Chances were, he would.

Dr. G was young and handsome, soft-spoken and kind. I was already intimidated. I sat in a squeaky chair in his office, the walls full of diplomas and Group of Seven prints, and I started to talk. He didn't interrupt me once. I brought it all out. When I was finally done, he looked at me and said quietly, "Wow, you are profoundly depressed."

Two days later, I overdosed and landed myself in the psych ward.

Chapter 2

My father appeared in my mother's life in 1963, in his threadbare fur coat. He was an American, or, rather, a New Englander, and he had found his way up to Montreal. The reasons for his move were not political (that would come later); after all, this was several years before Vietnam, and he was already 33. No, the reason my father left his beloved Boston and those Ivy League campuses was because his French Canadian psychoanalyst had decided to move home. And so, my dad followed.

Once settled in this new city, he attended services at St. John's Anglican Church, not too far from his apartment on rue Saint-Marc. This was one of the best decisions of his life, for it was there that he was offered a job as assistant to the parish priest (he had trained to be an Episcopalian minister in the '50s). And it was there that he fell in love with the much younger and very beautiful daughter of his new boss. Oh, all the young women at church were besotted with him, but he only had eyes for my mum.

They married in less than a year, my dad just 34, my mum a few days from her nineteenth birthday. Two years later came my brother Alan and a job offer in Rhode Island, an Episcopalian church needing a new minister. So, down to the US they went.

It was in the summer of 1969, at the height of so much,

that I was born, in Cambridge, Massachusetts. My parents had relocated to the area so that my dad could train to be a psychiatric social worker. Although he had a good position at Massachusetts General, he and my mum realized things weren't quite right around them. As a wee one, I took part in vigils and peace demonstrations around Harvard Square, me in my stroller, my older brother Alan holding on tightly to the rim of it, the horrors of the Vietnam War lost on us little ones.

And my mum was homesick for her family, so my dad started looking for jobs in Canada. He found one in Ottawa as a psychiatric social worker at the Royal Ottawa Hospital, or the ROH, the city's psychiatric hospital. I was two and a half when we moved back in March of 1972, settling on Edison Avenue in a neighbourhood called Westboro in Canada's capital city. My brother Jeffrey was born in 1973 and completed our family.

My father had the gentlest soul I've ever known. "Are you happy, Dad?" I would ask him when I was a young teenager.

He would smile, shrug his shoulders. "No, I am not sure that I am. It comes and goes. No one's life is completely happy, and mine is like that."

I found these conversations to be big and sad, and I felt helpless, wishing that I could make him happier. Looking back, I wonder if my dad had minor depression at times. And it made me wonder if it was the genes, what with my cousins and his grandfathers, who I write about later. Yes, definitely, there is a line there. My dad got off lightly, looking back at the whole mess from today. He was lucky.

My dad had many friends and was well-loved in my mother's family and beyond. Even with that, and the fact that he had a successful career as a leader in psychotherapy and marriage counselling, he was terribly eccentric. He had outrageous nicknames for us kids and would use them liberally in very public places. Shopping with him could be a source of embarrassment. It was common to hear him bellow from across the store something like, "Hey, Missing! Cardoons!" On elevators full of people, he would suddenly say in a funny voice, "Jocy—are you missing in action?" and I would die inside. Once, crossing a busy intersection on a walk signal, my dad froze when the blinking hand signal started up, not sure whether to continue on or go back to safety. He tipped forward, he pulled backward, the whole time his comb-over flapping in the wind.

I got my cookbook passion from him. My dad would sit on the living room couch with a beer or a scotch beside him, reading cookbooks. I understand why; it was his way of travelling the world. And when he decided on the perfect dish to cook, the kitchen would look like a disaster zone.

It was in the early 60s that he really got into cookbooks and cooking. Along with his fur coat and canned oysters (something my mother's family considered a bit out there), my father also brought to Montreal his copy of *Mastering the Art of French Cooking*, the stunning new tour de force by the then-unknown Julia Child, with Simone Beck and Louise Bertholle.

After my parents married and my older brother was on the way, my mother abandoned her teaching career and started a new one: that of mastering the art of French cooking. She was a natural. Our family never again ate from cans or boxes; we dined on braised tongue with caper sauce, Duck à l'Orange, and the occasional tripe stew. We were a family of three kids too embarrassed to have their friends over for dinner, who would stand in the kitchens of others, intrigued by the exotic displays of Kraft Dinner and Shake 'n Bake that lined the shelves.

***

Food wasn't my father's only passion. He was also seriously into gardening. Growing up, there were trips through the Ontario wilderness, when my father would suddenly interrupt his lecture on the natural history of the Canadian Shield and veer off to the side of the road. A plant had caught his eye, and it was time to take out the necessary tools and quickly (but gently) obtain a small cutting. I spent these roadside raids ducked down in the back seat, terrified that the Plant Police would show up and throw us all in jail.

But we always managed to elude the provincial police, and as the long summer evening grew into dusk, my dad would be outside, tending lovingly to his plants.

Unfortunately, there wasn't the right space and light for a vegetable garden. But that didn't stop him from enlisting the three of us kids to harvest fiddleheads in the lush garden along the front of the house. Once a year, we would gather little ferns, curled up like snails, to be turned into a wonderful buttery treat at the dinner table that evening.

The fiddlehead fared well in our journey to adulthood. Whether it's a quick lemony sauté or a parmesan-battered deep-fried treat, we three kids cherish the fiddlehead. It is more than a taste. It is a time. They curl up and are ready to eat for only a week or two every year. Their time is short, and as a result, the pleasure they bring is all the greater, all the better to be savoured and remembered.

***

I have often wondered how my dad would have reacted to my

ever-growing mental illness if he was still alive. Love, definitely. Always love. He would have supported me, absolutely. But he would have felt a lot of guilt. You see, both of my father's grandfathers had been insane.

***

It was the late 1800s, and Leon Austin Larimore had a mission to carry out. He was in a Missouri courtroom, arguing his case for divorcing his wife. He chose not to have legal representation. He was prepared. Leon wanted their son to stay with him, not with his mother. And then he produced it: a 10-page missive outlining the sins of his wife, all the affairs she had had, and how poorly she had treated him. The document went on and on. And what seemed straight and even to Leon was, in fact, just the ramblings of a man in the grips of a paranoid psychotic episode. He lost the case, lost his son, lost everything.

Several years passed, and Leon managed to get his life back on track. He courted a woman from Charleston, and eventually Jessie moved up to St. Louis to marry him. The union was a happy one. Leon's close friend enticed them to move to Alaska, where they would pan for gold. His friend had promised it would be high times. So, Leon and Jessie got on a boat on the West Coast and landed in Nome, Alaska, where they settled. A baby girl came soon, my grandmother, in 1902. Grainy black-and-white pictures show laughter, twirled moustaches, sled dogs, warm tents.

But things went off-course, the way things go in life. Jessie became very ill and died soon from TB. Leon's friend ran off with all the money they had made in the gold trade. Leon sent my grandmother to live with relatives in Los Angeles with a few of his possessions—an old cedar chest, a table, some silver. And then he headed to a Seattle motel, where he committed suicide by shotgun. No possessions except for the gun.

***

My father's paternal grandfather's story is quite different, and less clear-cut than Leon's.

George Wilbur Patten was born in 1843 in New Hampshire. When the time came, he and his brother signed up for the Civil War and were sent to the South to fight in the battle of Vicksburg in 1863. It was there that his brother died in action. George took it hard and was put on sweeping duty. The army called it "sunstroke." After the war, he wandered around, becoming a Unitarian minister. Still wandering with his family, he was in and out of hospital every four or five years with this "sunstroke."

I thought for a while that he might have had PTSD, and though he probably did, that wasn't the whole story. I think he had what I have. I think I got it from him.

Chapter 3

It was the third time that night. The third time that they had come in with their glaring lights, swooshing the curtains back, cluck-clucking and click-clicking. The pads of their soft shoes a predictable pattern of straights and turns, first bed one, then bed three, and turn and smile, bed four and bed two. And me, bed two, with the small light on, so inoffensive and such a big rule-breaker, me the rebel. Simply reading a book, slowly and with effort, the crime.

Jocelyn, they told me, *if you are going to persist in disturbing everyone, you have to go to the common room. Show some respect.*

Dragging my legs down the dimly lit hallway to the common room, I pass one room on my right. I hear the laboured breathing, probably Robin because he is so big. They have left their small bathroom light on. It gives them comfort, and it gives me comfort as I walk past. It seems warm and soft, what I would plug in when I was babysitting, then coming to their rooms later to watch them sleep, to kiss them on the cheek, to nod at the moon-shaped soft light plugged in beside the pile of books. Then the common room, the room with its pastel blues and pinks, reassuring flower pictures—but not framed in glass!—designed to be calming.

Uncomfortable vinyl chairs I can't find a good position to curl up in, too small for the couch, too big for the chair. There is a hum here, maybe the lights with their blueish tinge mixing with the soft sounds of sleep from behind me.

***

I had been in hospital for four days. The morning after that first overdose in February of 1995, I woke up to three or four men in white coats, me lying on a bed in the ICU, all of them looking at me with a mixture of concern and seriousness. My mother was there, and my uncle. The oldest doctor spoke, asked me many questions, but my brain was in such a fog that I had a hard time finding my voice. Finally, Dr. S. said that they wanted to admit me, that it would take about three weeks to get me up and dancing again. My mum and my uncle seemed to agree, so I did too. Frankly, it was a relief. Somebody was going to put a stop to all this mess in my head.

The first day was rough. I said goodbye to Mum and her brother. I was wheeled to the psych ward and deposited on a bed in a room with four beds. A nurse was waiting to do what was explained to me as intake. I answered a lot of questions, was weighed, was changed out of my street clothes, and was told that I was under close observation, which meant I would be checked on every 15 minutes.

Once alone, I lay down on my bed and tried to sleep, tried to get the horrible thoughts out of my way. The hours passed slowly. In the evening, my mum came and just sat with me. Ruby Tuesday was there too, giving me updates on my cat, Mickey, bringing me Sexton and Plath (did I see one of the medical students assigned to my case snigger at the pile of books?).

After that, when they were all gone, I started getting very upset. I started rocking back and forth, emitting a low moan. I did this for a long time. My brain was empty, with a blackness filling my head. My nurse came to sit with me, but I couldn't tell her what was wrong. She told me to hold on, that she had something that would help calm me down. She came back with a glass of water and a cup containing a pill, average-sized, round, and green. I swallowed it and lay down again, rocking back and forth. I decided to get Ruby to take back the books—this was not the romantic vision I had of depression, this rocking back and forth, this low cry gurgling up from my stomach. After a while, I felt a bit of a clamp on my brain, a dulling. My body was relaxing. And then I fell asleep. I don't know how long I was out, but when I finally woke up, the nurse was there asking if the medication had helped. I gave her a thumbs-up. The pill she had given me, that little green pill, was called Haldol, and that was the beginning of a love/hate affair that would last me to the present day.

***

The psychiatric ward at the Ottawa Civic Hospital was actually not that bad. It had two common rooms, a cafeteria, and a rectangle of hallway that went around the nursing station and med room. I tried to sleep as much as possible, but the nurses were always after me to get out of bed. I would invariably end up in the main common room, the one at the back, sitting alone in a chair with my feet tucked under me, silent and still.

Hanging around the nursing station were four or five elderly people, propped up in big chairs, some asleep, some crying out every now and then, dinner trays pushed to the side. And then the two hallways to the front, closest to the nursing station, each with no exit. These rooms all had single beds and were reserved for the most serious cases. I never walked there, just peeked. Sometimes yelling and loud cries came from these hallways. Many of these rooms had an orderly sitting outside, watching the patient and trying to manage them. Some orderlies got lucky and had a patient who was drugged into sleep and they got to read the newspaper, looking up at the patient every now and then. Little did I know at the time that, one day, I would end up in a single room in one of those hallways, with my very own sitter. But that would come in later hospitalizations.

There were others around me, statues on a vinyl seat. Occasionally, we would move a bit, adjust our position, look over at each other, an understanding. There was a young woman who twirled around us, singing a gentle song. She was in la-la land, I thought. There was a big guy having a conversation with himself, whacking his head with his hand as he walked around the unit. In a corner of the common room, there were three or four patients, laughing and conversing. I couldn't figure them out.

Yes, there were those who were depressed, manic, psychotic, all lost in their own worlds. And all had labels attached to them. Did I have a label stuck to me? Did I come branded? The fact is, though, that disorders never keep strictly in their boxes anyway. They like to climb all over the place, as I would learn. My labelling as depressed was to change and grow over the years.

Sometimes, a patient would make a run for it. Huddling in the corner of the common room, they would suddenly race towards the exit doors and dash down the stairwell, making their escape. But, they wouldn't get very far. The opening of the doors set off an alarm, and boy, the staff on the unit—the nurses, the orderlies—were fast! They followed the patient through the doors and down the stairs, a whole group of them. And, when the patient was returned to the unit several minutes later, they would get a shot in their thigh, of what, I didn't know. But, the patient always ended up going off to bed. End of excitement.

Every morning, we were pulled together in the TV room, pulled from our beds and the sleep we were hiding in. What a group we were! Most of us silent, others acting out a bit, as the voices in their heads told them to, still others yelling out questions to the staff, *When is the TV back on?* One morning, we learned about PRN medication. No, PRN did not stand for anything useful to us. It was an acronym for the Latin term, "pro re nata," and meant "when necessary." I had Ativan as a PRN. And Haldol.

Life took on a bit of a rhythm those early days. Shooed into the dining room at meal times, I would eat crackers and peanut butter, and make tea out of a plastic cup filled with tepid water. And worse were the washrooms. They didn't lock, and you often had to fend off an invader while you sat on the toilet. Often these washrooms would reek of smoke, some patients who were desperate for a cigarette taking a chance on a closed door. Three strikes and you're out, or so I heard.

In addition to the patients, there were a lot of nurses and four or five doctors, some with a clutch of students, some working solo. My doctor, Dr. S., had a resident doctor and a gaggle of students. They would come and get me once a day, taking me to one of the offices that lined the back common room. There they would pepper me with questions, noting how slow I was, how few words I used, how tired I was. They had put me on the antidepressant Zoloft the day I was admitted, and everyone was looking for signs of improvement. There were none. It would take time.

With the students and the two doctors, there were at least five or six people observing me. My fear of performing for an audience kicked in. Anxiety filled me, I wanted to hide from it, from all of them. But Dr. S. found me.

"You know," I said, trying to look him in the eye, "I think I am okay now. With the meds, with everything—it all feels good. I can go home now." Dr. S.'s face was blank. I couldn't tell where he was at with this. I continued, wobbling a little bit. "There is Dr. G. out there, and he and I can take it from here."

Dr. S. looked at me intently. "Okay, well Jocelyn, I am glad to hear you are feeling so much better. This is very different from yesterday afternoon. Why don't you leave it with me, and I'll get back to you in a couple of hours." He smiled, nodded his head, and left.

Where was he for all the hours that passed after our conversation? Was he watching me as I went about the unit, curling up on my bed? Were he and his team having a lively debate about my competence?

Three hours later, he came back and handed me a form. "This is a form 3," he explained. "It means you have to stay in the hospital for the next 14 days, or until discharge, whichever comes first." I was still curled up on my bed, not lending any confidence to my case. He continued. "I spoke with Dr. G. He said he doesn't know you well enough to vouch for your safety outside the hospital. And, I believe you have to stay here. I think you are still in a dangerous space, and there's a lot more we can do for you."

I was stunned. I hadn't even known that, upon admission, I was on a seventy-two-hour hold. But, two weeks? How did things get here, to being committed to a psychiatric institute?

What did they know about me that I didn't? I would have to act peppy, smile all the time, look happy and well recovered. That was the only thing I could think of doing, the only way out. Act peppy. Act normal.

***

The days passed by on the ward, and I was getting nowhere. My plan to look and act normal failed miserably. But on day 12, something happened, something changed. I didn't improve gradually. I improved suddenly, overnight.

I woke up early on this day, and felt an energy coursing through my veins, a buzz, a tingle, a bubbling. I headed to the hallway and started walking the circuit. Ten times around equalled one kilometre a big sign said, a sign that I had never noticed, my head always down, avoiding eye contact, avoiding my surroundings. But today was different. I noticed every picture, every door, every human in my way. I rounded the corner near the nursing station, and a nurse looked up, puzzled to see me up so early, walking at such a fast pace. But, as the day progressed, I settled down, sunk back into a solid lump, eyes staring blankly. My doctors seemed intrigued.

Around 4:00 a.m. the next day, I woke up again with great excitement. I leapt out of bed and started walking, started the circuit at quite the pace. The place was deserted, everyone still sleeping. I said a big hello to the nurse at the station and kept going, around and around. As the nursing shift changed at 7:00 a.m., I had many new people to say hello to, to greet with a big smile. When the doctors arrived and headed for the conference room, I greeted them as well.

My thoughts were crystal-clear, no longer at a sluggish pace, and they cascaded from my brain and down through my body. I could feel them. Everything was brighter. The soft-pink plant picture was now neon, the sofas a crisp and shiny black genuine leather. Everything was intensified in colour, with sounds coming through in dramatic waves. People seemed to be happier and more connected to me and my brain. I had no idea why my depression switch had flipped off, why I was suddenly so energized and happy. It just felt good. And at that time, that was all that mattered.

When Dr. S. grabbed me that day, I whirled around and laughed. "Sure, let's go, let's go!" I sang. I went bouncing into an office with him, where the resident and students were seated, waiting. All of a sudden, the questions started coming at me, but I was catching each one, throwing them up to the ceiling.

"Jocelyn," Dr. S. said, "things have really changed for you. Can you fill us in on a few details? One thing we wondered was if you've ever had trouble sleeping in the past."

"Oh, sleeping, yes, yes. It was hard, growing up, I had to steal my dad's Xanax all the time!"

"Have you had times when you were getting little sleep?" he asked.

I thought back to Ireland and my stay there a few years earlier, where I had such a wonderful time, and where I was always awake. "Maybe, sometimes," I said. I was getting bored with the conversation, and it was hard to sit still.

"You seem pretty happy right now. Have you had other times in your life when you were really happy?" This was from the resident.

"Oh, yes!" I exclaimed. I thought back to Ireland again. "It was really lovely, my happy time! Yeah, I know! And is this not fantastic, now?!" I looked at them all watching me, hanging on my every word. What was with this, this Spanish Inquisition? They were seeing how normal I was, I thought. I was no longer dragged down by horrible thoughts, whatever those were. I couldn't even remember them, and yet apparently, they were present less than 24 hours before.

"What about feeling powerful?" she asked. "Has that ever happened to you?" As she spoke, Dr. S. sat there listening, realizing that a mistake had been made, with the form one, the form three, with this whole time in hospital.

"Power!" I called out. "Yes! Like right now! You all sit here because of me. I have got you lined up!" I started to laugh at it all, at this strange dream sequence that was carrying on and on.

"Okay, thank you, Jocelyn," Dr. S. said. "You probably want to get up and do some more exercise. We will talk some more later."

They finally let me go, bursting out into the ward, out to walk the circuit, kilometre after kilometre. By the end of the week, I was walking 20 kilometres a day.

***

I started chatting with the willing, telling long stories about Mickey the cat, other things that were not necessarily so cohesive. A bit of rambling, but a lot of laughter.

I got involved in things. Played well with others. I learned to play pool, and I was terrible at it. A few years later, with my buddies from the cinema where I would work, I would go out shooting pool and drinking beer, and when my turn came, I used the psych ward rules, which included things like lifting the end of the table up so that the billiard balls rolled down a little bit, settling to my advantage.

One afternoon, a family friend came to visit. From her

squirming bag, she produced two little ginger kittens, adorable and cuddly. I played with them while patient after patient came to join me, awoken from their fog; kittens were passed around, and people smiled and giggled.

This went on for about half an hour. The change in people was incredible. But then the head nurse showed up. No animals on the ward! Everybody back to your places! No fun allowed! No healing moments! And my friend and her cats were shooed away.

***

Early one morning, I was told to go to the conference room, since I had a special meeting set up just for me. When I entered the room, I saw them all: four students, one resident, one head doctor, my nurse, my mum, and my uncle. I whooped it up, and shouted, "Party!" They stayed grim. What the hell was wrong with them?

Dr. S. asked me to sit, which I did with great effort, my knee bouncing up and down like a ping-pong ball. "We are all here," he said, "because we have determined your diagnosis. We believe you have manic depression, which is now called bipolar disorder." He paused as I started laughing. "Your reaction to the antidepressant sent you spinning. Look at you! Two weeks ago, you could barely speak to us, and now you are laughing and chatting away."

Then he started talking meds, something different from the Zoloft and the occasional Ativan. "We are going to taper you off the Zoloft and start you on a drug called Tegretol. Although Lithium is the standard treatment for bipolar disorder, it comes with a great deal of weight gain, and we don't want to do that to you. . ."

He carried on about Tegretol, how it was an

anticonvulsant, and it would stabilize my moods, protect me from mania, and from the dark times of depression. (Mania is an elevated state of mood, to varying degrees, often pleasant—but definitely not always—with lots of goodies: pressured speech, lots of spending, inability to get any sleep. Just go, go, go.)

"We really think you should go with this. It will stop your current hypomania (mild mania), but it won't send you down again. It will leave you right in the middle, at your normal setting." He tried for a laugh.

As the meeting broke up, I was filled with a sudden anger, which I used to lash out at my mum. "This is all your fault!" I hissed. But, underneath, I knew it wasn't. I knew that really, everything was my fault, that I couldn't handle myself around other people. That I just had to act a little more normal so they wouldn't put me on their crazy-sounding drugs.

First, there were some tests to rule out things like brain tumours and other neurological disorders that could throw off symptoms that mimicked bipolar disorder. I started Tegretol two days later, but soon developed a rash on my arms and legs. Dermatology came to see me; I was off the drug. Dr. S. came through with another one to try, another anticonvulsant called valproic acid, apparently weight-neutral as well. It was sold as Depakene in Canada, and Depakote in the US. It being called "weight-neutral" was apparently a joke. I later learned that Americans call it Depa-bloat. This was the drug that I was finally released on, six weeks later, with the pounds already creeping on, and a mood that was still shaky.

Chapter 4

My mother was a gentle and loving presence in my life. She was warm and steady, talented with kids (as I see in her role as grandmother today), energized and fun. When I was a child, we would go on nature walks, collecting leaves and twigs and pine cones to glue to paper and create collages. At Thanksgiving, my brothers and I would spread the leaves and cones on the dining room table to create a lovely fall centrepiece. At Christmas, we made popcorn strings and paper chains to go around the tree. And at Easter, we decorated eggs, pink, pale blue, light green, yellow. When my mum made playdough, she used the same food colouring to create vibrantly bright colours for us to shape and then bake.

When my brothers and I got home from school, she would greet us with snacks and tea and fun activities. Board games, finger-painting, reading, gallivanting outside, and in the winter, building forts in snowbanks (but never facing the street—we had heard stories of city plows covering fort entrances with their mountains of snow. Whether that was just an old tale, I don't know. . .).

We would cook together. I made some delicious things from a children's cookbook, absolutely wonderful. Oh, and the joy of making chocolate chip cookies with my mum, of trying a spoonful of batter, getting to eke out the last bits in the bowl before it went in the sink. Long trips to the library, loaded down with books on the way home. CBC News on at 5:00 p.m., dinner going, the smell of fresh bread. This was our chance to watch TV, which was small and black-and-white, unlike the televisions in other houses I would visit. Apples and a glass of milk. Maybe Oreo cookies, if we were lucky.

***

My mother's family had emigrated from Europe when my mother was a child, arriving on a ship one freezing winter day in 1949. They had settled in the forbidding countryside of Eastern Ontario, but moved around a lot, ending up in Montreal. Over the years, she and her siblings—there were six in all—grew close, a pretty happy bunch.

But all did not turn out perfectly as the six siblings aged. Depression and alcoholism run in the family, as well as anxiety. It had hit a couple of my mum's siblings; it hit Papa, my grandfather. His own father had foul moods and turned to drink. (That makes three out of my four great-grandfathers cursed.) And there is me and my own random love affair with alcohol. It flares up every now and then, this love affair. A few too many G&Ts, the rush in my head. Vodka Screwdrivers. Every now and then.

My mum is certainly one to enjoy a good G&T on occasion. In fact, while growing up, I saw her get a little tipsy at family gatherings, just as almost everyone did, laughing and dancing to ABBA or other similarly embarrassing music. Today, when we sit on the back porch, she nurses a glass of white wine, the free-flowing alcohol of the seventies and eighties slowed down to a trickle.

With her Order of Canada, her many years working in the philanthropic sector, her time in retirement thrown into serious volunteer positions, on boards, on committees, and her globe-trotting past, my mother is one of the most impressive people I know. Though she started working outside the home in 1981, her career really took off, it is kind of sad to say, when my father died. She was only 46. She is wise, smart, creative, outgoing, extrovert to my introvert. Intensely private. And, at times, she lives in fear.

I became ill when she was 48. And then my illness really took off. Yes, she lived in fear, fear of getting that phone call that I had disappeared, that I was dead in the woods on a walking path from my childhood. A phone call that said Jocelyn needed help. She had to go to the hospital, so get ready for some gruelling times over the next weeks or months. And she would rise to the challenge beautifully, visiting every day, dinner and treats in her bag, even when I was too out of it to want them.

The times when I was actively ill but not in hospital were probably the most stressful periods for my mum. We might have had arguments about what I needed to do in order to get better. She might have sighed over my huddled form on the sofa, wanting so badly for me to get better, wanting to make it right for her child. The worst was when I was psychotic. (Psychosis relates to being out of touch with reality. It includes: believing things that aren't true (delusions), and hearing or seeing things that aren't real (hallucinations).) This terrified her the most. The things that I could do while out of my mind. She worried for my safety, and sometimes even her own, though she knew that mental illness usually didn't bring violence along with it. No, if there is an element of danger, it is almost always the danger to self. (There are, sadly, exceptions to this.)

Today, when I experience an episode of psychosis, she handles it very well. We have had 25 years of experience and practice, many hard times, times of conflict, terror, and sadness. Things are much easier now. I am on a good drug cocktail for the most part, and I am much more mature. Things seem more clear-cut, and much of my old self is evident.

I understand her need to check in with me to make sure I am doing okay, but it can be annoying at times. If I am a little depressed, I try very hard to keep it under wraps, as I am usually feeling pretty vulnerable. But at times, I fail at this, fail at the cover-up, and my mum will pick up on things. Maybe three or four sentences are exchanged between us, and she might ask if I am feeling a little low, something that I hate admitting. My mother says she can tell when I am psychotic, when I am dealing with disruptive voices, when I am not straight in my thinking, when I am afraid. She has had a lot of practice at it.

It is normal for caregivers like my mum to be sad and feel loss when caring for someone like me. I know my mum had to adjust her thinking and expectations for my future when my illness started to cloud my way forward. For her to grieve for my future is a normal reaction for caregivers—parents in particular. How terrifying it must be to see a child veer off course, become withdrawn, anxious, sleepless, to lose touch with reality. It may be hard to get the person some treatment, and even with treatment, those with severe illness may never be the same again. Parents may have to visit their child at a group home, take them out on walks, trying to break through, unsuccessfully, into the lost mind, the ramblings, or the withdrawn behaviour. That is not my story, but it happens, and it is heartbreaking for everybody.

***

I was always aware that I lived in my mum's shadow, and to a certain extent, in my brothers' as well. Unlike them, I never had a career, let alone a hugely successful one. I didn't do the school thing, never got a serious job, never realized my potential. Yes, the comment I heard from most of the adults around me, including my mum, was that I had so much potential. When I was younger, I heard it as a phrase to get me going. You can do it, you have so much potential. And I heard it as a question. Why are you failing this, you have so much potential? And I hear it today, as a kind of sigh, a sadness. You just have so much potential, it's too bad that you never realized it. . . It is not enough for me to have my own private doubts about the course my life took. I get to hear it from others as well.

But nobody is angry about my lack of success in life, though they may feel a little saddened by it. Instead, the people around me have my mental illness as the culprit to blame. Simple and tidy. And, sometimes, when I get upset about all the misses in my life, they pull out things that I have in fact achieved, however small, and point to them, to say, *Wait, don't forget this.* They try to reassure me, but usually I think they have missed the mark. We all know the truth about me. *I had so much potential.*

***

My mum and I are great friends. I live in an almost-apartment in her renovated basement. I am hard on myself about that, about being my age and still living with my mother (let alone in her basement).

The situation isn't perfect for her, either. I am sure she didn't expect to be living her years out with her daughter right under her, providing her with financial support. We have both had to adjust, but I think it works.

When I am well, we spend every Saturday going through cookbooks (I have well over 200) and cooking apps, and dream up the menus for the following week.

"How about we use these two books this week," I said, holding up a fancy vegetarian book, and one on Middle Eastern food, by Claudia Roden. "There are some really good ones. I am thinking of the Thai Green Curry from this one, or the Phyllo Eggplant from here." I always choose the more time-consuming recipes, and I look upon them with love, much as my father had. I hand the books to my mum.

"Those do sound good," she said, after checking the recipes out. "I wonder what else is in here." She flipped through the pages of the Roden cookbook. "This sounds really good. Chicken baked with honey and almonds." She read the recipe out loud to me.

"Okay, that definitely goes down for the week as well." I now had three recipes. Four more to go.

As if she could read my mind, my mum said, "Don't forget we always have leftovers, so don't go too much farther. I wouldn't mind an egg dish, maybe a slow-cooked frittata."

I would always be a bit disappointed, as I had grand plans for all seven nights. I would end up getting four or five instead. But, she was right, of course.

We do a lot of grocery shopping together, hitting up market stands, bakeries, fish stores, grocery stores. We are getting to know the people who run them, and I always feel a bit embarrassed as we talk about what we should buy for the evening's dinner. Although I generally do not look disabled, I think people wonder what's up with me and why my mum and I are always together, how it is obvious that I live with her.

But she has saved me. I know this to be true. She has saved my life, she has provided me with so much support, she has kept the warmth from my childhood and turned it into a lovely safe zone.

She is now in her mid-70s. I know she won't go on forever, that she will grow old, that she will die. I will be faced with a life without her. I get upset just thinking about it. I cannot think past it. Sometimes, I feel okay when I agree with myself that there is always suicide after her death. When I consider that option, I feel better. That is when I think that I have value only when with my mum and won't have any need to keep living once she is gone. But, I know that is not true. There are other things that will keep me from killing myself.

Chapter 5

As a child, I was lonely. I felt like no one liked me at school, a miserable place where other kids bullied me. I have lived with vision problems all my life, and one of my eyes wanders, creating a real reason to tease me (especially when I wore a patch). Even one of my grade four teachers made a comment about my school photos—that it was too bad that my left eye had wandered in the photo, that it "ruined" it. That's a lot to set a kid up with. (These vision problems are getting worse as I age, and they affect both how I see, and how others see me. I have included as an author photo one that clearly shows my left eye drifting outward, my right eye looking directly at the camera. To put this out there, after years of trying to avoid family photos, is a big step, a big claw ripping into the shame I have lived with since I was a little kid.)

In the earlier years, I was also bullied about being American, "Yank, Yank, go home!" I didn't understand that, was not yet aware of the anti-Americanism that is fairly popular in Canada. I remember sitting at the dining room table for the evening meal, in tears as I felt so ostracized during the day. This is a memory that my mum does not share—she doesn't remember my early life in Canada as such. But I remember it all too well. Am I making it seem bigger than it was? Does my mum downplay it because she wanted me to be so happy? Maybe a little of both?

When I was 10, I switched schools, and the abuse stopped. I started making life harder for others, turning into a bully myself. I remember once my grade six teacher had to take me aside and talk to me about a classmate whom I had teased relentlessly because her breasts were developing. Later, two classmates confronted me. "Nobody likes you, Jocelyn," they said. The bullied had become the bully. Not unusual, but not something I am proud of.

My career as a bully was short-lived, a year at most, and then things switched over again. The transition to high school in grade nine was rough, but I was not alone in feeling on the outside, as everybody else was trying to figure out their place. A year later, I made friends with Ruby Tuesday, a friendship that took me out of school life, and the outcast label was firmed up as I became a teenager.

***

I believe my inside world, my world with my family, was delightful, warm, and cozy when I was a kid. It was full of playing outside till darkness fell. (There was a bellow to be heard throughout the neighbourhood—"Alan, Jocy, Jeffrey. . .time to come in!"—a similar call that went out by parents up and down the street. I can still hear it today, the one word: Alanjocyjeffrey! "Alanjocyjeffrey! Time to come in!") When we finally showed up, dirty and happy, ready for our baths and nighttime snacks, it was already 9:15 p.m. and the block had gone quiet. Raggle taggle kids, those Pattens.

Baseball and hockey on our quiet street ("Car!"), games of imagination played out behind our houses, in the spacious backyards of our neighbourhood. And we fought, as siblings do, tackling each other to the ground.

Inside, we had a space we called the playroom. This was where our TV was situated, for afternoon watching. Shows like *The Brady Bunch, Happy Days,* and *Gilligan's Island* were favoured. But the best had the creatures that hovered over our growing up in the seventies and eighties, the Muppets. From *Sesame Street,* and later through brilliant shows and movies, the Muppets definitely played a big role in entertaining us.

Those were the good old days, as they say. Another world, another lifetime. I am sure you can still play street hockey on Edison Avenue. But that looseness isn't around anymore, that sense of playing really hard, without devices around to grab our attention. It no longer exists.

***

Often, people living with mental illness come from unhappy homes, were abused sexually or physically, or never got a firm foundation to keep them steady in life. These facts in themselves do not cause mental illness, absolutely not. But, if one is genetically predisposed to a mental illness such as depression, for example, difficult times, or the memory of them, may tip one into an episode. Many conditions are like that, a mix of genes and environment.

Overall, my childhood was a happy one, though at school and with people other than my family, I faced difficulties. I wonder if this dark side, which continued up through high school, was environment enough to lay the groundwork for a genetic explosion.

***

My father made sure I knew the difference between baroque,

classical, and romantic music by the time I was a toddler. A bit older, I would follow the score to the Moonlight Sonata with my finger, and my dad would sit beside me as the record played, crack crackle.

"Listen to the first movement," my dad said. "It's adagio. Often, the first movement of a sonata is fast. This is probably the most famous movement of any of Beethoven's piano sonatas," he explained to me.

"Is it as famous as Mozart's Turkish Rondo?" I asked.

"Probably, yes," he answered. "More famous, I would say."

I went back to the score, the haunting music laid out for me. My dad would hum, pleased by my question. How precocious of me!

The first instrument I learned was the recorder. I became quite good and played in a recorder group, giving concerts here and there. Then, when I was 10, I started studying the piano, which stayed with me through my teenage years. I wasn't bad, and within the conservatory I was working in, finished my studies at an advanced grade.

Our evening routines included reading, oh so much reading, reading by age four, reading on my own, being read to. I loved being read to as a little one, snuggled up against my dad, delving into the land of fairy tales, the blue book, the red book, the orange book. Often, these stories would frighten me to my core, and other times I would be so saddened that I would start crying. My father would pull me closer, tell me that it was only a story. *The Hobbit* and *The Lord of the Rings* came next, and though I listened intently and was enthralled, I have to say that I preferred the fairy tales, preferred the tale of Beowulf, preferred my father singing ballads to me, even though they would often make me weep.

My dad would sing "Peggy Gordon," or "The Water is Wide," some of the Child Ballads. "Did you like that one?" he would ask after each. "Nobody dies. It's only a bit sad." He smiled at me. "'The House Carpenter,' that is very sad."

"Don't sing that to me," I said, a little worried. I snuggled into him some more. "Can I have another fairy tale?"

"But, Juice, it's past your bedtime."

"I am six!" My big-girl feathers were ruffled. "Please, one more?"

"How about another ballad?" he said. "I could sing about a sea captain and his fight to keep his ship afloat."

"Yes, yes, that one!" I just wanted to have more time with him, safely at his side, picking up on his pride as he shared his passion for folk stories and songs with me.

I also learned to appreciate and be creative in visual art from an early age, a cue from my mother's side of the family, which had several branches populated by famous artists back in Germany. However, music was, and is to this day, incredibly important to me, and if I had to choose between visual art, the written word, or music, I would surely choose music.

When I am actively ill, I lose the ability to focus on the written word. Reading is too much work when I am depressed and too slow and clumsy when I am manic. Music is seductive at first in its pull into its world. But gradually, it wants too much from me, a concentration I don't possess. I don't appreciate visual art when I am depressed, and when manic, I find that it overpopulates my world with its colours and lines, and only fans the flames.

***

I was in tears often through my childhood, and into today, in the privacy of my apartment. I've been very sensitive to other people, to animals, and situations around me. This sensitivity affects me still, as an adult, as I blink back tears, fighting to maintain my composure when I am hit with something close to me, something too beautiful or too sad. Even as a child, I had strong marks in compassion and empathy, which as an adult remain, partly as a result of my illness. Walk a mile in somebody's shoes, they say—I have done this many, many times. And that has allowed me to not get swallowed up in myself. Other people matter too, I see that, and yes, that can bring on tears.

Chapter 6

Two of my American cousins, daughters of my dad's only sister, have bipolar disorder. One is new to it. She is one of the many women who develop a mood disorder during menopause, and she's got it bad. I email with her every now and then and am sad to see her spiral out of control; long and drawn-out depressions, her psychotic-tinged manias. She fights it hard, harder than anyone would know.

My friendship with my other cousin is lovely. We talk a couple of times a week, and it is wonderful to get to know her. I first really met her at our Grandmother Patten's funeral in New Hampshire. We took the beautiful hike up to the monastery together, sharing mental illness notes. I was new to it, this being September of 1995, but she was five years older than me and had a long history with bipolar disorder. I remember growing up hearing stories about her, how wild she was, even at the age of 14, how angry she was, and that she was in and out of hospitals, with a whole year spent in one of them. It seemed so strange to me, yet at the same time I had a particular fascination with hearing her story. She has come a long way, just recently finishing her masters of social work, which I think is amazing.

The three of us share the same two great-grandfathers. It is interesting that the family's trade in bipolar disorder skipped two generations. None of my dad's siblings had it, my dad having minor depressions now and then, and we're talking minor.

***

Grandmother Patten lived in Peterborough, New Hampshire, a lovely town about eight hours by car from Ottawa. We went every summer for weeks at a time. In the early years, we went down for American Thanksgiving as well, but my parents didn't like driving in the mountains with bad weather, the date being at the end of November. The only other time we got to see Grandmother was at Christmas, when she would fly up from Boston and join us for Christmas celebrated with my mum's family.

Talking politics with Grandmother and her friends was a real sport, since she was a solid, old-school Republican. (How horrified by the politics of today would Grandmother be!) She decried (with a gleam in her eye) her eldest son's decision to live in Canada, we being a bunch of commies who banned smoking on airplanes and drove with our lights on during the day. And seatbelts! I remember her wearing a seatbelt, grumbling about it, smoking in the car on the way from the airport to Edison, the air blue.

Once we arrived at Grandmother's after the long drive, there were lots of things to do right away, like playing with her dog, checking out the ancient shed where the family Civil War wonders were, and picking raspberries. Straight away, the fruit to be brought back up to the house for dessert that night.

The surrounding countryside, the beauty of the place, with Mount Monadnock ahead of us and Pack Monadnock behind, and rolling farmland and just gorgeous villages in between, was unmatched in my part of Canada.

My mother enjoyed her holidays in the US as well, though it wasn't always a proper vacation. She had all the same things to take care of as she did in Ottawa. Although Grandmother always had a beef stew ready on the stove for us when we arrived from our long drive down, my mum did all the cooking after that. No cleaning, but a lot of time spent with her three young children—I am sure she just wanted sometimes to sit on the sun porch and read a book, nursing a cup of tea.

But we did have fun, all five of us and Grandmother.

Visiting with neighbours, and especially my dad's cousins who lived in nearby Massachusetts, was wonderful, though the time with them in the sun porch could be long for us kids.

"Jocy, I see you've lost a tooth! I hope the tooth fairy paid you a visit," my dad's cousin would say. She would ruffle my hair, announcing my tooth loss to the room. They had money, these relatives, as did the couple next door, with their rambling white clapboard house, facing off a field to Monadnock.

Grandmother always served up the same appetizers every time, canned sausages and jarred artichokes with toothpicks, which were my favourite. Sherry or sweet wine, and lots of coffee, which seemed very American to us, coffee all the time, even at dinnertime.

We would get restless when another pot was put on. "Go on, off with you," my mother would laugh as she poured out the coffee. The three of us were allowed to escape, burst outside, play a game of croquet, explore the woods out back.

Every time we were down in Peterborough, we would always visit the same two places. The first was the ocean in the southern part of Maine. I loved this the most, playing in the cold waters as long as I could, the smell of the sea mixed with wet sand and sun lotion. The second was the two-hour trip to Boston. My mum and I would be thrilled at Filene's Basement, looking through the amazing deals. We walked around Faneuil Hall, and then down to Newbury Street. My dad, in the meantime, had been doing family research at the New England Historical Society, which he called the Hysterical Society. My mum would laugh at that, but it was an "Oh, John" moment, just as when he got us kids calling Grandmother's cleaner Mrs. Sweeny Vacuum Cleany.

We rented a cottage on nearby Thorndike Pond (really a lake) some of the years, inviting friends and family to join us. Those were special days, and my brothers and I look back on them with fondness. Jeffrey fell in love with Jaffrey the dog (he broke down in wails when it was time to return home, leaving the dog, leaving his beloved cottage). Alan learned how to drive a stick shift, my cousin and I in the back seat, choking on our giggles, my dad patient in the front, Alan lurching us around the lake.

We had Grandmother, we had her eighteenth-century home to play in, the back acres with the raspberry bushes and woodland, some beautiful gardens. We had her dog, a black Shepherd who was strong, once pulling me along a road while I walked her, taking off into the field without me. There was the road on the side of the house that went on for miles with no end in sight, big cabins in the woods, with trailers and junk in the yard, people who my dad would call "Swamp Yankees" with a gleam in his eyes. And we had the history, since my father had traced our ancestors taking root in that part of New England, centuries ago.

My great-grandfather George, the same one with an undiagnosed mental illness, was born nearby in 1843. This astounds me. I've met many people who knew a great-grandparent, but mine fought in the American Civil War of the 1860s! The Pattens had long generations.

***

Many things in my life played out in my summers down in the US. The most important thing was that I was starting to become aware of my body. I was 13 years old, and the idea of dieting was already firmly rooted in my head. I tried to enjoy grapefruit every morning, measured out my steak in inches, ate lots of fruit. When I lost a pound or two, I was happy. Standing on the scales, checking out my new weight would give me a high—a high that I have sought out every year of my life since. But, that was when I was a tween. I wasn't even overweight, just a little prepubescent softness.

My daydreams seemed different when I was down there. I read *Seventeen* magazine and made copious notes about fashion for the school year, which I imagined would be a star turn. There were interesting men around, men that I would form crushes on, men I couldn't wait to see when we would make the drive down from Ottawa. They were all older—I found guys my age to be useless. No, for me it was always older men, like my second cousin, David. I played touch football with my brothers and him on Grandmother's front yard, and I was just in heaven.

These were good times, so long ago. I think it pleased my father that we could return to where his own family had roots, that we didn't turn our backs on the US with the knee-jerk reactions to all Americans that so many people have. Yes, we did meet many who were like the stereotypical ignorant Yank. But the ones who I hung out with were real flesh-and-blood people, smart, accomplished, playful with us kids. They were fascinating to us, these well-dressed neighbours, friends, and family.

They are all gone now; the family members have died, the house has been sold, the trips to Maine no longer a part of our lives. All that's left are the memories. Looking back on them, I realize these happy memories have served me well, coming before the storm of serious illness hit.

Chapter 7

My family was a lovely thing happening, the warmth and steadiness keeping all three of us kids happy and right side up. In the middle of my teenage years, however, I veered off course, went totally off the map into a cloud of turmoil. But that was not the case for my brothers.

Both Jeffrey and Alan were good at the school thing. They had happy social lives and were beloved by their teachers. After high school, they each moved to Montreal for further studies at McGill University.

And then it was all a whirl of schools and jobs and successes. Jeff took an interesting path to where he is now, a New York City wine merchant. And Alan is a professor of politics at Princeton University. Between the two of them, there are six nephews and nieces for me, great personalities who I always like being with. I try to be a wonderful aunt to them, even with them being so far away.

***

I think a lot about my maternal grandparents, Granny and Papa, who loved all of us, me and my siblings and all my cousins. We each had a lovely relationship with them, all 15 of us grandchildren, no matter where we lived. And I know every one of my cousins who grew up in Ottawa had special times with Granny and Papa, and then just Granny after Papa died in 1994. Each after-school visit, there would be tea, treats, and a big catch up. Both my brothers and I were lucky, since we lived just three blocks from them. We were older than the other cousins, and we had more years of visiting. We got to see them a lot. At the end of December, each grandchild in Ottawa, including those visiting, were treated to Christmas Eve, European-style, at my grandparents, a very special memory for us all.

***

In recent years, it is after Christmas that my mum and I pack our gifts into the car and head south to Princeton for five or six days. Jeff's family comes in from Brooklyn, and Christmas is recreated over New Year's Eve into the first of January. A new tradition for our family. And, we feast. A little bit of old favourites mixed in with new creations, though Alan's wife Matilda goes out of her way to make me great vegetarian food instead—some potatoes cooked with oil, rather than duck fat, some gravy without the pork drippings. We exchange presents, but that's mostly for the kids.

These days, our summer holidays are also very different, since we are now 12 people, two families of five, me the aunt, and mum as nana. We rent big houses, in Canada, New England, upstate New York. Not only are we a family of political junkies, but we are also a family of great cooks. Matilda by far gets a shout-out as the best cook in the family, and knowing the talents of the others, that is high praise. When we visit Princeton, Matilda and I will chat in the kitchen, me peeling potatoes as she works on elaborate missions to get the porchetta ready for New Year's Eve dinner.

***

There was one Christmas when my brothers came up to celebrate in Ottawa. This was before Matilda, the late nineties; it was Jeff and his then-girlfriend Natasha, and Alan, who was still teaching in Montreal. It was a period when I was not doing well, and I had my whole family there to witness and deal with it.

I remember the issue as being that they all thought I was psychotic, and my mum desperately wanted me to go back on Haldol, a drug that would clean out my psychotic brain if I took it as prescribed, if I actually took it at all. For some reason, I had discontinued it. I had my reasons, I figure, even though they weren't reasonable. Dr. G. was out of the picture since it was the holidays, leaving it to my family to figure out.

I sat alone in the living room, speaking quietly to myself, scared, afraid that people were building a case, creating a dossier on me. This was very frightening, and it didn't help that my family was trying to intervene, to make me stop thinking for myself. That was how it appeared to me, at least. It was very confusing.

There was fresh snow on the ground, and Alan, Jeff, and Natasha took me out for a walk in the dark, heading down to Puzzles, a sports bar on the main drag of Westboro. We found a table under one of the large TVs that were everywhere, game on.

"Jocy, Mum is really worried about you," Alan began. "She was in tears earlier. Can you not acknowledge just that one thing?" He was coming down firm, and I didn't like it. The voices that I heard in my head didn't like it.

"Okay, so Mum is upset, I see that. But she doesn't have to be upset. She only has to listen to me and my explanation. It's that simple. Take all the confusion away, see it from my perspective." I could be firm too.

"I think what we are worried about, Jocy, is the fact that you aren't taking your Haldol. It's the end of December, your doctor is off," Jeff said. "We all know that Haldol will really help you feel better."

"No! You think you know this. I don't know this at all. It is incorrect." I took a swig of my Molson Golden. "Of course I want to see Mum happy. Of course. But she has to meet me halfway."

"Well, maybe to meet her halfway is to take just a little bit of Haldol. Not the whole dose, I know you don't like that. But maybe take half the dose. That simple action would go a long way in making Mum happy." Jeff, as usual, was calm and laid-back. He made it all seem so simple. I thought of my mum and all the words between us over the past weeks. She was really angry with me, it seemed. But, I didn't know why she would have tears. That didn't make sense to me.

"I guess I don't understand Mum right now," I said quietly. I was feeling like I was slowly shutting down, the three gorgeous people there, confronting me, pulling at my weaknesses. What could I do to make them stop?

"So, have you discussed all this with Mum? Are you just out with me to fight on her behalf? Because I am done with fighting." I could feel tears coming. This was not what I wanted. My voices were frantic. *No Haldol, no Haldol, you big fat crybaby!* I gripped my beer bottle as my eyes watered and a tear fell. Natasha put her hand on my arm, and I accepted it—it was a dangerous move on her part, but it worked. I started to weep. I was in the middle of a room full of men talking at the TVs, and right there in the middle was me crying.

"I think you know what you have to do," Alan said.

"Meet Mum halfway, take some Haldol."

"Yes, we will support you with this," Jeff said. "We will make sure she knows that you are only taking half the amount of Haldol, and that that is the right thing to do."

Our table grew quiet. There were a couple of hockey games on, it seemed, and my brothers looked up at them. I was drinking my beer quickly. I wanted to get out of there, to end these treaty talks. I knew what I had to do.

"Fine," I said, "Fine. I will do that. I will take 10 mg of Haldol, and only that. If Mum wants me on 20 mg, well I can't do that. Halfway means half the Haldol." I couldn't believe what I was saying. "I'll do it. Fine. If it gets everybody off my back!" I pushed my chair back and got up. "I'll see you at home."

I took a circuitous route back to Edison. I didn't want to arrive home and be alone with Mum. And I didn't feel like talking to those guys anymore. Were they trying to trick me? I kind of felt like they were. I kicked the snow around, trying to quiet the voices by singing a song—"I'll Stand by You," imitating Chrissie Hynde, singing into the night. I knew that I would take some Haldol when I got home. I would make them all stand around me, I would pour myself a glass of wine, down the pills. Two round green pills, 5 mg of Haldol each. My own standby.

That was not a great Christmas, for my mum, for me. It was so long ago—I was 29 or 30? A whole other lifetime. I am relieved that episodes like that one are in the past, for the most part. I did have some real doozies after that one, though. One of them not too long ago, a little too close for comfort.

***

It is early 2018, and my mum and I are FaceTiming with

Alan's family. We talk mostly to the kids, and then Alan casually mentions he will now be chair of the politics department at Princeton where he is a professor, a position that would last for four years. I am so happy for him, so proud.

But I can feel something in the pit of my stomach, something dark. *He's fucking with you!* The alarm goes off inside my head, a torrent of voices. *He is trying to make you small, trying to hatchet you into the earth!* Why are my voices suddenly so violent? The voices that I hear constantly have been woken up, as they can be, put into use as terrorists in my brain.

"That's fantastic, Alan," I say. "Congrats!"

"Yes, great news!" my mum adds. She begins to pepper him with questions about his new job, and I try to listen to her voice while I deal with the words coming at me in my head.

You horrible excuse for a human being, my voices yell at me. *You have wasted away your time on Earth, completely wasted it away. They keep bounding ahead of you, you will never catch up! Not even close!*

I push back at the voices, stay in the present. I focus on my mother's face, her warm, happy face, the joy of celebrating such a success for one of her children. It is fantastic, Alan's news, my mother's face.

And I manage it, just like I always do. Oscar-worthy performances, my whole life.

It has been difficult to be in a family that is as accomplished and successful as mine. And sometimes it is even harder to hear that you are as intelligent as the others, and everyone knows you haven't realized it. Unfortunately, you are told, your illness, your disability, has robbed you of your own years of success. It is hard at my age to hear that. And though my brothers treat me as one of them, and amongst my larger family I am treated as my brothers would be, I know deep down that there lies a lie.

***

I think that in the early years of my illness, Jeffrey, three years younger than me, wondered if he would develop something similar. But both he and Alan were spared, leading normal lives compared with my bent-out-of-shape existence.

During hospitalizations, my brothers are regularly in touch with Mum. The last time I was in, early summer of 2019, Jeffrey flew up to check on both of us. During one of my first times on the ward, in 1995, both Alan and Jeff came to Ottawa for a few days. They had asked if we could get some space to visit as a family. We were given the conference room, where the doctors, therapists, and some nurses met around 8:30 a.m. to start off their work day. When we had our little gathering, I made wonderful drawings on the blackboard at the front, drawings to illustrate what was going on in my manic brain. We never erased the board; we left it for the team the next morning.

I know my brothers worry about their own kids, whether they are loaded with the genes that turned me into what I was in the earlier years, when things were rough, or even what I am today, with the bumps. But so far, so good, though it is early days, and the kids are just now growing into teenagers, a danger zone.

Over the past two decades, a pattern has emerged. On return from New Year's celebrations in the US, I become depressed or even psychotic. Like clockwork, really. Perhaps it is because I am around my family and spend a lot of time drawing comparisons, my own mixed-up life to my brothers' full, happy ones. But I would say that it is worth it, these trips down south. The few days I have with my brothers and their families are so wonderful. When I am right in the middle of it, I just feel complete joy.

Chapter 8

It was 1983 when I entered high school. I was 14 years old and had no idea what I was in for. Most of my grade eight class were floating around me, suddenly becoming very important in the sea of many new faces in grade nine. We hung on to each other for a bit, safety in old ways. But gradually, we started up new friendships and relationships as we moved from class to class, year to year.

It was in grade nine that I met Ruby Tuesday. I remember it so clearly. It was a track and field event, and we were side by side, both doing up our laces.

"Hi, I'm Jocelyn," I said, a little bit shyly. "I love the curls!" I motioned to my own head of twirling waves. "I've got them too!" We both laughed. It was the day and age of the perm, at age 12, age 13, and farther into our teens. That was the 1980s.

"Do you run?" my new friend Ruby asked me.

"Nah, I can barely get around the track." I laughed again. I was being sarcastic. "Shot put is more my thing. *Strong like bull, big like tractor*," I said, imitating a Russian accent.

"You're funny," Ruby said to me. And, then she was off, jogging down to her group of friends.

For the rest of the year, we smiled and waved when passing each other in the hall. But our friendship didn't develop beyond that in grade nine, that of cheery hellos and funny perm jokes. It wasn't until grade 10 that our friendship solidified and started down a tricky path as we grew up.

***

At the beginning of each year, we were all assigned lockers. In grade 10, I was given one between two girls I had never met before. I decorated the inside of it with Springsteen, early U2. Things that my brother Alan had got me into. There were pictures of models in clothes that I hoped to acquire, beautiful Laura Ashley dresses, sweaters from Club Monaco, funky blouses from L'Esprit. I visited those stores with Ruby when we were on solid footing as best friends, both of us having saved up our allowance so that we could drop an easy $150 on a top from Benetton at the Rideau Centre, our downtown mall. The third floor, where all the good (expensive) stuff was. Talk about privilege. It gives me a bit of a bad taste in my mouth today.

In the earlier days, I loved geography, art, and English, with its Shakespeare and its creative writing. There were the free periods in between classes that were meant for forays into the library, studying at a desk there. For those, I sat down in the hall, leaned against my locker, and listened to music on my Walkman, doodling in a notebook.

My grades were okay in grade nine—maybe in the seventies. Definitely much lower than what I was capable of. They were better in grade 10, when I made the honour roll. But it was all downhill from there, my teachers and parents wondering why such a bright young girl failed grade 11 math. Drugs? Alcohol? My parents wondered about those two things. And what about this new, sudden, intense friendship with a girl called Ruby Tuesday? Was she leading me astray?

I turned into a rebellious teenager, and my parents didn't know what to do with me. It is so hard to tease out what were the early signs of mental illness and what was just normal adolescence. I know this is true for so many.

***

When I was 16, my parents sent me to counselling at my request. I met with a lovely woman who talked to me about life and everything that went into being a teenager.

"You seem to be in a good mood compared to last Wednesday," Heather would say to me, or, "Did something happen to you this past week? You seem very quiet." She seemed genuinely concerned about my mood changes, which she could easily assess as I only saw her once a week.

"Yeah, Ruby and I are talking about moving to Montreal next spring. We're both beginning to look at the art of knitting sweaters." My voice was bouncy. "We're going to create really exotic sweaters and set up a shop on one of the funkier streets there, like Park or Laurier." I rubbed a spot on my jeans. "I know I can meet the man for me when we have it all up and running." I laughed. "Our own little empire." I truly believed these things were going to happen.

Then, the next week. "My mum is really on my case. Both my parents are convinced that I am being lazy. I am not lazy. I just don't know where to get started. I don't know, it's too much, I don't even know if it's worth it." My voice was soft, no bounce or laugh to it. Maybe anger, but that required energy, something I was low on that week.

These mood swings were mild, though, not pronounced enough to get me to a psychiatrist. And besides, wasn't this kind of mood vacillation all part and parcel of being a teenager? Looking back on those years, I realize that I had cyclothymia, a mild form of manic depression. The motor had been turned on. It just wouldn't get revved up for some years.

***

It was around that time that my life revolved completely around Ruby Tuesday. The two of us together, enabling each other, pushing all other friends aside. We were labelled snobby, were laughed at, were called druggies.

It was so bloody unhealthy, our codependency, but we just went with it.

We pulled each other down when it came to school performance. We hated it so much and spent half the time at our neighbourhood mall, Carlingwood, sitting upstairs at Sears, the little restaurant with coffee for me and an ashtray for Ruby Tuesday, her smoking a cry of defiance. When we showed up to our respective homerooms each morning, there would be pink slips waiting for us. Head to the office, head directly there, do not pass Go, do not collect $200. Usually with the vice principal, though sometimes we were hauled into the principal's office. "You have been seen at Carlingwood," he would say. "Your parents are being called."

And it wasn't just Carlingwood. Sometimes, we would take the bus downtown, stopping at the National Arts Centre bookstore, loading up on important titles by Hemingway and de Beauvoir. We cut class to further our cultural education, or so we thought. Other times, we would head back to my empty home and make chocolate chip cookies, eating most of the dough before baking, listening to Bob Marley, who had been introduced to me by Alan. (Older siblings are good for some things!) Often, our activities were quite innocent, but they involved breaking the rules.

"His face is getting redder and redder," I read. A note from Ruby in English class, passed quietly to me, one seat over. "I worry about him."

I giggled quietly. "Can't take much more of this today," I wrote my response. "Must get outside ASAP. Will you cut art again? I am cutting French and Phys ed."

I folded the note over, slid it in her direction.

"Will cut art, will cut school, will cut life!" was her note back to me. I gave her a funny smile and a thumbs-up.

Busting out of class, the two of us struggled into our winter coats and headed down to the river, crossing the parkway toward the beach, beautiful in the white wonderland. We fell to the ground, laughing, rolling down to where the cars were, the pain, oh, the angst of being, or, at least, of being a teenager, the melodrama, all so overwrought. We stopped to lie there, staring at the sky, not knowing where to go any more. We had already checked out; we would not be returning. Well, at least I wouldn't be.

I guess I was an outcast, as opposed to a rebel. I had been an outcast for the better part of my social life, something that, in part, was a result of my germinating illness. I think this mild bipolar illness had a huge impact on my friendship with Ruby Tuesday. And vice versa.

Ruby had always been a good kid, a self-described goody two-shoes. At the beginning of high school, she had high marks and a solid best friend. But a darker part of her was growing, her own rebelliousness, and she found good company in me, who was already far gone.

Ruby would say that in me she found a bit of an oasis, with my family life so different, new to her, embracing her. She remembers cottages, big meals, hearty discussions. I remember all that too, the good times woven through the pain. Those years in the eighties were special for her, if not for me.

She took up smoking, jean jacket draped over her skinny shoulders, and, with me, started to skip school. Her long, dirty-blonde hair was unwashed. For a couple of years she was in it, she was really in it, saying "fuck you" to the world. But it was me who followed her. I needed her to define who I was. Cutting class maybe was my idea, but I hung on to her every word, needing to hear them, to fill me up.

Ruby got back on track when she left high school, growing into the person she was meant to be. Something I feel I never got to do.

What pull, exactly, does Ruby have? It lasts into the present. Ruby is so open and friendly with others. I think she has a comfort in being herself that is attractive. She makes whomever she is interacting with feel like they are the only person in the world.

***

In grade 12, we both decided to switch schools, going to one with a semester system. We felt that schoolwork would somehow be lighter there, and we would have more time to hang out together. That school was, however, the place where our friendship would crack open.

We made this switch in 1987, our last year of high school. Ruby Tuesday started hanging out with two other students who were in some of her classes. Both young women disliked me intensely. They both felt I was an unhealthy appendage to Ruby, and my fingers had to be peeled off her shoulders so that she could find her way to safety.

In January of 1988, Ruby broke up our friendship once

and for all, in keeping with her new friends' thinking.

"I just can't take it anymore," she said at the other end of the phone. I was pacing my bedroom, starting to cry, pulling at my braid so that it hurt my scalp. "You are everywhere in my life, I can't turn around without bumping into you. Christ, you really need to back off!"

I was mystified by her anger. What were they telling her, her new friends? "I promise I won't be everywhere, then, I won't. I'll only be where you want me to be. Really. I promise." Did she know that I was crying? Was she crying? Probably not. "Just don't leave me, please."

She was wrapping up the conversation, I could tell. "Well, I know what I have to do. I have to stand back and reorganize my life. I can't do that with you hanging off my arm all the time." She was sounding firm. "And, I can't have contact with you anymore. Please don't call me again."

"No, no, please, don't go!" I sobbed into the phone, my scalp hurting. But she was gone, she had hung up. And I just lost it. I picked up my bedside water glass, and threw it at the door frame, shattering the glass everywhere. I was hardly able to stand up. I threw myself onto the bed, sobbing into my pillow. "No, please. . ." I cried. "No, please. . ."

My whole world had dissolved. I did not know how I could be again, all alone. I was at a loss. Would I be able to dry my eyes, walk downstairs, and eat a sandwich, all on my own, no Ruby Tuesday at all anymore? What would I do with myself, all alone?

The breakup lasted; it was very much in place. I did become depressed over those first months in 1988, trying to build up a life without Ruby. At the end of that February, out of the blue, she called me. She said she just wanted to check if I was okay.

Was that the only reason she phoned?

I asked this, hoping she would tell me she wanted to get back together again.

"Yes, that was the only reason," she said softly. Well, I threw out words that I was fine, that I had moved on, and not to call me ever again. I got off the phone, sobbing, like it was a happy dream one has, only to find out the sad truth upon awakening. But, this made me decide to forge ahead. I started feeling a little stronger. I planned to reinvent myself as a single, individual person.

All the way through to the winter of 1989, a whole year, we stayed apart. I was working at a popular toy store and living with my parents. My life had a gentle ebb and flow. I was not the happiest, but I was getting by. It was around this time that I received another phone call from Ruby.

"How are you doing?" she asked me. Her voice was gentle, it felt real.

"I am doing just fine." I stopped and waited. What was she going to say? Why was she calling?

"My aunt died," she said.

"Oh no, I'm so sorry," I said. "That is so sad. How's your mum with it all?"

"She's having a tough time," she said. "Listen, do you want to go for a coffee or something?" She paused. "I really miss you. I think of you a lot, and wonder how you're doing."

I couldn't believe what was happening. What was I to say? I pinched my arm. Was this real, or was it just another dream? Apparently, it was real. We agreed to meet later that day. I was ecstatic! No matter how well-adjusted without her I had thought I had become, I was still under her spell.

***

I don't think I cracked that nutshell until she moved to the UK to be with her boyfriend in 1996. Ruby Tuesday would be out of my life for four years or so, though we figured out the Internet and email and corresponded regularly. I visited on a few occasions—times when I would also see my brother Alan, who was teaching at Exeter, after finishing his studies at Oxford—and met her baby girl, who was born in 1998.

They—Ruby, her husband, and their daughter—moved back to Canada in 2000, settling in an old house about three blocks from Edison. We would sit on the porch at night, after their daughter was asleep, and sip red wine and talk about life, enjoying the warm air and the constant buzz of crickets.

And today, with a second child, they live a happy life out in the country, west of the city. I am in that life, but I am not the centre. I wouldn't want to be, now, ever. During the four years that she had lived in London, I took on different friends, had a boyfriend named Stagger Lee, was hospitalized on numerous occasions, and changed jobs. I grew into myself, stronger than ever, happy to email Ruby, to visit her on occasion, but to be completely separate. I think Dr. G. helped immensely with this, worked out the kink of my neediness, created a person that, despite growing illness, could stand alone in herself. He erased any trace of a personality disorder that I might have had, helping me use my full self to fight off my demons.

It took that 4-year break in our friendship, and a restart, to achieve the close-as-sisters-but-in-a-healthy-way friendship that we have today. And whenever we go to a coffee shop, a bookstore, or an antiques shop together, no matter what I add to the conversation, the owner will invariably turn to her and direct what they say to her. It is something I have come to expect, and I am fine with it. Her personality is a little more magnetic than mine.

I visited her just recently, in the country house in Almonte. When I arrived, I parked and then went to the top of the hill to spot them. They were just coming up along the path, Reggie the dog weaving in and out of the space between them. Ruby had a hat on, a jacket, and baggy trousers tucked into hiking boots. She had a wood stick in her hand, and her hair was down. They were all smiles and greetings, tea being made immediately, all of us getting caught up.

***

I often wonder what impact this toxic friendship had on my illness. Did the wild intensity of it destabilize me at a critical time in my youth? Ruby was very much part of my illness at first, in 1994 and 1995, sharing an apartment with me in Ottawa's Glebe neighbourhood, having to call an ambulance on several occasions. But earlier than that, as we blazed through our teens: How would my illness have been different if I had never met her, never had that needy, codependent friendship? A relationship that was beyond the usual intensity of relationships in one's youth.

These days, I talk to Ruby maybe once a week or so, text with her more often than that, and see her every couple of months. We have figured out what is comfortable for us, finally, after all these years.

Chapter 9

I now know what it's like to fall asleep at all the wrong times. During his final years, in the late eighties, with plenty of drugs in his body, my dad would drift off when company was over, fall away to sleep, only to be awakened by me yelling at him. Or at least speaking loudly. But yelling is what I remember; whether that is something confabulated or not, I will never know.

In front of The National on CBC, or even better, CNN with all its breaking-news urgency, I am now the one to drift off to sleep, sedating drugs running through my own blood. Sitting beside my mum, she will call out to me to wake up, to which I will drool out the words, "I'm not asleep." Finally, I will admit it, and get up and go to bed properly.

Why was I so harsh on my dad? Was I embarrassed, afraid to look at our guests and their reactions to my dad's drowsiness? Was I worried that he was having a stroke right then and there? Or was I angry with him, angry that he was dying and didn't seem to be doing much about it?

***

Back in 1979, we knew little about the disease that would hijack my father's body for the rest of his life. His doctors worked to keep up with his illness through the years, to stay on top of his shredding aorta, his weakening heart. He had a good medical team, and in retrospect, he got a lot of time here on Earth, some good years, certainly more than was expected.

I was nine when he had his first surgery, and 22 when he died in the fall of 1991. His first episode—a heart attack that led to bypass surgery, which exposed an aortic aneurysm ready to blow—uncovered the family disease that felled his own father in 1942.

At the age of 12, my dad witnessed my grandfather's collapse on the family farm outside of Boston. They were burning some brush out on the land, and my dad had to run for help. My grandfather died later in hospital, and my dad always felt guilt that he had been so helpless at the time, that he had not run fast enough. As the oldest child in the family, he should have been the one to rescue his father, to keep him alive longer than the hours he ended up having. I know that stayed with my dad his entire life. But there was nothing the doctors could do—the aneurysm was fatal.

I would have loved to take away my dad's sense of failure. I know all too well the complicated emotions that surround the illness and death of a parent.

Growing up, after that first event in 1979, I lived with an anxiety about my father's declining health and what felt like his imminent death. It was a steady presence in my life. It was an anxiety I shared with my two brothers, Alan having been just 13 during the first wave and Jeffrey only 6, though it expressed itself in different ways in each of us, even to this day. It was an anxiety that lasted the 12 years until my father's death.

My mum struggled when my dad ended up in the hospital, struggled with her own feelings, all the while trying to stay positive for the three of us kids. Granny and Papa stepped in, as did uncles and aunts, and close family friends.

The community stepped in, neighbours and bosses and mere acquaintances. Throughout my father's bouts of illness, on and off during those 12 years, we experienced such love and support—it was nothing short of amazing, and in retrospect, I realize how truly blessed we were.

After the first heart attack in '79, my mum wrote my teacher, offering an explanation as to why my behaviour might be off. This teacher gathered my class in a circle and read the note out loud. I died a million deaths.

During my teenage years, I would often lie in bed, thinking about my dad and how long he had to live. If he could just make it to when I was in my thirties, I would pray, then that would be okay. He would see me grow up, get married, have children, have a career. He would see me happy. And he would be happy. We would still play music together, talk about things we were interested in: geography, history, food, family. I could accept his death at that point; I would be at an okay age to lose him.

***

The spring of 1988 was a particularly rough time in my father's life. He had several conditions that needed quick treatment. He had had a series of small strokes. His renal arteries had aneurysms in them. But the most serious was a large aneurysm they found in his aorta as it runs through the abdomen, and it was a significant one.

The best vascular surgeon in the city was to do the surgery to repair it, and he happened to be an old family friend. That made it particularly difficult for both him and my father, and the two men talked it over for quite some time. And then it was suddenly a go. My mum stayed with my dad as he was being prepped to go into surgery, until they wheeled him out of his room and into the operating room. In the downstairs cafeteria, my uncle sat with me and my brothers and Granny and Papa. He explained the procedure to us, breaking it down so that we were able to see the gravity of the situation. He told us that there was a chance my dad would not survive the surgery.

I remember how frightened I was. It was 24 hours of sheer terror. We saw him afterward in recovery, and I didn't like to see all the tubes and monitors he was hooked up to, his yellowed surgery skin. He was not out of the woods yet, apparently; the next day or two would be critical.

***

My grandparents were celebrating their fiftieth wedding anniversary at the very end of that April. The whole family, all the aunts and uncles and cousins, was getting together at an inn in the lovely town of Gananoque to mark the occasion. It was a month after my father's surgery, and he was given a tentative green light from his doctors. He could attend the party but had to stay as sedentary as possible. Rest in his room a lot. I remember how weak he really was, how he still had a ways to go in his recovery.

It is amazing to me that my dad got an extra three and a half years of life after that surgery. These were months that he almost lost. Time with his wife and kids, time with friends, time at work. These were all bonus months, as far as I'm concerned.

My brothers and I live in the shadow of our father's illness. All three of us undergo screening on a regular basis for the family curse by way of an echocardiogram, checking our aortic health. Climbing into our fifties, we feel it more urgently.

***

In September of 1991, Ruby Tuesday and I stuffed our second-hand hatchback with a load of things, including little bottles of vinegar (for french fries), maple candy (for gifts), and a whack of Canadian cigarettes. There were thousands of kilometres stretched out ahead of us and many months to explore them, the established, storied routes that circled around the US. This would be the ultimate road trip.

Why did I think I could do this? We had plans to do some waitressing in California once we got there. How long did I think I could be gone? So fresh off my dad's recent spate of trouble, his hospitalization in the middle of that summer for a failing heart—how could I just drive off like that?

For his part, my dad was thrilled that our first destination would be the southern states. His mother's family came from there, mainly Georgia and South Carolina, but he himself had never been. He loaded me up with genealogical materials, graveyards in Charleston, old portraits in Augusta. And he was thrilled that we were going to travel through Appalachia, from where he got so many of his legends and folk songs.

We bought Dylan's *The Basement Tapes* in New Hampshire, and it went into heavy rotation, along with our carefully curated music tapes—a collection we had been working on since the beginning of summer.

***

It was in Athens, Georgia, that Ruby and I got into a massive argument. Over what, I do not recall, but I do remember it was very intense. When I went to bed that night, I was unable to sleep. I started to cry as I lay there in the dark, so hard that I was hit with visual waves of sadness wiping over me. This was not about Ruby and our fight. What I was seeing while I wept were spotty images of my dad, images that seemed to move in time and place, back and forth, all the way back to when I was a child. A sense of my father washed over me so intensely, I could barely breathe. It was tinged with such sadness and what felt like regret—regret and loss. Somehow, I fell asleep, and when I woke up the next day, the visions were gone.

We ended up in a youth hostel in Memphis several weeks later. Our plan was to stay a while, then take Highway 61 down to New Orleans. On the first night in Memphis, we went downtown to hear some music on Beale Street. That was a lot of fun. The next day, after a day of kicking around various places, checking out some ducks in elevators and recording studios, we stopped at a liquor store to get a few bottles of wine. Falling into conversation with two of the clerks, we were told to go to the other end of the city to hear some "real" music. We had made friends at the hostel with two American women who drove a Volvo station wagon, and an older woman from Germany, and the five of us headed out to the bar later that night.

Feeling suddenly very far away from Ottawa, I excused myself to make a call home, and went into the doughnut shop that shared the parking lot with the club. Ruby came with me. I asked the waitress if I could use the phone to make a quick call and was handed an old rotary-style phone that barely stretched onto the counter, in the middle of all the patrons, all of whom were staring at me.

It was Jeffrey who answered and accepted the collect call. His voice sounded strained, pinched. "We've been trying to reach you," he told me. "We've been leaving messages at the hostel—didn't you get any of them?"

"No, I don't think they're very good with guests there." I was more than feeling far away now, now I was filled with dread.

"It could be any minute," he said quietly. "He's in the hospital, and he could die at any minute."

"Oh my God," I said, stunned.

"You have to come back right away. Go to the airport, and Mum will pay for a ticket. Just go now."

"Where is Mum? Can I talk to her?" I asked.

"Just go to the airport now," was all he said.

I hung up the phone, turned slowly to Ruby, the sounds and faces of the diners around me melting away. "We've got to go. My dad is going to die. We have to go right now." I started to break down. "I can't go back in there. I can't face all the people. Go, go, tell them." We were outside again, I was walking to the car.

She was inside the club for an eternity. I leaned against the car, no tears, just dry heaves, waiting for her. She finally came out, our purses in hand.

"Okay, let's go," she said, slipping behind the wheel.

"I am so, so sorry. I hope you told them that. I feel like a real pain." I was watching her as we got on to the main road.

"No! Don't say that. There is nothing to be sorry about. We just have to figure out how to get home."

"I am not flying home, that's for sure. Oh, God, I'm ending our road trip! I am so sorry. This means it's all over. Only one month. Fuck."

Ruby got out of the car when we were back at the hostel, heading up to pack our things and pay for our stay. I pulled out our road atlas, the interior light on in the darkness, trying to figure the best route home. Nashville, Louisville,

Cincinnati, Detroit. Then into Canada, where I could relax a bit, still hours to go, but familiar territory, the hurdle of the US behind us.

"I gave them hell," she said as she got back into the car. "They knew the whole time. Assholes. 'But it's our policy,'" she mimicked.

I lit up another smoke, showed her the route home. "I will have to call my mother soon, she's expecting me to fly home. I don't even know how to fly home from here. At least two flights I am sure, and I am sure the whole trip would be hours and hours. It's just better to drive." At least we were doing something, we were moving—no sitting around in airports for ages.

Nineteen hours later, I dropped Ruby off at her parents and drove the familiar streets home. I walked in the front door and saw a large number of family members in the living room, dining room chairs pulled out for service. My mum came to me, breaking down. "I've been so worried about you." She had stayed up all night, insisting that I call her every hour so that she knew where I was, that I was safe. "Of course, you'll want to go see him right now," she said.

***

I had 17 days with my father. He had been given a death sentence—maximum 6 months, all of them in hospital. He needed a new heart, but the surrounding tissues were like thin slices of cheese and trying to sew the slices would never hold.

We never talked about him dying, but I knew that he was utterly terrified. He had not made his peace with it. That, above anything, breaks my heart.

We got the call during the night: "Come to the hospital

right away." We were greeted with, "We worked on him for 33 minutes. Nothing more could be done." I kissed his cheek as he lay there in his hospital bed.

The next morning, Alan was on a plane home from England, and family and friends gradually filled our house until there was almost no room left.

***

Sometimes I think it is a good thing that my father never saw me grow up. But when I express these thoughts to others, they react strongly. They tell me he would have loved me through anything, including a serious psychiatric illness. That he would have been proud of me, despite my missing every major milestone along the way.

This is what they tell me. And given who my father was, I know it is true.

Chapter 10

All the way up into my early twenties, I remained a virgin, which was a source of great inner humiliation and pain. All those years, I had never had a boyfriend, never danced with a guy at high school dances. I had had many crushes, serious crushes, but unrequited love was always the card I drew. Since the age of 13, every time my family went down to the beaches of Maine and the beautiful town of Peterborough in New Hampshire, I would fantasize about a mystery man, a marine biologist or an ornithologist. It would usually be someone older, handsome, and sexy. One who would find me hot and beautiful and impossible to resist. But alas, it never happened.

Looking back, I see darker elements in my life that may have contributed to my sexual innocence. I had been sexually assaulted twice, once when I was six, the other when I was 20. I think those two events set me up for a brain full of confusion and doubt about my sexuality and my ability to handle sexual situations. I am better now, today, though in order to enjoy sex, I must be either high in mood, or high on alcohol. I know that that is not right, it is not healthy. It does not sound 'better.' But, it seems to be the only way for me.

When I was six years old, I was playing at a local park with my two friends from down the street. We were mucking about in the sandbox when a man approached us, scruffy in jeans and a lumberjack shirt, hair brushing his eyes.

"Come with me," he said to me. "There's something cool I want to show you." He held out his arm, flexing his hand so that I could grab it.

Being trusting and probably a bit curious, I went with him into the rundown building on the southern slope of the park. We walked down a couple of hallways, past studios and workout rooms, and went into the men's washroom.

I kind of hesitated. "I can't go in this room," I said, doubtful.

"Nah, you're with me, so it's okay," he said.

The next part is a bit hazy in my mind. I have some basic memories, some images, but no dialogue to go with them, no photos to explain. I know he was sitting on one of the toilets in a stall, and I was on his lap. I remember his fingers, his hand, and I remember his mouth as he kissed me on the lips. Very murky after that, the next thing really is walking out into the sunshine, holding his hand, and being reunited with my friends.

And then I did a terrible thing. I said to the man, "Why don't you invite them inside with you? They need a chance too."

The man shrugged, said, "Okay," and motioned for the others to follow him. I played in the sand, trying to make myself as filthy as I felt in my head.

They came back soon, too soon, I thought, and the man took off. "So, what happened?" I asked my friends.

"Oh, we looked at the kiln and saw all the pottery ready to go in," one of them said. "Then he said we had to come back and talk to you."

"That's it?" I asked. I don't even think I felt relief for my friends. Instead, I felt anger. Why just me? Why couldn't he have done those things to the others? It somehow didn't seem fair.

Today, when I look back at my six-year-old self, I can forgive her. But it took a long time to get to forgiveness. For many years, I thought I was manipulative and slightly evil. I didn't understand why I had done any of the things I did that afternoon, but now I do. What had happened to me was awful, and I didn't want to be the only one to have to make sense of it. I was only six. I was scared and scared of being alone in it. At least, that is how I justify it now. That's all I've got.

When I was 20, in the spring of 1990, Ruby Tuesday and I hitchhiked around Europe for three months. It had been a bumpy ride in terms of our friendship, but the trip was amazing, from my family in Hamburg to the poverty of Eastern Slovakia, the beauty of one month on the Greek island of Naxos, and time in Eastern France. We were hitchhiking from northern Germany toward Paris to catch our flight back home when at a rest stop we took a ride with two men on their way to Brussels. One of them, Pierre, lived there, and the other one, his cousin Marcel, lived in Paris. Tracy Chapman was playing on the car stereo system when we got in—I still can't hear the song "Fast Car" to this day without my stomach turning a bit sour.

When we arrived in Brussels, we agreed to stay with them for the night, so we dropped off our stuff and headed out on the town. We dined in the historic centre and went bar-hopping. We communicated in French, which worked for all of us. It was adding up to a fantastic night, but Ruby did not hold her liquor very well, and after vomiting on the tiled entrance to the apartment when we got back, she passed out. Pierre pulled out of the evening too and headed to bed. That left me with Marcel.

"How about some wine?" he asked. "I have a nice white here, from Burgundy." He held up a bottle to show me, began to open it. Bringing the wine and two glasses over, he sat beside me on the sofa. The television was on, but muted. It looked to be music videos.

We started drinking, adding to the wine we had already had while hitting up the bars earlier in the evening. I had a first, a second, a third glass. Marcel kept opening bottles, and I kept on drinking.

"Wow," I said, "I think I'm getting drunk!"

Marcel laughed, so did I. "What do you think, baby?" he asked, moving closer to me. "You are very beautiful." He reached his hand out and brushed my long hair off my face.

"I'm thinking that I need more wine!" I said. More came, it was flowing steadily that night. Marcel kept stroking my hair. I tried to stay sexy, fanning his fire.

He came closer. "Je t'aime," he said, "Je t'aime." He kept repeating this, leaning over to whisper it in my face. He went in for a kiss, a lingering one on my newbie lips. He sat back and laughed, saying, "You are driving me crazy! You are so, so hot." He came in for another kiss, tilting my chin up with his fingers. It was all becoming very real, very quickly. Soon, we were flat-out kissing, which felt so scary to me, setting off panic alarms inside my brain.

This has to stop, I thought. *This can't happen.* I started to pull away.

"Marcel! What are you doing?" I asked, still trying to sound sexy. My head was spinning from the wine, from his touch. It was getting hard to coordinate my arms and my hands; bringing the wine glass to my mouth becoming difficult to execute. I put the glass on the table, and put my arm over his shoulder, figuring out how to kiss him back. It felt good, his kisses, but I had nowhere familiar to place them. That file simply did not exist.

"Je t'aime," he cooed in my ear. He moved in even closer, placing his hand on my collarbone, rubbing my neck and my shoulder, using his fingers to slide my bra strap down my arm.

I giggled when he started kissing my neck. It tickled, it felt so good, and it felt very, very frightening. One thing was leading to another. Soon, he was fondling my breast, his hand under my blouse—how it got there, I didn't know. I broke away, trying to get out from under his weight.

"Hey Marcel, we've gotta stop this," I said, trying to laugh at the situation, but my words were slurred from the drink. He was now practically in my lap, working at the buttons, telling me over and over how much he loved me.

"Hey, let's stop this!" I said, feeling pinned by his weight, his head moving down my body, kissing me. "Let's stop this now," I said. But he was using both his arms now, pushing me off the sofa, onto the floor.

"Je t'aime," he murmured, sliding half of my top to the side. He was now completely on top of me, he was a big guy, he weighted me down so that I couldn't move.

"Stop! Please stop!" I was trying to say, pushing at his chest, trying to get him off me. He started kissing me again, shoving his tongue into my mouth, moving it around in there, taking away my ability to form words and speak. I was suffocating under him, and I couldn't breathe through my mouth. So, I bit him. I chomped down as hard as I could on his tongue, and I tasted his blood immediately.

He yelled out, no words, just an animal-like cry. His right hand came down towards my head, striking me at my temple, at the side of my face, hard. "Fucking bitch!" he spat out at me.

It was at this point that Ruby walked in, and when she saw us both lying there nursing our wounds, she didn't say a word, just turned around and left. I got up and ran after her, struggling into my top, and exited the building to the front steps. Ruby was standing there with Pierre, and I could tell she was not happy.

I started crying, tried to explain what had happened. Tried to defend myself for being topless with a man I had met the afternoon before, operating on alcohol fumes. It didn't look good, I knew, but still, I had to explain, explain how I got in way, way too deep.

"That wasn't me in there," I said, pulling in the tears. "He was all over me. I couldn't stop him!" Was that true? Did I not giggle at his touch, with all my come-hither smiles? I was still kind of drunk, but I looked at her pleadingly. She had to understand this, she had to tell me, *Hush, hush, it's okay, it wasn't your fault*. She had to say that lie to me.

Instead, it was Pierre who leaned over and rubbed my shoulder. "Let's get both of you on the way to Paris. I can drive you south a bit, to a rest area, where you can hitch a ride."

Ruby was loading our bags into his car. "Maybe we can even see part of the city," she said to me. I could tell then that she wasn't mad at me, that she felt kind of bad for me. And, just like me, she was confused.

That afternoon, we ended up at a truck stop 40 kilometres north of Paris. I made Ruby call the number Pierre had given us from the payphone, to apologize to the two men. To tell Marcel how terrible I felt about the night. That it was all my fault, and I was so, so sorry. And then, I sat in the shower for over half an hour, water pouring around my shoulders, wiping emotional grit away. I was unable to cry. You see that in movies and on TV, the shower after an assault, but it's true; the shower was the only thing I could think of. I felt charred.

We made it home two days later, and my mum met us at the now defunct Mirabel airport outside of Montreal. Driving back to Ottawa, Ruby was all chatty in the front seat, whereas I remember sitting behind my mum, staring out the window, feeling flat, feeling nothing.

I feel for my 19-year-old self. She was a beautiful woman. She was a flirt. She loved to drink. But she didn't ask for it. Any of it. Or, that is what I mostly think. I know it is the correct thing to think, it is the thing that I would say to anybody else in the same situation: "You were not asking for it." But when it comes to my own truth, I sometimes wonder. Surely, I had led him on. Surely, I had been playing a game that only women could handle. And I had definitely not been a woman. It is too bad the trip ended as it did. It had been a wonderful time that now is forever tainted.

Chapter 11

A year after my dad's death, in 1991, when I was almost 23, my family went on holiday to Italy. We rented a house outside the town of Montepulciano, an ancient house of stone with farm buildings on the grounds. The caretaker met us there. Romolo spoke no English but loved to talk. He looked around at us and seemed to ask where our father was. We all stood still, heads down. My mum, my two brothers, me. Finally, I looked him in the eye and said solemnly, "La Papa es morte." He understood right away. My grade nine course in Latin finally paid off. I think I used all the romance languages put together when I declared that my father was dead. It was the first time in months that I had made such a declaration.

We had a wonderful time in Italy, exploring Rome, Perugia, and Tuscany. Afterward, we headed north to Hamburg, where we had a tiny bit of family left on my mum's side. And then we drove straight to England, crossing the Channel to Dover by ferry. Our destination was Oxford, to celebrate Alan's graduation, having earned his masters degree in philosophy. Over the days that followed, things were all a bustle with the ceremony and honours and parties and celebrations. My three grandparents were there. So was Ruby Tuesday, who was working as a nanny in London. Some of my mum's siblings were there, my aunt and a few cousins.

We visited an old family relation, and during tea, I excused myself to use the washroom. I saw that there was a scale in the little room, so I weighed myself. This being Britain, and this cousin being very British, the scale was not in kilos or pounds, but in stones. Fortunately, I knew that one stone equalled 14 pounds. I weighed in at nine and a half stone. That meant that I weighed 133 pounds. I was stunned. All the eating, the drinking—how could this be? I was happily amazed.

***

After Oxford, we all went in different directions. I went to London to stay with Ruby Tuesday before I made plans to carry on to Ireland. She was on holiday herself, the family that she was nanny for away in France, and she had this splendid house in Clapham all to herself. Although London was not new to me, I definitely saw a lot of interesting things with Ruby that I never would have as an "ordinary" tourist. I got a taste of her London: little tea bookshops, puppet theatres, pottery shops, small "ethnic" neighbourhoods. It was fantastic. This was in July of 1992 and my twenty-third birthday, and as a gift, Ruby handed me two tickets to Dublin, a single for me and a return for her. I had been hoping to work in Ireland, had plans to look when I got there. So exciting and terrifying. Little did I know that the next months would be the best of my life. And little did I know that I would be experiencing my first clear-cut episode of mania.

***

The taxi from the airport into Dublin showed a city waking up, the rougher neighbourhoods in the north, where I imagined U2 once hung out, the maze through the centre, and finally our B&B in Rathmines, south of the Liffey. After depositing our bags, we went exploring. I realized I loved Dublin, but I did not want to live or work there. I felt crowded in by the city and longed to be out in the countryside in some romanticized version that I had of rural Ireland.

I had obtained an Irish work visa back in Ottawa, and it came time for the interview with the employment counsellor in Dublin. I was fairly nervous but knew what I wanted, and she was easy to be with. We talked about her trip to Canada, where she visited Toronto and Vancouver. We joked about the fact that they were about 4,000 kilometres apart. Ireland, she said, was much more compact. However, she noted, the jobs outside the city were coming to an end now as we moved closer to the last days of August. People who had worked at resorts and restaurants would be heading back to town soon. I must have looked crestfallen, because she lowered her voice and told me to hang on for a minute. While she was gone, I thought of being barkeep somewhere in Dublin, pulling pints for locals. Although that would probably be pretty fun, it just didn't sit well with me.

She came back 15 minutes later. Again, she lowered her voice. She told me about her friend Samantha who lived in a village on the West Coast. She was looking for somebody to staff her shop and look after her young son. This would all be under the table; Samantha would give me room and board, as well as an allowance each week. I accepted the job immediately. I had four days to prepare.

I was elated when I met up with Ruby afterward. We

combed bookstores and read travel guides, looking up the village of Roundstone, in a faraway place called Connemara, in County Galway. We checked out buses and planned my route. And then we went shopping. I bought a waxed jacket that I ended up loving for years. I got proper boots. When it came time to leave, Ruby and I parted ways with promises to keep in close touch. She left for the airport, and I grabbed my bus, destination Galway City.

***

The bus cut straight across the country and took five or six hours. We drove through the outskirts of Dublin, past rolling greens with horses, and towns not as pretty as the towns I had seen in England but still nice enough. All new to me, which was the whole point. A place to stop and get food, potato chips, and a water, and several packs of smokes. I liked Silk Cuts, purple. Back on the bus, more towns, scenery, encampments of Irish Travellers. Finally, we arrived at the Galway bus depot. It was there that I switched to a bus headed toward Clifden. I wondered vaguely how I would know where to get off, but I wasn't too worried. I would figure it out.

Roundstone was hard to miss. The bus stopped at the pier, and there were many people mucking about, waiting for friends or family. I grabbed my bag from the luggage compartment and scanned the crowd for a blonde woman, early thirties. And there she was, suddenly, Samantha, with her long hair and the seventeen-month-old boy in his stroller.

She lived down the hill in a small development that was built inside the walls of an old monastery, the tower remaining, which was where she had her shop. I had my own bedroom, one that had views over the harbour and the mountains beyond. I went for a long walk that day. Connemara was the most beautiful place I had ever seen, and I had been to a lot of places. There were the 12 mountains, The Twelve Bens; there was the Roundstone bog, where many who were lost had perished; and the wild, wild Atlantic crashing against the rocky shore. I crossed between two grazing cows and stood on the rocks with my arms outstretched, face to the sun, the seafoam spraying all over me. This was the place for me.

Samantha and I agreed that I would work five days a week, that some of it would be in her tourist curios shop, but most of it would be taking care of Peter, her little boy. I would receive 60 Irish pounds a week, plus room and board.

The first evening I was there, the whole village was celebrating the twenty-second birthday of Jed, a local carpenter who worked with his father. And I was invited. Such hospitality these people showed, what I believe was a true kindness and openness.

Samantha's wealthy family owned a house on a beach, right beside a cemetery. There were no neighbours as the season was over. I was sent there with little Peter to give his mother some space so that she could be creative. Two men were summoned to bring their van round and take me and Peter, plus all our gear, out to the beach house. Pat and John were so helpful, lighting me a turf fire, checking the gas for the cooker, and helping me set up the little guy's room. Afterward, in my room, I brushed my long hair out down my back, pulled in close to the mirror to check myself out.

Not bad, I thought.

I went into the living room, where I found the two guys sitting with a bottle of whiskey, a toasty fire roaring in the large fireplace.

"Are you in for a drink?" John asked. "We're just kind of making ourselves at home here. Hope you don't mind!"

"Not in the least," I said smoothly.

They poured me a glass, and the three of us fell into easy conversation. They shared stories about their fellow villagers, gave me the history of the more prominent ones.

I was feeling very warm, inside and out. I was so incredibly drawn to Pat, the quieter of the two, the feeling nearly ran me over. I had never experienced anything like it in my entire life. It was pure desire, and it was in real time, for someone who was actually living and within reach and wanting me back. Never before had the stars lined up as such for me.

John filled my glass again, and looking at Pat, excused himself to do some work in the kitchen, though I am not sure there was anything really there to work on. All three of us knew that it was simply an excuse to leave us alone together, me and Pat. I held up my glass of whiskey, Pat held up his, and we toasted the night ahead. I was smiling a smile that I knew was sexy, and our conversation became ragged, like panting for breath.

"Should we head up to my room, give poor John some space?" I said, my eyes dancing, my lips puckered for a kiss that was yet to come.

"Let's go," Pat said. We both stood up at the same time, and he put his hand on my back to guide me, and the touch was startling, yes, like electricity, but still different. Another first for me, the touch of a lover.

In the bedroom, I acted as if it wasn't my first time; I had seen enough movies, read enough books, heard enough stories, that I could manage that. I was flying along as we progressed, using my long hair seductively. When we were joined together,

I was feeling completely in control. This was my game.

And in no way did I feel dirty or disgusting. It was pure bliss, the way it was meant to be.

So, there it was, the loss of my virginity in a beach house in the middle of Connemara. Replaying this event in my today brain, I cannot think of anywhere better where I could have been deflowered.

***

The next man in my life was Phil, a thirty-nine-year-old Anglo-Irishman from Dublin who loved to head west in his blue Jeep every weekend, the smell of money drifting off him wherever he went. I met him at O'Dowd's, by the turf fire in the back of the pub, passing Jed and his sharp blue eyes on the way there.

Phil and I fell into conversation. We talked horses and horse racing, which was his father's realm in County Meath. "I had wanted to be a jockey," he told me. "But, I was too tall. By this much," he showed me with his fingers—a centimetre, max. Yes, he was kind of short.

"One of my uncles is really into horses and horse racing," I said. "The two of us used to hole ourselves up in my grandparents' place, upstairs with the TV." I could smell the bratwurst Papa would cook on his little hibachi in the back garden, floating up into the room. "My uncle told me all about the races," I continued, "The Kentucky Derby, and The Triple Crown, Secretariat and Man o'War. It was pretty neat."

Phil was full of surprises. Sometimes he would show up in his Jeep, ask me to get in, and take me closer and closer to the mountains. When we would finally stop at the base of one, he would grin and suggest a little walk. Another time, we borrowed someone's currach, rowed out to a deserted island, and took up residence in one of those quaint whitewashed cottages, green paths and animals all around. In fact, the next morning during breakfast, Jack the donkey came in through the open door.

Jed and I hooked up while I was with Phil. Not that that stopped me and my wonderful sexual energy. Over my three months there, I slept with quite a few guys, more than making up for my late start. Looking back on my promiscuity, I realize it was part of what was turning out to be my first manic episode, for which a highly charged sexuality is a very common symptom. I didn't know that at the time, didn't know it for quite some time, but there it is. A manic episode that I experienced as a glowing, solid-gold energy. I didn't wreck anybody's life, thank God, but I could have wrecked everything if it hadn't come to a sudden end.

Oh, the energy I had. Pushing the stroller the couple of kilometres from the beach house into town to pick up groceries. Following the school bus as it crossed the bridge onto Inishnee, an Irish-speaking island with a white horse framed beautifully by sea and mountains. Waiting for the bus to take me into Clifden, Connemara's largest town, to go clothes shopping. I hailed the bus, pulled the latch and door open, swung the stroller into the hold, slammed the door shut, got on the bus, paid the driver, and took a seat, the whole time with Peter on my hip. At home, my anxiety would have prevented me from doing any one of those steps.

Why was I so self-assured and smooth? How did I let the anxiety fall away like that, in fact not even considering that it could be there in the first place? I was a different person in so many ways. It was lovely, but I couldn't keep up with it. Mania does that to you.

The energy was taking a bit of a toll on me. I was finding

it hard to settle down, to stay still. I was knocking back three or four pints of Guinness every night and would lie awake for hours with a pounding headache. When I took Peter to the travelling doctor for an ear infection, I scored a script for a benzodiazepine to help me sleep. I went through the bottle quickly and had to ask the doctor two more times for more until he said no. Then it was on the bus to Clifden, visiting a doctor with the same story for the same prescription. When I wasn't with Peter, I was hitching rides with the locals, climbing castle ruins believed to have once been owned by Gráinne (Grace) O'Malley. And so I hitched into Galway City, where there were two doctors who each gave me a prescription. I filled them in separate pharmacies before hitching back home.

My stay was punctuated by a trifecta of village parties, the first being Jed's birthday bash. The second one was in October, with the Galway Hookers—beautiful boats with rust-coloured sails—racing out in the bay. I had hung around all day with Ian, an SCTV Chicago man who had me laughing all the time. We got our pints from O'Dowd's and then crossed the street to drink them along the harbour wall. I went through three packs of smokes that night, my voice left hoarse for three days. Later, the village filled a huge room, and gorgeous music was played. An old man stood in the middle and sang a song in Irish, his voice hitting each note with precision, despite my anxiety for him. Ian and I took the bus into Clifden that night, a bus that had already done a tour of villages and hamlets across southern Connemara. It was a Saturday, which meant disco night, a ritual that would last until two in the morning, then the chip stand, then the bus back to Roundstone and beyond.

Ruby Tuesday visited in the second week of November.

She flew into Shannon, rented a car, and drove to Galway City, where we met up at a bar. We had a fabulous time, me showing her all the places that meant something to me, all the places of profound beauty. Looking back at those weeks, and listening to how Ruby describes them today, I was behaving in what some would call overly friendly behaviours. But, there was nothing wrong with that, and Ruby chalked it up to me being in a very, very good mood.

***

While Ruby was visiting me, it came to be the first anniversary of my father's death, the tenth of November. I felt a long way away on this day, and very alone, even though Ruby was there. Before I met up with her, I gave my mum a call from the office upstairs at Samantha's, knowing it was early for her.

"Oh, sweetie, it is so good to hear your voice. Things are not good here," my mum said into the phone. "I was in emergency all night." She paused. "You have to call back in a couple of hours, give me some time."

I was completely confused. "What do you mean, Mum?" I asked, on guard. "Why were you in emerg? What's going on?"

"I was crawling around, vomiting blood, in such pain. They got me to the hospital. They did a couple of tests, and it looks like something is wrong with my kidney. I am just about to go for another test, and we'll know more about it in a few hours." She sounded withdrawn, maybe a bit scared, something I had only heard in her voice a few times in my life. "Okay, so phone me later. I am so sorry. How are you doing today?" she asked. "I know what today is."

We chatted a bit more, and then I headed out the door to

meet Ruby at her B&B. I was upset but managed to put it aside. We took a road that meandered through the bog all the way into Clifden, where we stopped for lunch. After some nice smoked salmon and a pint, we took a gorgeous road out of town, circling alongside the water, with stunning views of mountains and islands. Toward the end, when we went around a bend, I couldn't believe it. An English-style red phone box in the middle of nowhere. It was time to phone my mum back.

This time, she sounded fine. She had Papa and Granny over, they were apparently helping her out, though why she needed help was still a mystery to me.

I stared at the water down the bank, calm, not the wild ocean that I had grown to love so much. "Okay," I said, "How are you? What's going on? You sound so much better!"

"Jocy, I am sorry, but they found a tumour on my kidney. They're pretty sure it's cancer. My parents are here, my brothers are here. And you, you should think about coming home."

"I should go home," I repeated, not really understanding the weight of what she was telling me. "I don't know, I don't know how to do that. But, of course. Of course I will come home." I needed more to go on. "What will your treatment be?" I asked. I didn't want to ask what the survival rate was for her kind of cancer. Was it 50/50? Better? Worse? But, those questions didn't feel right, at least not then.

"We don't know yet. It sounds like surgery is the first thing. We don't know from there." She grew quiet. "I'm so sorry, Joc, the boys have to finish their studies. It's really only you, and of course I want you here."

We spoke for another minute or two, talked about her buying me a ticket from Dublin to get home. Alan was working on his Doctorate at Oxford, and Jeff was in first year at McGill in Montreal. They couldn't go home yet, they would have to wait for Christmas break.

I looked out and saw Ruby waiting in the car for me. What was it about road trips with her that lead to phone calls and terrible news? I got in the seat beside her, looked her in the face, and burst into tears. "It's cancer," I cried. "It's kidney cancer. I have to go home now, I have to be with her." She leaned over and put her arm around me.

"It will be okay," she murmured. I knew that she didn't have any backup for this statement, but it was what I needed to hear.

***

My last night in Roundstone was the night of the third village party—I don't remember the occasion. Jed and I had long since broken up, and I was feeling like shit. My mood had come way down after my mother's news and the fact that I had to leave. And my glands were all swollen, and I swear I was running a fever. I walked out of the party after all my goodbyes and took in the night air, that smell of turf fires that I wished I could bottle, the moon aglow.

The next day, I took the trip back to Dublin, had dinner with Phil, and crashed at his place for the night, asleep within seconds. He drove me to the airport, saw me off on my Aer Lingus flight to London, and waved at me as I went through security, his face pressed up against the glass.

When I got back to Ottawa, I hugged my mother as hard as I could, and then I went to see my GP. Mono. The kissing disease. How fucking ironic.

Chapter 12

It was lovely to see my grandparents when I returned from Ireland. They were so supportive of me and of my mum as she went through surgery to remove her diseased kidney. There were some tricky weeks in there, waiting for the pathology report: Had the cancer spread?

It hadn't. And my mum had screenings over the five years that followed and remained cancer free.

In mid-December, Alan returned from Oxford and Jeff from Montreal, and we were all together again, more or less. But, still, it was a very muted Christmas.

We passed into the New Year, it was now the winter of 1993, and I was 23. I felt somewhat low, I moped around, not sure of where I was going, but with the knowledge that I probably had to get some sort of job.

My mum and I loved to go to the ByWard Market in the centre of Ottawa to visit the seasonal displays and check out all the fun shops. One was the most fantastic kitchen store I had ever been in, all light and glass and beautiful shapes. While we went through checkout, I noticed there was a help-wanted sign at the cash. I made a mental note.

Once home, I immediately began work on my CV. I didn't have much for it, but I hoped it would do. I dropped it off at Domus the next day and crossed my fingers. The store was empty, except for quite a few staff members congregating around the cash, gossiping and chatting—I found it very intimidating to introduce myself and hand the envelope over in front of them all.

I found out later that they had opened the envelope immediately, as soon as I walked out the door. They noted my work in Ireland and found it very interesting how far I had gone with my piano studies. They had already begun gossiping about me, and I didn't even work there, at least not yet.

I got the job. I began my employment as a clerk in the back of the store, learning all about pots and pans. It took me a while to get my bearings, not only to figure out my work routine, but also my fellow workers and all the attachments, dating, flirting, and fights that were going on between them.

One of the guys downstairs in charge of shipping and receiving was a man with a thunderous laugh, to be heard throughout the store whenever it rolled out. Stagger Lee had cheeks craggy with acne scars, peroxided hair cut super-close, multiple piercings, and several items of jewellery. He was a big guy, and he cut quite the figure in his black leather coat, almost intimidating, except for the imaginary sign on his back with "Sweet Puppy Dog" printed between his shoulder blades.

I didn't know it, but I had just met the love of my life.

Stagger Lee and I began hanging out together a lot. We went for coffees together, waited at bus stops together. Later, we would go for long lunches, breaking all the rules of respect for our co-workers with our intense lateness, arguing over who had better taste in books. We would walk the streets of Lowertown, then up along the canal toward the Glebe, turning the discussion over and over. He mimicked my voice if it was turned up in anger, making me even angrier. But it wasn't a real anger. It was part of our relationship, an intensity of emotion that surprised us both, part of the way we got along on all levels.

He asked me out to dinner several weeks after my initiation into the loves and laws of the kitchen store. I asked a new friend what his request meant. Were we just going to hang out as friends at this expensive restaurant? Or was this a date-date? I decided to find out for myself.

We met at the restaurant, all white tablecloths, napkins, multiple glasses, and flatware. Stagger Lee was wearing a black suit and a crisp white shirt with a funky tie—of course, the eccentric tie. I would have expected nothing less. We awkwardly ordered from the menu. He bought me a red rose from the travelling rose peddler, and I felt even more awkward. This was definitely a date-date. Afterward, I drove him to the venue where he was working set-up for a punk show. He asked me whether I would go as his guest. He settled for a kiss, a quick one that he initiated. I sat in the car for a while after he had gone, perplexed, concerned I had set something up that was more than I could handle.

***

As we walked the city after work, our conversations would ramble. Stagger Lee told me all about his time at the Ontario College of Art & Design in Toronto, and the music scene that he had been into. His '80s music was so different from my own, as he was 6 years older than me. I spoke of Ireland, of my childhood, we compared notes on the deaths of our fathers. I introduced him to the world of a foodie, and of course, we talked about our cats. We would collapse in laughter over the slightest thing. I claimed to have an old soul, and his was a new soul. He claimed the reverse. More fighting, our little act.

We walked through the Market, up and across the canal to Elgin, over to Bank through Centretown, into Chinatown, no destination in mind.

"Hey, you want Thai food?" I asked him, finally giving us a place to land. "Siam Bistro farther up. It's really good."

"That sounds great," he replied. "How far up is it?"

"Another couple of kilometres. But I think it's going to rain soon, so maybe it isn't such a good idea," I said.

"It's not going to rain, my little one," he said.

"Yes, it is going to rain, and don't call me that."

"You don't like 'Little One'?" He started singing loudly, an ode to a Little One. People on Somerset Street were giving him funny looks. *Whatever*, I thought.

"Can't you see it in the clouds?" I persisted. "And feel the wind that's cropping up? It's all in front of you."

"Nah," he said. He had stopped singing. "Those are not rainclouds. It's just a nice sunny evening. Let's leave it at that. Why do you always have to be so negative?"

"You know nothing!" I stood there. "Those are cumulus clouds gathering ahead of us, and they will bring rain. Want to bet on it?"

"You're on! How 'bout if it does rain, I'll buy dinner." He was using his finger to poke me. "Poke, poke," he said.

I shook away. "You're on! If it doesn't rain by the time we get there, I will buy you dinner."

Over the next 20 minutes, the sky started to turn dark, and the wind started in earnest. We still had a ways to go. I was feeling pretty solid. Ten minutes out, the raindrops started. I started to sing, gleefully, I started to sing "Singing in the Rain" as we hurried along. And when we got to the bistro, I ordered the most expensive seafood curry on the menu.

***

Stagger Lee never backed down on wanting us to be a couple. There were times when he was pretty straightforward about his desires.

"Because, Jocy, I want to be with you. You know that, you know that we are perfect together. Why can't you see that?" We were walking in the snow, a soft gentle evening, and he was trying to hold my hand.

"C'mon, let's not do this again," I said. At times, it was annoying, his constant declaration of love for me. And trying to hold my hand—what were we, 12? This was our pattern. We were so close, but our friendship would sometimes veer into more romantic territory. He would sing Al Green to me, he would tickle me, he would empty his heart for me. But, I always put up a wall. I didn't want our relationship to go any farther than the slightly confusing place it already was.

He told me that the day he first saw me, he had gone home and said to his mother that he had met the girl he was going to marry.

How do you live up to that?

***

We took road trips, sometimes with Ruby Tuesday but usually just the two of us, me doing all the driving in my mum's car. This would have started in the summer of 1993, my first summer at the store, long before my illness started up in earnest. We played CDs, me trying to get him into Dylan, him testing me out on Marilyn Manson. Although Marilyn Manson was a bit of a stretch, I certainly did appreciate and grow to love many of his musical choices. He sat at my computer, downloading his huge collection of music into my iTunes, leaving me with everything from Icelandic moody to West Coast grunge, blues, jazz, and hip-hop. More than that, everything but metal, which I never did like.

Conversely, I tried to get him into "classical" music, a music for which I had such a passion. We would sit down in the living room, me making him listen, without interruption, to Beethoven's Kreutzer Sonata. How about Mozart's Jupiter Symphony, or maybe even some Dvořák? Or the easy-to-get-into nocturnes by Chopin? But I don't think that music made much of a dent in Stagger Kee. You can't love it all, I guess, though you can try it on for size.

He introduced me to so much stuff that I would never have known without his tutelage. Not only whole genres of music, which I ate up, but artwork, different galleries, a tour of his artist friends. Stagger Lee didn't just have artist friends. He was an artist. He rented studio space in a warehouse in the neighbourhood of Little Italy. He had his sketchbook, always. I remember one small one at Domus, small enough to fit into the pocket of his great black coat, filled with wondrous, dense doodles. He gifted some of his artwork to me, still on my walls today, my favourites.

Stagger Lee took care of me whenever I had an episode. He would visit me in hospital, walking the halls with his platinum pompadour, singing. He made friends on the ward, patients who would later stand in line at Domus, recognizing me, recognizing him. He always made me laugh, no matter what. Laughter was heard a lot in our relationship. He was a truly funny guy.

***

There is this wonderful photograph, taken by Ruby, of

Stagger Lee and me examining a map, folded out on top of the hood of my mother's Volvo. He is wearing a black hat and a big, burly black sweater. I am in my striped red hoody, my hair back in a ponytail. There is an old, small white church behind us with the word Letterkenny above the door. I have my hand on the map, my finger tracking our spot.

I was still living with my mum. There was a casserole of cookbook author Deborah Madison's best mac 'n cheese waiting at home on Edison. I had cooked the béchamel and grated the cheese, boiled the pasta and assembled the gratin earlier that day before we left. But it had been my first béchamel ever, and I screwed it up. It didn't thicken, no matter how much butter/flour mixture I whisked in. No matter how Julia Child I got on it. With a roar, I took the pot and the sauce down to the basement and threw it all over the ping-pong table. And started again. (Today, people search me out to make the white sauce. I have damn well perfected it.)

On that lovely day, the three of us, thick as thieves, had lunch in the main restaurant in the Polish village of Wilno. Sure enough, we feasted on pierogis and stuffed cabbage. Would we have any room for the dinner I had prepared?

***

Several years later, in the early summer of 1996, we continued with our explorations of the small roads around Ottawa. And finally I gave in. Stagger Lee had worn me down—the presents, the flowers, and more importantly, the amazing time that we were having in each other's company. We looked like a romantic couple, we did things like a romantic couple. We just weren't a romantic couple. At least, that's what I thought.

There were several weeks in there that my mum was

away at conferences, leaving me alone on Edison. I was back there again, since Ruby had left for London to embark on her new life; it was my base. I was high (it was early June). I had seen Dr. G., and we talked about ways of calming me down, no doubt some increase in whatever medication that made me chill. But I was not totally chill; I was happy and flirty, inviting Stagger Lee to come live with me for those days on Edison.

The stereo was blasting with lots of music, and I made him watch as I danced and sang along to "Thunder Road." I grabbed his hand and pulled him up beside me, forcing him to dance.

"Hold on a sec." I laughed. "I'll be right back!" I ran to the kitchen and poured myself another vodka orange. I stood there a minute at the counter, said out loud to the room, "Let's do it."

I went back to him and the music, to our dance, fortified, and yes, flirty. I leaned in and gave him a kiss on the mouth. He was totally surprised. Pulling back, he said "Hey! Hey, where did that come from?" He laughed. "I like it."

More kissing, our bodies getting closer and closer. I felt giddy, sensuous, powerful. I took his hand, led him up the stairs, down the hall to my bedroom, singing more Springsteen to him as we went. And finally, Stagger Lee won out. We had sex. I felt things that were new to me, emotions mixed in with the physical reactions. Why hadn't we done this before?

The next 10 days were lovely. Our togetherness was growing every day, my hypomania blooming. We spent time at his family cottage on the Ottawa River, cooking fabulous meals and making love on just about every bed in the cabin. Not that we confined it to beds.

But we ran into an issue. He told me I was his girlfriend, and that was what he would call me. And he wanted to tell everyone, announcing our coupledom to his friends and family. I was not so sure about that. I was enjoying my time with him and felt no need to label our relationship as one thing, to nail in the rules and regulations.

We fought as we normally did, and I initiated our very first break up, a pattern that would take place over years to come. We had this intense friendship, and when we introduced sex to it, the result was fabulous. I was happy, really happy, but I think that scared me. For some reason, I couldn't just let myself go. I couldn't allow our relationship to swallow me up. So, I broke it off.

God, how I did adore him. Right through to 2007, we were the real thing for each other. He took me to his childhood home; I met his mum and siblings. I took him to New York City to have a holiday with my own family.

And so, we continued on. We would break up and still be with each other at all times, our conversations intensified. Over one long weekend up at the cottage when we were 'just' friends, I surprised him.

"I want in," I said to him as we sat on the porch, music on loud. "I want back in."

"I don't think I understand," he said. His hair was in a long phase, tied up in a big knot, and his eyes were genuinely curious.

"I want back into our relationship. You've been right, and I have been so wrong all this time. It really is you, you that I love. I want in, I want you to marry me." I had taken his arm, looked straight in his eyes. "I love you. I want to be with you forever."

He accepted my proposal.

Later, back in my apartment, we talked weddings, guest lists; we were going to do something very non-traditional. We made music playlist after playlist. Our theme song was Lou Reed singing "I Found a Reason" from the album *Loaded*. We sang that to each other, slow dancing to it. He serenaded me with it.

But I was getting too wrapped up in our love. I was in that danger zone of happiness. And so, I called it off, called off the whole thing, including our friendship. He was crying, sobbing tears of sadness, tears of anger. This time, it took a good while to get our friendship back up and running. I know I hurt him multiple times, which pains me today.

Towards the end, towards 2007, I was living in an apartment back in Centretown, and Stagger Lee would come over after work, and we would have our routine every weekday without fail. God, how I loved this time. We were technically not together in a romantic way. We were not sleeping together, at least. But we had a lovely relationship. He would get off work—he was working at Canada Revenue Agency as the taxman, for which he was entirely unsuited—and would call me to take my order. A big bag of Ruffles, plain. A bag of peanut M&Ms. Maybe a pack of smokes, if I was low. And then we would figure out dinner. Order from the Shanghai? My usual, broccoli fried rice, a couple of spring rolls. Getting full. There was a pause in *Law & Order* reruns—or other shows we were half watching—and we would go to the gelato store, get a whole entire container each. People watched us, this fat couple going all-out on the ice cream.

He would look after Buddy and Finny when I travelled. (Buddy and Finny were the cats who had joined me after Mickey had died.) The last trip he stayed over was when I went to India. During that time, he met somebody on a dating site. I knew he was on this site and had helped him write his bio. This woman seemed to really have caught his fancy as he focused in on her, gobbling up their relationship. I was truly happy for him, though I knew that would mean our get-togethers would be over. Our relationship would change once again.

I never did meet his girlfriend. She was apparently threatened by me, my status as such a close friend and ex-lover. But they were serious. He moved in with her that fall, the fall of 2007, and I never saw Stagger Lee again. The last I heard, they had moved to the Maritimes and started a family.

Chapter 13

As I continued to work at the kitchen store, things grew serious as far as my illness went. Dr. G. saw me through the deepening lows over the years, the highs that continued to grow. I had intense depressions, breezy hypomanias. Insomnia was a problem; when we started treating it, we had no idea what a struggle sleep would be all the way up to present day. Lack of sleep seems to be a pattern no matter what kind of mood state I'm in.

I would take the number 16 bus from Edison to Dr. G.'s office. It was timed perfectly, dropping me off outside his building with 10 minutes to spare. I would shout out my depression during my appointments. It flattened me; it had me lying pinned under its weight. We worked at drug treatment. I tried many psychotropics over the years but ran into an allergy problem during this surge. I drank, had a definite drinking problem. And Dr. G. followed me down every rabbit hole I scuttled into, using "talk" therapy along with the meds, psychotherapy to become so important in my life.

He was new at this too. I got started with him early on in his practice. And I am still there, the only one left from the early days. I think Dr. G. learned from me, grew with me, especially in those years. He had to—I put him through his paces. There was severe depression, hypomania turning to mania, psychotic symptoms, anxiety, alcoholism, all coming fast and all hard to treat. It was very intense. That is definitely how I experienced it, but was unable to name it. Until now, that is.

I experienced tastes of full-blown mania behind the wheel of a car, driving fast, distracted, gesturing to the hills and small roads around me, overwhelmed by the beauty I was seeing. And after, it was time to work on my sleep, to make sure I got at least six hours a night. The high was put out of its beautiful misery with Thorazine, used as a major tranquilizer, to knock it out of me.

I fell into a routine of serious depressions, treatment-resistant, over the late nineties, nearing the end of my twenties. And then the psychotic symptoms, before they turned into full-blown psychosis, watching the raccoons.

I tried to get on CPP disability around then, in 1998, but was turned down. My illness was serious, but the cinema where I was working at the time had said they would happily keep me employed around my episodes. Now, of course, I am happy that I was turned down. I had many years at the cinema afterward, a positive experience.

***

These were the years when I was in and out of the hospital. I always had faithful visitors, mostly family, Ruby, Stagger Lee, and some friends from work. At first, I would fight it during the early days of any given trip to the psych ward (I was always on a form), but after a while, I would just give in, and let them change my meds and do whatever else to help me get back out. My hospitalizations were always stressful for my mother, trying to keep up with me and the bizarre changes I would go through. I knew she got plenty of support from family members and friends, and I would feel some relief.

My doctors worked with lithium, added to my other meds, which created a shaking, bloated, tired me. I attended a lot of occupational therapy when I was an in-patient, where I was to work on projects so that my focus skills could be assessed. I remember just playing with Plasticene, not able to do more than rubbing the dough into little balls. But obviously that changed, and I got better.

***

In the middle of all this, I had to pack up my stuff from the apartment Ruby and I had shared. She was moving to London to be with her boyfriend, and I was moving home. I was very worried about that—how would I be without Ruby? How separate would I be able to be? I had new friends from the kitchen store. Maybe that would balance it all out.

I tried to stay sober on the night before she left Canada. We had moved everything out of our apartment, cleaned it spotlessly. She was driving her parents' car, and we had pulled up to Edison.

"You going to be okay?" she asked me. "I'm really going to worry about you."

"No need to worry," I said for the umpteenth time. "There are telephones, there is my new computer. . ." I trailed off, not entirely certain that I believed myself. "So, you will go now, and I will go inside."

"You really have to be careful, Jocy," she said. "I worry about all the alcohol. It's too much. And with your meds, it's not good." She was saying this gently. I almost started to cry but held on to it.

"I'll be over in London to visit as soon as I can. But for

now, well, let's just turn it all off. Things have sort of come to an end here, and I would feel better if we could just say goodbye, and I could get out of this car." I said all this, knowing it was true.

And then we said goodbye, a quick hug, and I was back on Edison.

***

Soon after Ruby moved to London, the psychosis started. A few hours here, a few hours there. Nothing really big, but still alarming to me, my mum, and Dr. G. At this point, my experience with psychosis was only during a mood swing, when I was depressed or manic. Obviously, this was not caused by Ruby's departure, not at all, and fortunately, she wouldn't have to have a psychotic flatmate. She had already lived with me while I spun out of control on alcohol and depression—that was enough.

I would hear things that weren't real. I suddenly had a presence in my life, different people talking to me, filling my head. But I couldn't see them, no matter how I searched. Were others hearing these same things? I didn't dare ask. Sometimes I would hear one voice, but usually there were two or three, talking to each other, talking to me. Mostly, they just commented on me, coming across as cruel, or sometimes scary, when they made the world a dark, unsafe, paranoid place. But as was usual back then, they acted in concert with my depressive thoughts, echoing all the negatives in my life, narrating my days during an episode.

And I was starting to struggle with mania, unpleasant mania that went too far. Mania that would reach psychotic territory, which was often pretty scary. At the point of manic psychosis, my voices would stretch up to a level that made sorting other people's words out truly difficult. Sometimes, I felt on top of the world, powerful and entertaining. And yet, other times, the rush of it all was sending me down a dangerous line, my head spinning too quickly to be able to put the brakes on, my voices screaming at me, the sleepless nights endless.

On one occasion, in the spring of 1998, I found myself back on the psych ward, feeling rough and unruly. Dr. S. was on my case again. We were not getting along.

"Jocelyn," he said to me. "Because you are not co-operating, I am putting you on a form again. I don't want to do this. I want your stay to be voluntary, but you don't seem to be open to that option." He was very serious.

I stayed still, looking away from him. "Fine, that's fine with me. Do whatever you want. I obviously don't get a vote in this."

"I am going to have to get you a sitter. Do you really want that?" He was pushing me.

"Whatever," was all I said.

Later, after 10 days or so, Dr. S. and I had another unpleasant conversation. "So, we are talking about getting you off a form. Do you really think you can handle yourself, with your mood? I think you are pretty manic."

What was he talking about? "I am not at all manic," I stated. This idea sounded crazy to me. He was making a whole bunch of shit up.

"On a scale of 1 to 10, where would you put your mood, with 10 being really manic?" he asked me. He had another clutch of students in the room.

"Six," I said. "A nice, steady six."

"Well, I am not sure about that," he said with certainty. "I would say you are at an 8, maybe even 9. You are high up there. You know, normally you are dour, you are introverted, you keep to yourself. I understand you have had a couple of altercations with other patients. And you appear to be hearing voices. That is not a 6."

What could I say? To argue with him would only strengthen his case against me. He had all the power. I left the room feeling like a trapped animal.

It was during this hospitalization, the first time I was in that single-room corridor with my very own sitter, that a very vocal woman kept me up at all hours. She was howling profanities at the orderlies and the nurses; I could hear them discussing restraints. When I did walk by her room, I was shocked. There was a beautiful, 40-something woman, her hair in place, totally normal looking, swaying back and forth as she stood facing her sitter. I could hear another rush of profanity as I walked away down the corridor. It gave me a complete shock to see her, looking like she belonged in a business suit, her mind completely out of control. And I was only two rooms down.

Chapter 14

I am washing my cup at work, and the thought of swallowing pills plows through my mind. I dry the cup, turning to face my colleagues at the cinema where I am working.

"Should we make more coffee?" I ask. I know the smile on my face is a bit weird, but it was all I had. I walk to the coffee machine, put in a new filter, dump in the fresh bag of coffee, slide it in, press On, make sure there is a coffee pot in place. I feel robotic.

"You in for pizza?" one of them asks. I am staring at the coffee as it drips down. "Hey, hello, pizza?" My colleagues are looking at me with curiosity.

"Yeah, sure," I answer, the same weird smile. "Just running to the washroom. I'll take whatever on the pizza, no meat." I walk around the candy bar, across the lobby, into the washroom. Am I walking funny? Do they see it in me as I go by? Do they know what I am really thinking? Once in a stall, I rest my head in my hands, the full weight of dangerous thoughts hitting me in my solitude. I need to die, I need to die. But, no, I need to go back out there, I need to play-act.

Later, as we tuck into pizza, I am hit again, another wave filled with pills washing over me. I chatter away, pretending to listen, as I think of suicide. While I do the simplest of things, making coffee. Because once you have tried it, once you have tried to end your life, it is never far away, the option. It pops in at the most unusual times, as well as the obvious ones.

Try to stay and look normal. Get through it, get in the car afterward, and put hands to face, wallops of tears. Or, when walking, hold it in, hold it in still, wait till arrival at the flat, wait to let it go.

***

At the end of 1997, when I was 28, I started working part-time at an independent cinema on the edge of downtown Ottawa. Stagger Lee had wandered over to the ByTowne after he was fed up at Domus. I had been let go from the kitchen store over a year before. I followed and was honoured to find a place amongst the group of eccentric personalities working there.

The ByTowne Cinema premiered a bunch of arthouse and foreign language films every month, as well as carrying some more mainstream ones in repertory. I absolutely loved working there. Best job ever. Before I became a shift manager, there were three shifts open to me. One was candy bar, one was cash, the other was usher. I loved working as usher; I got to watch the films playing during my shift. I saw so many films (many multiple times) over the 10 years I stayed with the ByTowne. I remember the raw energy of a packed house during *Run Lola Run*, the mystified faces after *Dogville*, the silence in the auditorium following *The Pianist*. It was an incredible education for me, in film and in the ways of the world.

I made some friends there. The projectionist (with whom I would later have a fling), several colleagues who had been there longer than me, several who were newer. We would go out after our shifts to pubs in Sandy Hill or to bars in the

Market. My life was led in the late hours of the day, the early hours of the morning.

In the last three or four years of my time there, when I was in my midthirties, I worked with some colleagues who were really into playing poker, long drawn-out games held at the top of the auditorium after the last show let out. Leading up to the game, though, we were a good crew. During busy, often sold-out shows, I, as manager, would make sure that everybody did exactly what they were supposed to. We worked really hard, took it very seriously. But during the slow times, and particularly after work, we played.

The liquor store was two blocks away and on weekends stayed open until 10 o'clock. The cashier, the person who had cashed out and was finished, would take orders and money down to the liquor store—just in time—and pack a couple of bags of goodies for those of us still working, as well as their own drinks of choice. Off-duty staff and former staff began to show up, waiting for the last customer to exit the theatre, which meant it was playtime.

The long table was pulled out, stray chairs found their way, chips were sorted and counted, drinks were poured, and finally, that first cigarette was lit. Pure bliss. We used cups filled with water as ashtrays, very carefully, as we knew we weren't supposed to smoke inside.

"Okay, pay up, everybody. Three bucks to play, winner takes all," someone would say. We passed around the popcorn bowl, throwing in our loonies and toonies, someone making change for a twenty. Tunes were put on, everyone enjoying those first sips of alcohol.

"Okay," I would say. "Texas hold 'em. How much for blinds?" We dealt the first hand.

"Oh, I am all in on this, baby," the projectionist would say after a couple of drinks, a bit of a swagger.

"I call!" someone would challenge. The music played in the background, the cigarette smoke drifting to the ceiling (getting lost in the big auditorium), and the 10 or 12 of us filled ourselves up with alcohol as our fortunes rose and fell. And, at the end, someone would walk off with over 30 bucks. Not bad for a night of fun.

***

For a while, we got passes to other movie theatres—the chains—to see free films, which was a huge bonus. A friend from the cinema (who was the general manager at the time) and I went to see Moulin Rouge together. Giddy with delight at what we had just seen, we asked the manager there if we could watch the first 20 minutes again of the next screening.

The times that I was hospitalized during my tenure at the ByTowne never jeopardized my working there. My mum would phone the owner of the cinema and explain the situation. *Jocelyn is in the hospital again; it won't be for long.* He would react with kindness and tell my mum that I always had a job there.

Favourite movies: *An Angel at My Table, The House of Mirth, The Long Day Closes*. Yes, *Run Lola Run*. (I took my Granny to see that!) There were some films that had me going backstage, down to the boiler room, suddenly missing from the cleanup crew. I had gone down there because I needed to sob, needed to react to the film I had just watched.

***

I sang ABBA's "Dancing Queen" full throttle as I sped along the highway on my way to the cinema. I was neck in neck with a little red car, saw the driver look over at me a couple of times. He can hear me, I suddenly realized. They all can. They all can hear me, I thought. This was the third or fourth episode of mania I had had over the previous year or two. It was the spring of 1998, and the first time I felt people were in my head, a theme that would play itself out over and over again during psychosis as the years went by, leading up to present day. In this instance, I was experiencing what was called thought broadcasting. I turned the song up and shouted at the top of my lungs, serenading the other cars through their radios. This was thrilling—I was reaching people in a way I never had before. I kept it up, still humming ABBA when I entered the cinema doors.

Later in that shift, I was in a washroom stall when all of a sudden I heard two colleagues say something about me as they lounged in the office. "Have you noticed that Jocelyn looks like a lithium capsule?" one of them said. "Yeah," the other replied, "She's got the right kind of yellow going on."

How bizarre, I thought. *Why would they say that about me?* It seemed cruel, given how I struggled under the weight of the drug. I didn't know what to say to my co-workers for the rest of the night.

I worked at the cinema while high and while extremely low and always got through it. I worked at a punishing rate, absolutely punishing. Dr. G. would tell me that I was unbelievably strong, strong enough to fasten a sort of normalcy to my actions and statements and get by, just get by. I don't think I believed him at the time—today, I would agree with him, would make the same comments myself. But it hurt me, denying my illness, fighting it so hard. I took prisoners, but the prisoners were always me.

***

The run of *Crouching Tiger, Hidden Dragon* at the cinema over Christmas 2000 (it had been released in Canada in mid-December), was mania time, and I had to take Haldol to calm myself and keep the psychosis, which was becoming more common in my highs, at bay. However, the Haldol made my legs stiff, so to counteract that, I took a drug called Cogentin. Unfortunately, Cogentin, which is used to treat Parkinson's disease amongst others, can cause something called anticholinergic toxicity syndrome. There is a little mnemonic used to capture what this syndrome looks like: hot as a hare, blind as a bat, dry as a bone, red as a beet, and mad as a hatter. Which perfectly summed up my state whenever I used Cogentin. And it was during the Christmas run of Crouching Tiger that my manic self became even madder than a hatter.

I was whisked off the quick work of ticket sales and made usher for every single shift I worked, since that job entailed the easy work of ripping tickets and watching the film. I saw *Crouching Tiger, Hidden Dragon* a total of 9 times, sometimes twice in one day. Each time, it was new to me, as I couldn't retain anything I saw on screen (or off screen, for that matter) for more than a couple of minutes. In fact, when the film was brought back to the cinema sometime in the spring, I had an usher shift and was all set with a groan to watch it for the tenth time. But it was like I was watching a new movie, a beautiful one with twists and turns and love and betrayal that I was seeing for the first time.

***

My favourite apartment ever was on Argyle Avenue, the Windsor Arms, a classic 1920s building across the street from the Museum of Nature. Apartment 520, a one-bedroom. Finny and Buddy, my two little cats, were my mates there. This would have been the early 2000s.

In addition to usher shifts, I was now working as a shift manager. It was a good walk home from the cinema (after I triple-checked that I had properly locked the doors, and lit that first cigarette), a couple of kilometres long. On my walk home, I would stop at a small grocery store on Elgin and buy pasta, cream, parmesan. Sometimes I would buy some endive and braise it before adding the cream, a twist I loved. Sometimes I added bacon too, this being between vegetarian phases. Liz Phair on the stereo, cooking slowly, getting drunk on white wine, just pleasantly so, smoking too much. *Sex and the City* on TV while I sat on the sofa, managing the bowl holding the huge amount of pasta. Yes, I was hungry all the time, and had gained a lot of weight, my clothes getting tighter over the months.

***

From the kitchen, the couch looks like a shimmering golden mirage. A quick leap and I am standing on its back, face pressed against windows. Outside stands the castle, the Museum of Nature, all that has been this natural world gathered together just across the street. I scream, "I am a dinosaur! I am a volcano!" Shoes are found, keys stuffed in a pocket, and the elevator is deemed too slow as I race down the five sets of stairs. Outside, the cold air hits me, my eyes pop, my lungs expand, I am made for moving quickly. I scurry over the snowbank, and then another one, and then another. I trip twice, but this has me laughing, and then I feel a sudden bolt of fear that I will never get up. The museum generators hum a tune of ancient feet leaving giant imprints in the prairies, of islands springing up off the coast of Iceland, the rumble of tectonic plates, even the very faint sound of the Earth's rotation. I stand perfectly still. Yes, yes, I can feel it. I am turning, we are all turning, the dinosaur skeletons, the stuffed caribou, the apartment building, the neighbourhood, the whole world. From my left leg I feed all information available to humankind into my brain and let it flow back out my right, back into the Earth. I am rooted and connected, and it is all so wondrous and beautiful. The beast in my stomach has moved to my chest, it is pushing pushing pushing, and I know that I must give birth to it. That I must cry out the beauty of the world, sing to the stars, envelop my arms around every living thing around me and wrap them in my glow. Share with them what I know, show them that it is okay because I have the key, and they can follow me to the middle of the Earth, and all will be understood.

Suddenly, there is a firm hold on my shoulder. I shake it off, I scream that I won't fall down, that I get up, that bolts are just bolts and you ride them out. Voices come at me, voices mix with the voice of God, and I fight to keep things clear. The wholeness of the universe is in my stomach, I hear this, I know this, but I also hear other words. Words from underwater. Words that include drunk, crazy, police, freezing cold. I shake loose and run toward the greying stones that form the walls around my brain. I am going to scale them; I am going to leave the shoulder shakers behind; I am going to take my place high above ground and command my post as a proud and indomitable eagle. And I will take flight.

Chapter 15

I used to love the trickle of scotch down my throat, the swoosh of red wine in my mouth. Sometimes, I would mix the scotch with some red Dubonnet. It was sticky and sweet and very, very easy to drink. As was fruit juice mixed with vodka, rum, or gin. It was especially easy in the warmer months, when the alcohol flowed more generously and I could get away with more. Because I was all about tricking. Frankly, I was all about lying.

I drank very, very heavily from 1994 well into 1996. I hid bottles everywhere. I went to different liquor stores all over the city, embarrassed that it was a daily event. I drove drunk. I lied a bit; I lied some more. And it was getting worse. It was also getting trickier, since I had moved back home with my mother, who kept a close eye on me. Ruby had moved to the UK, and I couldn't afford the apartment on my own.

I was drunk a lot of the time, at work at the kitchen store, on the bus home, at home. Stagger Lee would take me aside at Domus. "You reek of alcohol," he would tell me, warn me. But, I still kept up with my vodka, believing it didn't smell of anything. My mum, as usual, and to this day, was on the front lines and was the one I always hurt the most. I had to try and control the drinking when I was with her. I relied on tricks to get the booze in me. I kept several bottles of wine in my bedroom closet and one on the go in the kitchen. I would make an excuse to go upstairs, I would say, "I need to grab a sweater, I'll be right back." I would go to my room, grab a bottle, and take several giant swigs. Back downstairs, I would sip my wine, refill, sip, and repeat.

After my mother went to bed, I broke out the vodka and orange juice and drank until I could barely get off the couch, watching *Law & Order* reruns. I hid the empties in my bedroom closet, big bags of them that I took periodically to the dumpster behind the 7-Eleven. Clang, clang they went as they got pitched over the side of the giant blue bin. A moment, where, with the sound, I let the whole world hear my shame.

***

Over one weekend, with my mum in Toronto for work and the place all to myself, I got seriously drunk and eventually passed out on my bed. I woke up around four in the morning and thought I smelled smoke. I flipped on the lights and went all the way down to the basement but found no source of the smell. Sleep again, a few more hours, and then a struggle to get up and get ready for work. I was headed for the kitchen store, so this must have been 1996. It was winter, I remember that so clearly, and as soon as I opened the front door, I was blown over by the smell. Marshmallows roasting over a campfire, doused with water.

I exited the house, turned my head, feeling a shock. The house next door had burned down. All that was left was its shell, dripping into the snow, that smell of wet, burnt wood heavy over everything.

There was a small crowd of people on the street, at the end of my neighbours' driveway. As I walked towards them, a woman in a big fur coat practically leapt on me.

"You! Are you only out now?!" She was shaking her arm at me. "It's on the news, you know, I found my way here. Where were you?!"

"Is everyone okay?" I asked, trying to shake her off. She was hurting my head, so hungover at 9:30 a.m.

"Jocelyn!" It was my neighbour coming to me.

"Is everybody okay, are you okay?" I asked him.

"Oh, why didn't you hear us?! We tried to phone 911, but our phone was melting. We came here, we pounded on your door. Why didn't you answer?"

I felt a blow to my gut, a solid punch. I struggled to speak. "I am so, so sorry," I said. "I am really sorry. I am such a heavy sleeper." I worked hard at looking him in the eye. "Is there anything you need?"

He shook his head. "The Dories have been helping us. We went to them after you." He shrugged his shoulders and headed back to his driveway.

I unlocked the car, threw my bag onto the passenger's seat. As I got in, the fur-clad woman glared at me, and shook her head, tsk tsk-ing me. All I could do was drive away.

***

Finally, I went to the ROH to get treatment. The intake nurse showed me a U-shaped curve and pointed near the bottom of it. "You are here," she said. "And you can stay here, or you can go back up the curve on this side. It's up to you."

I signed up for sessions, three nights a week. I promised to go to AA, which I did, once, drunk. The first session at the Royal, I said nothing. I walked home from the hospital, my brain jumping all around, suddenly aware that I was coming upon a liquor store. And I made a snap decision. I would stop there. As soon as I realized what I was going to do—it didn't feel like I had much choice in the matter—my whole body shuddered with relief. What did I want to get, how could I smuggle it into the house? I went up and down the aisles, feeling my anxiety floating away.

"Hey, how are you?" an employee stocking sparkling wines asked me. "You looking for the vodka?"

My heart jumped into my throat. I was so embarrassed—I had been noticed. I thought I had been spreading it out over four or five liquor stores, the vodka and the wine, so no one could catch me. I was wrong.

"No, I'm good," I said to him, exiting the aisle as quickly as possible. I went to the vodka wall and grabbed a medium bottle, taking it to the cash with my head down. Outside, a man was singing "Free Falling" when I exited the store. I found a toonie and flipped it into his open guitar case.

"You have a great evening," he said to me. I felt him stare at my knapsack, stare at the bottle tucked into it. Did he know what kind of an evening I was planning?

I never went back to the ROH.

***

I am not alone in having used alcohol to temper the damage my mental illness was doing to me. It is quite common. In fact, it is often difficult to tease apart what is illness and what is alcohol. What comes first? Does the drinking cause depression, or is it that the depression influences the drinking? I am sure those early years of my sickness were made worse by drinking as heavily as I did, and I feel such relief and gratitude that it is no longer an acute problem for me. I wouldn't have survived this long if it had been. Many are not so lucky.

I continued drinking, off and on over the years, spasms of

alcohol abuse that never went full-blown, thankfully. And now, I rarely drink. When I do, when I drink that first Screwdriver or G&T, I get a rush, and I want more and more. But I can stop. For now. It is entirely possible that one day, I won't be able to stop. So I no longer give myself the opportunity to come upon that day.

***

After the failure at the ROH, I coasted for a while, soused in vodka, probably reeking of it. But I decided once again that I was going to quit drinking, sometime that early summer. It was costing too much money, involved too much trickery, and had both my doctor and my mother concerned. So, on the day of my decision, I got up out of bed, a little shaky, got ready, and got the bus. Work was fine, I went home, survived the night without alcohol.

The next day the same thing, but after work I caved, and stopped to buy some vodka. Once again, I felt a rush of relief, that special relief. All would be good now. I cradled that bottle in my knapsack for the entire bus ride home. I piled the marketing bags onto the kitchen counter, but made myself a little vodka and orange, a little Screwdriver, before I started unpacking them. I went out to the porch, on my second drink now, and smoked several cigarettes.

It's good, I thought. *This is good.*

Time to cook, this time a spread of Indian vegetarian dishes with some festive rice. I was in the mood for a little Stevie Wonder, and I cranked it up so that his song filled the entire downstairs. I didn't know when my mum would be home—pretty late, I imagined—but the cooking felt really good. The third drink poured, another cigarette on the porch.

I danced all over the kitchen, singing too loudly, as I stirred the spiced spinach and tasted the chickpeas.

Another drink—I don't know what number I was on. I minced some ginger, still singing, when a thought suddenly crowded into my head. *Why are you doing this, you loser?* I shook my head, shook the sudden invasion out of my brain. I scooted over to the frying pan, tossed the ginger in, gave it a stir. *Oh, just go to hell,* I thought. *Have another drink, you loser!* Why? I was having fun. I turned off the stove and stood in the middle of the kitchen. I noticed the CD was skipping, and for some reason, this hurt my head, hurt my thoughts. *No, no, no, no,* I said in my head. *You're not going to go there.*

I turned the stereo off. I was getting pretty drunk, but the nice tipsy rush had been and gone. Now, I was alone with my suddenly negative thoughts, unable to process them with any clarity. Things were turning darker in my head, in the kitchen. *Wow, you are really doing this sobriety thing, you big fat fuck.* I shook my head, trying to make sense.

I had to pee. I waivered to the washroom, slammed the door open, bounced off it with my shoulder. *You can hardly walk, you fuck!* I rinsed my hands, patted them dry, pulled my hair back, looked at myself in the mirror. I had such bags under my eyes, and my cheeks were grey. *You're disgusting.* I opened the cupboard door, and moved my drug containers around, searching. I didn't know what I was looking for. A benzo to chill me out? No, something harder, something harder, I was thinking. I picked up the lithium, put it back down. Grabbed the valproic acid, held it up. What will this do to me? "*Go for it!*" My words were slurred.

I took the container into the kitchen, which was shuttered down now, and poured myself another drink. *Here's to you, kiddo,* I said in my brain. *Here's to you blocking it all out.* I opened the container and shook a few capsules into my hand. I put them in my mouth, swallowed from my Screwdriver. *That's it, nice and easy.* I poured some more capsules into my hand, threw them up to my mouth. *Oh, for fuck's sake!* I started cramming them in, all the valproic acid. I took big sips of my drink, cramming and gulping until they were all gone. *You're so pathetic.* Then I sat on the living room sofa, waiting for the blackness.

This was my third overdose, the first that was serious, and the last for a good 20 years.

Chapter 16

And if my allowing myself to be brought here confuses you, if you think for one minute that I am singing one song and dancing to another, then you have not been following along. Stick to the facts. That's what I have to tell everybody. They are clear and crisp and lay cold and unblinking on the snowbanks that lined the drive here. I pressed my nose to the glass and nodded at each, and as each passed, they would slip under the car and up into the back seat and down my stomach. I feel them still; they have not melted, despite the heat in this room. There are hundreds of them, and they tell the story of what has happened to me, what was done to me in the beginning, what must be stopped.

I will open my mouth round and wide, and each fact will come slipping out, only to attach itself to the blank wall that faces our chairs; there they will remain hard and sharp and be beautiful and powerful and all-knowing. And all I will have to do is point and say, here, here is all that you need to know. Here is where my doctor refuses to look, and here is what my mother does not accept. But you can see it, I know you can, and you can understand what the truth is. You can stick to the facts. You will recognize the danger I am in and order that I be removed outside the city limits, far from the grey grip of the pill-pushing death angels. Gone, wiped off their video screens, the metal disc in my brain growing weaker and weaker with every moment. Come spring, it will be mere dust, and one morning I will stand up and sneeze, and it will all be gone.

***

"Schizoaffective" is a scary word. Anything with the word "schizo" in it is. Basically, the diagnosis of schizoaffective disorder describes a melding of symptoms of a mood disorder, be it bipolar or unipolar, with symptoms of a psychotic disorder, such as delusions and hallucinations. It has a rather complicated set of criteria in order to make the diagnosis, and the disease varies from person to person. For a person to be diagnosed with the illness, they have to experience clear episodes of an affective (mood) disorder, with psychosis existing for part of the illness. This is not unusual. Mania is often psychotic, with delusions of grandeur, or paranoia, or anything, really. Psychotic depression is less common but happens in severe cases. My research finds that for schizoaffective disorder to be diagnosed, there must be episodes of psychosis that are stand-alone, not part of a mood swing.

The National Alliance on Mental Illness (NAMI) in the US makes it clearer than I have. Their web page on schizoaffective disorders states:

"In order for a person to be diagnosed with schizoaffective disorder, a person must have the following symptoms:

- A period during which there is a major mood disorder, either depression or mania, that occurs at the same time that symptoms of schizophrenia are present.

- Delusions or hallucinations for two or more weeks in the absence of a major mood episode.
- Symptoms that meet criteria for a major mood episode are present for the majority of the total duration of the illness.
- The abuse of drugs or a medication are not responsible for the symptoms." (www.nami.org)

Confusing? It's a lot to keep track of. How many weeks of this, and how many weeks of that, and when do they mingle and when do they separate? It must be difficult making the diagnosis in someone. I know I find it difficult to stick to the program.

***

I hear voices all the time. They never leave me. In the shower, folding laundry, falling asleep, or out with a friend. They are always there, humming along. Usually they are background noise, and I can ignore them and carry on with regular thinking and conversation. When my mood changes, however, or I slide into a psychotic episode, the voices come racing forward to the front of my brain, yelling at me, at each other, making it hard to focus and engage in conversation. But that is only in episodes of illness. Usually, the voices just hang out. I am used to them.

It's not just voices. I also have a running sense of paranoia as I go about my day. I have to be vigilant, screening every thought, holding each one up to the light to see if it's real or not. It is particularly intrusive when I am driving a car. People in cars around me are trying to get at me, to get into my brain. I hold these thoughts up and place them in the "ignore" category. It can be exhausting.

The running voices and sense of paranoia are symptoms I have, but they are not necessarily routinely found in people with schizoaffective disorder. I have them all the time, and when I slip into a real episode of psychosis, these two symptoms intensify and cross that border between sanity and insanity.

***

It was during a hospitalization in 2000, when I was 30, that I was diagnosed with schizoaffective disorder. I was in because I had been feeling increasingly paranoid, worried that people were after me or trying to kill me. This was not related to a mood state. I had thought that the best way to deal with the threat was to kill myself. I was being driven out of my own life by faceless shapes moving about my brain.

I was under the care of Dr. S. again, someone I was by now very familiar with. He was looking at something different from his first encounter with me in 1995. Back then, I was depressed, then manic, and the diagnosis was clear-cut. Subsequent hospitalizations also supported the diagnosis of bipolar disorder.

But this time round, things were different. Yes, I had a symptom of a mood disorder—I wanted to kill myself. But this symptom could be pulled out of that diagnosis and placed instead squarely in the context of a psychotic disorder, since it came from disordered thinking, not a mood swing.

Dr. S. had told me, way back during my first hospitalization, that I was lucky to have bipolar disorder rather than schizophrenia. He told me I could go places, wherever I wanted, that the illness was relatively easy to control, and it shouldn't hold me back. He explained some of the symptoms of schizophrenia, and I had agreed I did not want to go down that road.

But in 2000, there was some confusion about my diagnosis. I was presenting with symptoms that were mostly psychotic, not at all affective, like one would expect from me.

A week in, and it was time for a family meeting. My mum and I met with Dr. S. and his team. We were in one of the back offices again, seated around a long table.

"So." Dr. S. laughed a little, trying to ease the discomfort everyone was feeling. "Here we are again. Another get-together to discuss where things are at with you, Jocelyn. I am glad your mother is able to join us." He smiled at her.

"Why are we discussing anything?" I said this slowly, feeling heavy under the antipsychotic drugs I was on. My brain was further scrambled by the intense distrust I was feeling for this man in the moment. He was clearly trying to control my mind with drugs, and now with turning my mother against me.

"Well, Jocelyn, I think it's time to talk about your illness. More specifically what kind of illness you have. You know, you have been quite different these past few days than you were the last time I saw you. You are definitely not manic, and I am not sure that you are depressed either. Does that sound about right to you?"

"I am absolutely not depressed," I answered. What was he looking for? Where was this going? Was I being set up? "I am really manic, ha, ha, ha."

"It is good to see you still have your sense of humour," Dr. S. said. "What we want to talk to you about is an illness called 'schizoaffective disorder.' Those words might sound a bit scary, so let me explain. You currently have a diagnosis of bipolar 1 disorder. But, and I've consulted with Dr. G. about this, right now you are in an episode of psychosis. You have been for the past month or so, according to him. I know you understand what psychosis is, and that you have had psychosis in the past. But, this time it's different. You have delusions, you are hearing voices. Your behaviours have been a bit bizarre, frankly. But the difference is this time you are not experiencing any affective symptoms. You are not high, and you are not low. We think we have your medications all set for your mood disorder. But, we now think you have schizophrenia, and we have to focus on finding a treatment for that."

"I don't understand what you are saying," my mum spoke up. Her face looked funny to me, pale and slightly distorted. I began to laugh. "Are you saying Jocelyn isn't bipolar? Are you telling us she has schizophrenia?"

Dr. S. wasn't paying any attention to me, with my off-centre giggling. But he seemed to be very patient with my mum. "Yes, but the terminology is a bit different. Jocelyn has both bipolar illness and schizophrenia. The two of them together are called schizoaffective disorder. We now believe the correct diagnosis is schizoaffective disorder, bipolar type. So, yes, this does mean she has schizophrenia." He smiled again. "This is completely treatable with medication. But, it might take some time to find the right one, and we don't want to rush it."

After the meeting ended, my mum sat with me quietly. "This is a lot to take in, isn't it? How are you doing? You must be a bit scared." She leaned forward and caressed my chin.

Schizophrenia was all I could think. *Schizophrenia.* My mind went back to the discussion Dr. S. and I had five years earlier about bipolar disorder being easier than schizophrenia. Was he giving up on me?

***

When I got out of hospital, I fell back into my weekly meetings with Dr. G. He agreed with my new diagnosis of schizoaffective disorder—I certainly met the criteria—but disagreed with what that meant for me, and all of those receiving this serious diagnosis. If you looked at it along a continuum with affective disorders on one end and psychotic disorders on the other, you would see that some people are closer to a mood disorder, while others may present with something very close to schizophrenia at the psychotic disorder end. It varies from person to person.

I am closer to the mood end of this continuum—I have bipolar disorder and feel it the most. However, my mood disorder is joined with symptoms of a psychotic disorder, mainly delusions and hallucinations, and that leaves me with the diagnosis of schizoaffective disorder. I do not have full-blown schizophrenia, even if Dr. S. insists I do.

When I want to quickly label my mental illness for someone else, I usually call it a "kind of bipolar disorder," or "bipolar plus." That just seems easiest. It is okay for others to think about extreme mood states; I know where their thoughts will take them. To explain schizoaffective disorder—well, that I rarely do, except here, on these pages, where I have the time and space to put forward my case.

Schizoaffective disorder is a lonely diagnosis.

***

Whenever I have a psychotic break, I tend to fall into my usual pattern of heightened paranoia, an exaggeration of the mild symptoms that I live with every day. When I drive on the highway, I believe my thoughts are being fed into other drivers' radios. Those other drivers are trying to scoop out my thoughts or even my brain. I am being watched and followed. There are cameras everywhere, following my every move. In fact, I have a personal webcam that takes in all of my movements. It is not safe! Doesn't everybody know that? Doesn't it worry Dr. G. that his waiting room is tapped, that when I am "safely" in his office, they are at the door, trying to come in? That I worry for his other patients, that they may be subjected to the same observation, the same attempts at hijacking their brains? And what will happen with the little chip that they have inserted in me? How will we ever get that out?

I cannot tell you the number of times, ever since that diagnosis in 2000, that I have walked into Dr. G.'s office expressing the thoughts and feelings that I have just described. I have gone through it countless times, like clockwork. I will start to be a bit suspicious, and I will see a sign of some kind that confirms and reinforces my crazy beliefs. I might get honked at when I am slow to go forward on a green light. Or I will receive a phone call from the pharmacy about a delivery that afternoon. These "special signs" lead up to too many people in my space, people surrounding me and intending harm.

It is at this point that Dr. G. will increase the dose of my antipsychotic medicine. "We don't want this to escalate," he will tell me. "I think we've got it just in time," he will say. Sometimes I do not know what he is talking about, since my psychotic thoughts can feel as real to me as my regular thoughts, and I don't know the difference. When he tells me I am experiencing psychosis, I am baffled. I hear his words and think maybe he is a little bit crazy himself. But I do what I'm told. I take the extra meds, and after a week or two my disordered thinking clears up, I realize what I had been saying, and I feel embarrassed. Dr. G. tells me not to beat myself up over it, that it is all part of my illness. (I often have a depression after a psychotic episode, which is very common.) After a couple of weeks, when things have returned to normal for a while, we taper the drugs, and I carry on.

***

I have been hospitalized roughly 10 times over the span of the past 25 years. The first three times were due to serious depression and the overdoses that happened as a result of them. But the past seven or so times were not as clear-cut. Suicidality, in a sense, was part of each episode, but these thoughts did not come from depression. Instead, I felt that I had to end my life in order to overcome some sort of psychotic situation. Like when I came home from Paris, when I felt insects squirming inside of me. I needed to get rid of them and planned to drink a can of Raid in order to do so—an action that would have been lethal. More recently, after one of my favourite cats died, I heard her call to me, instructing me to throw myself off a highway overpass and join not only her but also my dad and grandparents, people who were waiting for me while living an idyllic afterlife.

Sometimes during a hospital stay, I would be so wound up that I got my very own room and my very own guard watching over me. I tried to plot my way out but realized I couldn't do anything. I was always on a form of some kind, stating that I was a danger to myself, so I couldn't just check myself out of the hospital. I would pace the bit of hallway while in these single rooms, pace like a caged animal.

Later hospitalizations focused very much on medication, slowly titrating a new drug, bit by bit, waiting to see the impact on me—will it hold my mood steady? Will it clear up psychosis?

Usually, we would get close enough, and I would be discharged from hospital with the real work ahead of me. Drugs do play a role, absolutely, but they are not the only tool in that box of treatments. Psychotherapy—basically "talking it out," as it feels on my end—is absolutely crucial to my wellness. Yes, other things like relaxation techniques or simply going for a walk have many benefits. But it is the weekly sessions with Dr. G. that really help put things into perspective, help me understand where a mood might be going, or how a broken chain of reasoning might be reworked. Understand when anxious thoughts may take up too much room in my brain, leaving not much room for other ideas. And, he helps me try to understand why he sometimes talks about us having different interpretations of events.

I read *Surviving Schizophrenia* by Dr. E. Fuller Torey and found great reassurance in its pages. He writes about all aspects of schizophrenia, symptoms, causes, diagnosis, treatments, and includes guidance for families. I took what was relevant for me and for my family and felt a great sense of comfort I didn't think was possible.

But my favourite book about living with schizoaffective disorder is *The Quiet Room* by Lori Schiller. She lived through a truly harrowing illness. I have such respect for Schiller and her family members, who also get a voice in this memoir. She ends up doing okay, finding the drug that helped her fight her demons, while understanding the work she would have to put into her recovery.

In grimmer times, I would read and reread these books.

They would make me feel stronger and not as alone. My path forward seemed just that much easier to navigate, walking along with those who had come before me.

Chapter 17

I weighed 150 pounds, which was positively skinny for me. I fit into old jeans and a new leather jacket and paired those with lace-up boots and a purple silk scarf. My hair was long and wavy, and I must say, I looked pretty good. I felt confident, and my step was sure. I was happy. It was in that frame of mind that I went to Paris with my mum for two weeks, in October 2002.

Although I had by then been on quite a few trips to Europe, this would be my first time in Paris. And it would also be my first psychotic break outside of North America, despite how well things had started off. In fact, I had no clue that my life was going to take a drastic turn for the worse.

My mum had some work that would take her to Brussels, so we planned the trip around that. I would not be accompanying her to Brussels but instead would remain in Paris for the three days that she was gone.

We rented an apartment in the sixteenth arrondissement and had good fun getting to know the neighbourhood—we put some quality food in the cupboard, from grocers, patisseries, boulangeries, wine stores, and little markets all up the hill along cobblestone streets.

We'd chosen the sixteenth arrondissement for a reason. It was there that my maternal great-grandmother was born. To her grandchildren she was known as Momi, probably as a result of my oldest aunt's attempts to say Omi, an affectionate term for Oma, which for German speakers means grandmother. She was the daughter of well-off German Jews who were in France doing business in the silk trade for richer relatives. So, Momi wasn't French, but she sure felt it, especially when the family decided to move back to Germany when she was 10. She always maintained her love for Paris and its trees, despairing that Hamburg had none.

Many walks brought us to the neighbourhoods of the Marais, Montmartre, the Latin Quarter, Montparnasse, and some indoor and outdoor markets. We visited art galleries and museums, walked along the St. Martin canal, and sat for a drink in the Luxembourg gardens. The Arab World Institute was fascinating, and my mum looked out over the Seine while I bought a gorgeous ruby ring from Afghanistan. And the food we sampled along the way came from all corners of the Earth and was utterly delicious.

Just sitting outdoors in a café was nice. The whole world walked by as we sipped our coffee.

"I feel like spending," my mum said to me. "Let's hit up some clothing stores."

"Okay, what do you want to look for?" I asked her.

"Anything really. Something Parisian, European. Will you look for things for yourself?"

"Absolutely!" I said. "Maybe some more sweaters? Some more jewellery?" I felt so light. The weather was perfect, and I leaned back and let the sun caress my face.

There were many little stores for us to do our shopping, on little side streets, on bigger streets and walkways. I picked up a lot: flowing blouses and tops, sequined jeans, beautifully printed skirts. I fit into it all back then. These pieces now sit in boxes in the furnace room next to other boxed skinny clothes, refugees from a distant era, not even close to fitting me anymore. But I keep them, just in case one day. . .

***

It was after my mum boarded the train to Brussels that things started to unravel. I was on my own. That first evening, I enjoyed a half-litre of red wine at our local café, sitting outside to watch the people pass on by. I smiled to myself and smoked cigarette after cigarette. I was totally unprepared for what would soon hit me.

My first big outing by myself, the next day, was to the Opéra Garnier, with its Chagall frescoes decorating the ceiling. It was bad timing: the house was dark, except for a pool of light illuminating the workspace on the stage. Several people were there, pieces of paper scattered around. I was so disappointed. I wandered around the building a bit longer, returning to the viewing section before leaving. I was treated! The lights suddenly went on, and there were the frescoes beautifully laid out ahead of me.

As I travelled Paris by myself, I was more and more caught off-guard by the various plaques and signs designating sites as a place where Jewish children were rounded up and sent to Auschwitz. Signs that two hundred people were shipped in cattle cars to the big camps in the east in train stations, on museum walls, and on the walls of former schools. There were signs throughout the old Jewish Quarter in the Marais, as well as places where you would least expect them.

I had not come to Paris expecting the City of Light to be full of Holocaust reminders. When Ruby and I travelled to Poland in 1990, we had visited Majdanek, a concentration camp on the edge of the city of Lublin. I was prepared for it, prepared for what we were taking on. Of course, actually visiting the camp went far beyond anything we may have thought we were prepared for. I had been disturbed for days.

That afternoon, I decided to visit the Jewish museum. After I had paid entrance, I took an English audio guide and started my tour. Halfway through, I came across a section of black-and-white photographs dated 1942, 1943, 1944, pictures of people standing in groups, luggage by their sides.

And then I saw it. A picture depicting a small group standing outside a synagogue, brought together so that they could be sent to the death camps. In the middle of the photo was a young woman with long dark hair. She appeared to be alone and did not have any luggage. As I studied her, completely transfixed, I realized I was looking at a photo of myself, taken so long ago.

I was quietly shaking. It didn't make any sense—how could I have ended up in this photo display? How could I be pictured all the way back in the 1940s and yet be standing here in the twenty-first century? I wanted to find somebody else in the museum to look at the photographic evidence and explain it to me. Explain how exactly I could be two people at the same time and yet be just one.

Gradually, I was able to shake myself off a bit, and I left the museum with all sorts of thoughts and images swimming in my mind. On the metro ride back to the flat, I felt great confusion. Old people were staring at me. It was clear that many of them recognized me from wartime. They were trying to figure out how I got to be there. I was doing the same thing. A shock to us all that there I was alive, in Paris, still 33 years old.

I finally arrived back at the flat. To my horror, outside our building were piles and piles of shoes. Men's dress shoes, women's high heels, little running shoes, all on top of another. I had to walk right by them in order to get to the front door. I safely made it up in the old elevator, spilling into the apartment, rattled and upset.

I closed the curtains and poured myself some wine, hands shaking. I knew what the shoes meant and what they were trying to do to me. Scare me off, frighten me out of the city. As I sat on the sofa in the living room, the thought that this was not all real did cross my mind. That maybe my brain was tricking me, leading me down a path that I had been on before, a path through a terrifying jungle of disjointed thoughts and feelings.

I decided it would be smart to have a nice, relaxing bath in the fancy tub in the apartment. I turned on the hot and the cold water and waited. But instead of water coming out of the tap, bugs came. They came pouring out, ugly little cockroaches that swarmed the tub, crawled on walls and fixtures. I quickly stepped out, closed the door, and stood in the hallway breathing rapidly, dizzy and frightened. Wait a minute—this was not some passing psychotic trip; this was not my brain on fire. Shoes on the street, bugs in the bathroom. This was real. And I was all alone, which was how they wanted me.

I don't remember how I got to sleep that night. I probably took extra medication to knock myself out. But somehow, I slept.

The next day, drinking my coffee at our café, I felt nervous about others around me. I couldn't look anybody in the eye, since the fear of recognition was too strong. I decided to go back to visit some outdoor markets, check out some cemeteries. Anywhere where I wasn't confronted with my newly realized past. The pile of shoes had disappeared, had been taken by the garbage men, no doubt. But I was still watched, still stared at, not just by older people, but the young as well. They all seemed to know something, a big secret I had not been let in on.

My mother finally came back from Brussels. I felt somewhat safer with her around. No more bugs in the bathroom or in the kitchen, where they had been swarming just that morning. I stayed cool, acted cool, acted even. Somewhere I knew, somewhere in my brain, that these thoughts, the bugs, the shoes, were altogether something different and had to be hidden from my mother. At least I had that modicum of awareness left in my being. And so we left Paris.

It wasn't until we were at the airport that last morning that I drew up the strength to talk to her about what I realized was the new me. I remember where we were sitting very clearly—she was an elite Air Canada member, so we were allowed to relax in the lounge. It was there, waiting for our flight to be called, that I summoned the courage to break the news to her.

"Mum," I said, leaning toward her, "Mum, there is something I have to talk to you about." I stopped, my mind reeling. I couldn't keep going, couldn't explain it. But I tried. "You see, I am not the person you think I am, though the person I really am is kind of mysterious to me too, so it will be totally confusing to you. I am not sure I can explain it." My voice grew steadier with each word, each phrase. I definitely had to explain it. I needed it to make sense not only to her, but to me.

"There is this picture in a museum. I went there on my own, and when I saw it, I realized the picture was of me. Me in 1944." My mum was looking confused. "I guess I am living a double life, and now I am not sure if I am good or bad, a victim or something evil."

"Jocy, what on Earth are you talking about?" my mum said. There was tension in her voice. She leaned forward and touched my hand.

"Oh, Mum, I don't know." I began to cry. "There were all these shoes outside our place, there were bugs in the bathroom. They're after me." I was really crying now. "But I don't know who."

"My God, Jocy," she said, clearly shaken. "You aren't making any sense. What happened to you while I was gone?"

I could not answer. I could recite the facts as I knew them, but I could not answer. What had happened? It was all so confusing.

"Oh God, they were everywhere. These bugs, just everywhere. And everybody knows me. Not here at the airport, but back in the city. I couldn't go anywhere without being accused. Oh, I don't know, accused or met with surprise, I just don't know."

I seemed to strike her down in size a little bit with each thing that I said. She was getting smaller and smaller in front of me, shrinking back in horror. And it was horrible.

"Are you going to be okay on the plane?" she asked. "You are really worrying me. We are calling your doctor the moment we land." Her words felt harsh, though she said them gently. She had found a tissue for me, and I was drying my face.

"Okay," I said in a whisper. "Okay about Dr. G. Maybe he can help."

***

I was hoping that upon return to life in Ottawa, the bugs and the people would leave me alone. Instead, the Nazi bugs—for I had realized they were Nazis—burrowed deeper inside my gut and inside my chest. They stayed there, they didn't try to crawl out of my throat and mouth. But I had to do something about them before they took over my entire life. Which, by then, had already happened. I didn't know it at the time, could not see it, but I was getting sicker and sicker with each passing day. But all I was then was hungry and scared, like half of me was departing and the other half was arriving, but the transition between the two was never seamless. There was always overlap, and sometimes even gaps.

I worried about my two cats, about my mother and grandmother, about anything and anyone who could be at risk by hanging around me. The Nazi bugs might hurt them, hurt them all, and no matter how hard I tried, I knew the dam was going to burst.

In a state of extreme fear, I decided that I would need to drink a can of Raid, the bug killer that had been around for so long. At the same time, I would take a knife and cut open my chest, like the zipper scar my father had after his open-heart surgery. I would also slash my gut to relieve the pressure there. It all seemed cold and clinical (unlike the heat and the mess that it really was). But I knew it had to be done.

The day of my big decision was a Tuesday, the day of the week I visited my psychiatrist. (Sanity somewhere underneath, working away? A trace of it, even?) I was eager to share my feelings about Paris, about the plane trip in business class, with the glasses of champagne that greeted us.

I told him about the notices all around Paris. "Those signs were there for me, for my eyes, maybe my eyes only, I am not so sure. I mean, others could be going through exactly what is happening to me now, at any stage, really. . ." I remember the weather wasn't nice that day. I was wearing a warm jacket, and I bounced my foot up and down. "But all of us, we each have to figure out what to do about things."

Dr. G. didn't look confused, didn't seem to be surprised by what I was saying. "And I guess I have figured out what to do with my problem. I have to fix this Nazi situation tonight." (To play it back in my mind today—if I hadn't been so confused, if things hadn't been so dangerous—it's almost comical.) "Bottom line is that I have my anti-bug measures laid out for me, and I will be enforcing them tonight."

My mum had come with me, since she was worried about the state I was in, and was in the waiting room. Dr. G. went to get her so that she could join the conversation. She came in and sat on the leather sofa. I don't really remember what was said from that point on. I kind of drifted off. I certainly remember the word "hospital" and the phrase "danger to herself." And then we were off, off to the hospital that, thanks to Dr. G., was waiting for me. I felt anger, but at the same time, I felt very calm. I did not resist. That makes me wonder if I knew a little bit about what was going on, had almost planned it, though I think that was a bit too organized for me at the time, given where my brain was at.

And by that point, I was clueless. I did not know which fact was more important, which word was somehow significant to their ears. But the doctors seemed to think it was all serious, whatever I said, and that warranted a stay in their psychiatric ward, a place with which I was now very familiar.

Weeks later, after I had been released, Dr. G. and I tried to put all the pieces together. Why had my brain gone sidewise for two months? Why, in the middle of such a wonderful trip to Paris, would I veer off course? What crisis of identity was so powerful as to cause such a bizarre and dangerous reaction? It is not surprising, however, as psychosis can hijack any of my thoughts or emotions. The feelings I felt when visiting the Jewish museum, and the constant reminders of the Holocaust throughout the city, had mixed with complications of my mixed family history that I feel to this day. The results were brutal, and almost killed me.

Chapter 18

It was several years later, in the fall of 2007, that my brother Jeff and his wife Natasha gave me a call. Did I want to relocate?

"Relocate where? To Brooklyn?" I asked, both of them on speakerphone.

"We're thinking of opening a kitchen store in Williamsburg and thought you maybe wanted to come along for the ride. You would be perfect, you know," they said to me.

"Along for the ride. You mean, work for you?"

"No, not just work for us. Be a partner with us and Josh and Steph. You would own a third of the business. You and Natasha would be in charge."

I thought about this for a few minutes. What an exciting offer. I was living with my mum and working at the cinema. I was losing steam there, that's for sure, but had nothing ahead of me. "When would it start? When would I move down, if I decided to do this?" I asked.

"We're thinking sometime in the summer. You could move down here in May and be in charge of the buying. Lots of fun, Jocy!" They both laughed.

"Okay, initial reaction: very interesting. But, I obviously have to think about it. Wow, this is so new, so all of a sudden. I have to wrap my little brain around it."

"You'd have a lovely apartment; we would make sure of that. You would be close to your nephews here, and in Princeton." They were dangling carrots in front of me.

And, so, after much thought, I took them up on the offer. But I had one caveat: every second weekend, I would fly up to Ottawa to see Dr. G. and be with my mum and grandmother. I simply couldn't leave them.

After a winter spent visiting Ottawa-area kitchen stores to make notes, I drove down and landed in Brooklyn in the month of May, a permanent move. But, every second Friday afternoon, I would head to LaGuardia and board a direct flight to Ottawa, Air Canada. No longer on Ontario's health plan, I had to pay Dr. G., whom I would see on the Monday, $125 for 40 minutes of talking and med prescribing. It was worth it. I would fly back to NYC early Tuesday morning, just in time to work the day in full.

It was never going to work, I look back and see that now. The fact that I had to fly home twice a month was an indication of that. But at first, all was fun, setting up shop, visiting lighting stores, tile stores, and paint stores. We enjoyed all that went into smashing down a wall and adding shelving and fixtures in the space we had rented. We chose a mustardy yellow for the walls, a dark wood for the shelving units. One trip into Manhattan was just to choose three or four sizes of paper bags, very chic, with our name imprinted on one side: *Whisk*. That was a lot of fun, almost playing at make-believe.

Having had the kitchen store experience, I was in charge of stocking Whisk. I was holed up in my new apartment (right in Park Slope, too expensive, but very nice), going to distributors' home sites, scrolling through products in catalogues, talking to reps and having coffee with them. It was a good feeling.

Natasha and I would meet over a beer every couple of days to go over my inventory list that added up to $135,000. Cut, cut, cut. The word from Jeff and our business partners, Josh and Steph, was to bring our stock numbers to $110,000. I had no idea how to do that but would head up to my little office space and cut down the numbers and amounts, knowing that the first shipments would be cash on delivery before we could set up terms with the various companies.

Finally, I wrestled with the numbers and met their demands of lowering the inventory. It was a thrill to meet up again with the reps, this time to place orders. Although I screwed up at a lot of things while living in the US, I did manage to populate the store with a good base of products. Yes, we would learn what was popular, what was missing, and what was a total failure, but the core was good and hasn't changed to this day.

Park Slope certainly was a source of eye-rolling when mentioned to other New Yorkers. So full of itself, so self-important, so marked by perfect schools and well-off hipsters. The neighbourhood grew up on a large hill alongside the beautiful, wonderful Prospect Park. It was great to see so many people of so many different backgrounds congregating around little grills, having multigenerational picnics there. I truly enjoyed being in that park and felt strongly that it should be exempt from any eye-rolling reputation. The whole world was there.

***

We set up shop in the Brooklyn neighbourhood of Williamsburg, which was still a pretty hip place back in 2008 (hipper, and younger, than Park Slope). A lot of bizarrely dressed people populated Bedford Avenue and surrounding streets when I was there. I couldn't go out to grab a coffee without being passed by young women dressed as a cross between Pippi Longstocking and Raggedy Anne. They were decked out in intensely red ponytails, striped tops, jean skirts, thigh-high boots, and bizarre makeup. And, of course, many, many piercings. As they walked quickly down Bedford, these women would hold their gaze up, staring straight ahead, pretending to be confident and so sure of themselves. Who knows what was really happening behind the chic façade.

Williamsburg was also home to many Hasidic Jews. Not so much in our part of the neighbourhood—though you could hear the sirens from the Yeshivas every Friday from where we were, 10 minutes before sunset. No, it was mainly in the southern district, where the Hasidim carried out their daily lives, pretty much ignoring us and our ways. They were a real, exotic mystery to us. As, I am sure, we were to them.

Our space was owned by a lovely couple of old hippies. Natasha and I watched the process of building out our site and together ran our errands to set up the details.

Williamsburg was a half-hour subway ride away from Park Slope. You could hop on the F train and head into Manhattan before changing to the L train heading back to Brooklyn. This limited the amount of walking one had to do but took longer. The other choice was to pick up the G train, with a drop off about 500 metres from our corner. I would stop and get a latte on my way in, a nice routine.

Gradually, though, as the months went on, I had it with the Metropolitan Transit Authority. The time spent riding the trains was feeding some of the paranoia that would later be my constant companion. So, I started calling for cars every morning, leaving it up to 20 minutes before I had to be on site. And then, after we opened and I worked nights, I would walk up to the car service window, wave lightly, and a car would soon show up, getting me to my flat in under 20 minutes. Twenty bucks, each ride. A lot of my money went to this.

I became depressed over these months. I would sit on my sofa, drinking Limonata and smoking cigarette after cigarette, being comforted by Buddy and Finny. I would ring up my mum, talking to her in tears, feeling so far away from home. I would fall asleep on the couch, sometimes relocating to the bedroom, though not always. Rinse and repeat.

It felt good to finally earn an actual salary, though—$50,000 US a year. Welcome to adulthood. I was rich! However, this money eventually went to my twice-daily car rides and my plane trips home.

***

In August of 2008, my mum came down to visit and inspect the new digs. I liked my flat, and together we arranged vases and pottered bowls, my mug collection, and all my CDs. The fact that half my boxes were left unpacked in the backroom months into my stay told a story. The fact that I kept my psychiatrist and flew home twice a month just added to it. I don't think I ever was truly there. Just half my brain, half my body.

We toured the Whisk site—this is where the cash will go, this is where the pots will be, back here are the cookbooks. We had enough stock that it wasn't hard to imagine what the end product would look like.

One morning, as Mum and I took the train into Williamsburg, we sat in a quiet spot in the nearly empty orange and yellow car. She had had dinner with Jeff and

Natasha the evening before, and they apparently had a big talk about me.

"So, do you think you are working hard at the store?" she asked me, as the train swayed to and fro.

I didn't know where she was going with this, but I was immediately on high alert. "Yes, I do. I am working very hard. We're almost open. Why?"

"Well, Jeff and Natasha shared some concerns with me last night."

"What do you mean?" I asked, picturing the three of them trading stories about me over a leg of lamb and a bottle or two of wine. "What kind of concerns?"

"There are times where you appear to be, let's say, hesitant. Like showing up on time, for one," she said.

"That's not fair! I am always on time!" Christ, where was this going to go?

"Well, then I will tell you what they had to say." I know she wanted the truth to be spoken, but it was going to hurt nonetheless. She began to tell me about their conversation.

"You come across as lazy. You start work later and leave work earlier than Natasha. And it feels as if the real responsibility rests squarely on her shoulders, and that you don't seem to take the work all that seriously. She has her own work to do, but she also has to check yours. You are slow, somewhat disorganized, and you make mistakes. You are forgetful."

I couldn't believe what I was hearing. My mother continued. "We are wondering if you are more disabled than we actually realized." That one was particularly painful, since I didn't know what behaviours they were referring to.

There was more, but it hurts to remind myself of it. I don't think Jeff and Natasha were all that upset about me and my work, they had just felt good discussing it with my mum, someone close to the situation. And, this was my mum's way of shaking me, of giving me a head's up. There we sat in the subway car, tears streaming down my cheeks.

I wrote these points down immediately upon arriving at work and have carried that notebook around with me wherever I have lived, a reminder of what I had been down south, the pain of what I was like to work with. I didn't really disagree with all the points; I knew they were basically true.

Weeks later, I would confront Natasha, reading back the words that had been spoken that night, that I had written down. She didn't deny anything—we both knew each point was true, but it still shocked Natasha that those words had reached my ears, that I had written them down and had worked quietly ever since. She had assumed that I was a bit depressed, which I think was quite possibly the case.

In fact, I was growing more and more depressed as the weeks went by. I want to be clear: Natasha and Jeff were a pleasure to be with, supported me fully, and were very kind to me. I chose to keep my growing illness from them, which was my own action, and I think it was the wrong one. I should not have shut down when I got sick. I should have let them into my illness—maybe things would have ended differently. Unfortunately, it is the choice I always pick whenever I start in on an episode. Shut down. Hide it. And that, frankly, often leads to my own undoing.

***

There were two absolutely wonderful things that happened while I was there. One was the birth of a new nephew for me, Jeff and Natasha's second child. I got a phone call at one in the morning on November 8, 2008. My services were needed!

I actually ran to their apartment, where Natasha was having very close contractions.

They phoned me a few hours later. It was a boy. When my first nephew woke up, we had a quick breakfast, and then we headed to the hospital. Taking some pictures of the entire family, I left them alone and had a bagel by myself in the cafeteria.

The other was the election of Barack Obama a few days before. The three of us adults watched from the apartment, cheering each win, every battle where Obama came out on top. We pulled out the champagne after they called Ohio, trying to be quiet, as their son slept in the room beside us. When I walked home that night, cars whizzed around me, blaring their horns, crowds of people gathered, laughter and cheers. What an epic night!

***

Writing this chapter has been painful and hard. The way I behaved around Jeff and Natasha still makes me cringe to this day and I think always floats around whenever we are together, probably killing any opportunity for a lovely, close relationship with them. I blame myself, and it hurts. My brother only wanted to make me happy. He saw me floundering up in Ottawa, no path ahead of me that would engage my mind and creativity. As he and Natasha talked it over every night, it became the right thing to do: invite me to co-own this little dream of a business.

After working with me for a while, they figured that, once past the stress of opening, I would slide easily into the role of manager. I would be able to supervise staff and control stock amounts. It would be much simpler for me when the store had been open for a few months.

In late January of 2009, I asked Jeff and Natasha if I could have a meeting with them at the restaurant next door to Whisk. The next morning, as we sat there nursing our Americanos, I screwed up the courage to deliver the news.

"So, I know I haven't been great with things. I'm sure you already know this, but I have to put it out there anyway. I am moving back to Ottawa at the end of April." I really wanted a cigarette.

"What?" They both gasped. This actually seemed like a surprise to them. I thought they had read me long ago, that they were expecting this.

"I am not doing well down here. You know that. I go home twice a month—and yes, I call that home. I made a good start at it, but for some reason, I just couldn't keep that up. I can't even learn the stupid payroll system."

"But Jocy, you are just getting back in your groove again," Jeff said.

"Well, this is not the life for me, unfortunately. I am really, really sorry. Honestly, I thought you would be relieved."

I had curled inward tight, depression rocking my nights, not even doing my job well. Yes, I was good with the staff, and I could gently sell things to customers. And I started up the huge hit: loyalty punch cards. I think they still do that in the store today. But my work had remained sub-par, and Jeff and Natasha deserved better than that. I worked the rest of the winter into spring, just barely getting by, putting on a great show whenever I was working at the store.

I still couldn't face the subway after my shifts, would walk up to the car service window, tapping on the glass and waving at the man behind the desk. And, at the end of April, I packed my things up and moved back home.

The whole affair was bittersweet. It clouds my memories. It prevents me from hanging the famous New Yorker map of the city, much as that makes me laugh. That is a shame, and I probably carry around thoughts that are exceedingly negative. But that is the way it has all spilled out. Hopefully, someday the weight will be less.

Chapter 19

A few years later, a visit to Brooklyn one particular American Thanksgiving married my paranoia to my reality. Every Friday of the holiday weekend, it was our custom to walk down from Park Slope to the neighbourhood of Fort Greene, where we would play soccer, tennis, and view the Manhattan skyline from the big hill in the park. There were always people going by, every which way, getting some exercise to counter the turkey fullness that still hung on from the day before.

I sat on a bench, watching the tennis players. I played with my phone and chatted with my sister-in-law Matilda. We were the only two in our party not partaking in physical activity of some kind.

It was after lunch that I decided to head back to Park Slope. I did get some exercise walking up the long hill along Sixth Avenue, headed for Jeff's place on Ninth Street. I sat on their stoop, resting after my exertion. When were the others coming back? I decided to text Jeffrey, but I suddenly realized I didn't have my phone. I began to panic, taking every single item out of my bag, emptying it out. Shaking it. That horrid, sinking feeling weighed down my torso. I looked up and saw a gaggle of Pattens heading toward me. I stood up.

"Do you guys have my phone?"

"No," my mum replied, echoed by all in her group. "Are

you sure it isn't in your bag? You have so much stuff in there."

I ignored that last comment. I was feeling dizzy. Dizzy and frantic. "I have to go back to the park. I think I left it there. It's on that bench, I'm certain. I have to go."

"Let's take Mum's car. I'll drive." Jeff went in and grabbed the keys off the front hall table, and we got going.

"Go faster!" I ordered him. "You could have made it through that, the light just turned yellow!" We found a spot to park and headed straight to the bench. Of course, it wasn't there. I don't know why I felt it could have been. We hunted the place, all the other benches, the whole area around the tennis courts, even peeking into a couple of garbage cans. No luck.

When we got back home, I picked up my bag to go through it again. But, my oldest nephew spoke up. "I think I have an idea," he said. "Why don't we check Find My Phone to see if we can locate it? Is it an iPhone?" He pulled his computer to the middle of the counter and got to work.

"What's your phone number?" he asked, opening up an app, typing as he went. "There it is!" A map had pulled up, and he pointed to a little green dot on it that was pulsating. "That's your phone." It seemed like magic to me.

The dot was on the edge of a green space on the map, the park that we had just scoured—exactly where I had been sitting. "Let's go," Jeff called. "Natasha, can you come with us? We need your eyes."

"Wait," my nephew said, holding up his hand. "It's moving."

We all crowded around the small screen, watching the dot head east so slowly, block by block. It stopped, again in a green space, a small park with no name. That was it.

"Okay, let's stay on the phone with you," Jeff said, "and you can tell us if there is more movement." We got back into Mum's car, this time with Natasha as navigator, and headed back down the slope.

The park seemed to be completely lined in metal gates and bars, it being dark now and the grounds closed. Somehow, I hauled myself over one of the gates—the other two had leapt, it seemed—and we each took different sections of the grounds to search. It wasn't easy. The park was larger than I had thought, and there were many paths, many benches, and a few garbage cans. Natasha used her phone to stay connected with my nephew, who was holding the position of air traffic controller on his laptop.

"You're right there," he told us. He was also tracking Natasha's phone and comparing it to my blip. "You are literally on top of it," he said. Right below us was a grate covering a manhole. My heart sank—somebody had trashed it in the sewer system. I walked around for another few minutes, kicking up the ground.

"Jocy, guess what!" Natasha called out. She came up close to me, her face almost in mine. "Hold out your hand," she said. "Just hold it out." This seemed a bit strange, but I did what she told me. "Here it is!" she said, pushing the phone into my outstretched hand. "It was over there on that bench," she motioned to the bench right beside the manhole. "I just took one last pass, and there it was, right in front of me. I don't know how I missed it."

"Oh, my God. Oh, my God," I said, giving her a big hug. "You found it! Oh, my God, I don't believe it!" I held the phone in front of me, making sure. What a relief to have it back. I was never happier to see it.

My life was in that thing.

***

A few days later, when my mum and I drove back to Canada, I began to have an odd sensation. Something was not right, and I was very confused. Who was following us? Why? It wasn't my usual psychotic symptoms that come on after some visits to my family. This was *really* real. My mum could back it up. The bleeping light on the computer screen, tracking me down.

The days after I got home were terrible. I couldn't shake the blips on the computer screen. They were tracking me by tracking my phone. I tried not to use it, not to carry it with me. But that didn't seem to help. I was still being followed.

I was upset at Dr. G.'s office. Upset about what had been put in motion down in Brooklyn. He spoke gently to me, which I felt was off—why wasn't he angry with these people, why wasn't he fiercely protective of me and my safety?

It took longer than normal to set me straight. At first, I refused the higher dose of Haldol. Just another way to follow me. But the psychotic break was taking me down, keeping me from sleep back on Edison, rearranging my thoughts and my words. I grew confused about the simplest of things. What did my friend just say? What did she really mean?

Finally, I accepted the increase in the Haldol. Over the next few weeks, I started smoothing out my brain. I slept. I showered. I emerged from my room on a more regular basis. I stopped fighting with my mum. And, finally, I could understand what was happening to me for what it was: a blip of illness.

Dr. G. and I talked about it later. It certainly was bad luck for my phone to go missing. I was lucky that my nephew was able to track it down. I saw my phone move around, walk a couple of blocks, rest on a park bench. That computer was really, in real life, tracking it down, at least for an hour or two. But, later, that phone became my own personal blip, and I was followed wherever I took it, even though the hunt for it was long over. Yes, I was nicely set up, set up for a bout of psychosis. It couldn't have been more perfect, playing into my terrible weakness, paranoia. It was kind of eerie. We almost laughed, me and Dr. G., sitting there discussing it, shaking our heads. What a story.

Chapter 20

It was funny how fast it all went. Lightning-quick, dry storm, electrical activity across the river at night. Across the river to Quebec, to the town of Gatineau, and further inland, the town of Buckingham, where I had never been, not until the summer of 2017.

I was giving up. Online dating was sucking me dry after a year of misses and fumbles. It just wasn't working. Until Marc, who was sort of an afterthought, squeaking in under the door at the very last minute as I was closing down my account. He sent me a note at the end of July, around my birthday. I studied his profile thoroughly, trying to figure out if he would hurt me, or if I would hurt him. But, there was only one way to check. I started a chat with him.

He was a widower, was 6 or 7 years older than me, was hidden by his bushy beard, and looked relaxed in a Hawaiian shirt and jeans. He lived in Quebec and worked at a midlevel government job that was, as he described it, soul-sucking. (How familiar this sounded. Shades of Stagger Lee. . .)

Favourite activities: nothing physical. No cycling in fancy riding outfits for him. No $300 hiking boots, perfectly kitted out at Mountain Equipment Co-op. He had a love of exploring towns, villages, and countrysides that seemed to match my own. He had a dog and several cats and drove around in an old, tired van. And he moonlighted at a fancy downtown hotel as a parking valet. A lot of material to work with. He was very interesting.

In person, Marc was just like his profile made him out to be, except for an added layer of eccentricity that I was not prepared for but took in stride, following him down the rabbit hole. My birthday was visible on my profile, and he had obviously noted this. Before we went into our chosen restaurant, he took out a guitar and played "Happy Birthday" quite pathetically. I was not expecting that either, but thought it was quite charming.

***

It was our third date, the third night in a row. "Pitou!" Marc said to his dog, rubbing her neck. "What a good girl, yes, a good girl."

"What does that name mean, Pitou?" I asked. We were in his van, driving aimlessly around the city, haunting the neighbourhoods on the periphery of downtown.

"Ahhh, it means nothing, really," he laughed. "It's French slang for dog, basically. It's not really a name." We were getting closer to his hotel. "Okay, Pitou, be good for your friends." He opened her door, and the dog jumped out and over to this really skinny valet, who bent down and stroked her.

"We'll be fine," the valet said, "Now, you two go and have some fun. . ." He winked at me and laughed with Marc. I think I even giggled.

I had been drinking hard lemonade and cider while we were driving around, alcohol with so much cloying sugar that I was amazed I went through so many cans. Definitely tipsy. The two of us settled into a booth in the bar, drinking beer and eating fries with truffle oil.

"You're thinking about having a smoke, aren't you?" He was teasing me. I was smoking so much around him, more than normal, but obviously couldn't light up in a public space. "Don't worry," he said, "It's all under control. I have a smoking room all lined up for us. You'll be able to light up as much as you want."

"Hmmm," I said. "Hopefully we will be doing better things than smoking."

"Well, let's go up, then." He signalled the waiter.

"Yes," I looked at him. "Let's go."

The next morning, we stumbled over to a diner, where he had a big breakfast and I had lots of coffee, excusing myself for a cigarette in the alley.

***

We were getting along just fine. He liked to have Pitou with us, so we were always driving to his place in Buckingham to collect her, me sucking back cans of sweet alcohol. When he ran into his place, a couple of cats would come out, and I patted them and tickled their chins. With the dog on board, we would drive around aimlessly before ending up at the hotel. (Marc never had a drink during these escapades, and, in fact, I don't remember him being much of a drinker at all. However, for me it was dangerous territory.) During these drives, we talked the whole time, nonstop really, finding more and more that we had in common. We laughed and joked; Marc had an excellent sense of humour.

He was a former military guy and loved to take part in veterans' activities, like the crab dinner in Gatineau that he took me to at the Legion. We danced alongside the other couples, a thrill I had never had before, or since. All completely normal, with other completely normal people.

He had ADHD and was all over the map. And he was late for everything. So, I started giving him a "false" time for him to shoot for, something much earlier than was needed. And still he was late. (Dr. G. told me about some of his patients with ADHD, who have no sense of time. They have an appointment at two but are not there yet. Dr. G.'s phone will ring, and a new message will come in at ten after two: "Hi, Dr. G., I am way out across town, and I think I am going to be late.")

***

Marc always wanted to check out thrift stores. I know lots of people who loved hunting for a bargain, but it had never really grown on me. However, I humoured him. But one day he went in for a cribbage board and came out with six or seven other things. I did wonder why he needed three teddy bears and a stack of colouring books.

It was after blitzing the shops, sitting in the van about to leave, that I asked him. "Marc," I said quietly. "Are you a hoarder?"

He didn't look at all surprised. He gave a funny little laugh and said, "Yes, I am. How could you tell?"

"This, here, today," I answered. "The fact that I have never been inside your house. All the presents you bring me. Your entire van, almost like you are living out of it."

He agreed to show me his house, something I knew was very difficult for him. He was making himself extremely vulnerable. When we arrived there, we stayed in the driveway, in his van, Marc rubbing his face in the tension.

"I've lived here for almost 25 years," he said. "With my wife, with Joanne. But, she was really sick—cancer. She was housebound for a whole year, she didn't go anywhere, she was too sick. And, when it was time—" He paused, looking for words. "When it was time, I called an ambulance, and the paramedics came and took her. But they made comments about our house. And, sure enough, afterward I got a call from the city. And the fire department. They came and investigated; they gave me deadlines. Even the SPCA. Clean up, or lose everything."

He didn't look at me. "When is the deadline?" I asked.

"I don't know. I don't keep up with it, I don't listen anymore. But, it's soon." He took the keys out of the ignition. "C'mon, let's go," he said.

The front porch sagged, with an absent railing that made me nervous as we walked up to the entrance. When he opened the front door, he asked me to wait outside as he moved things around so that I could get in. A powerful smell of cat urine hit my nose. Yes, I think that that was the first thing. And then it was the visual. The sheer volume of stuff as I squeezed down the hall into the living room.

Piles of papers and magazines that were taller than me. Record players on top of speakers on top of tires, mail and paper bills littered every bit of floor space that didn't hold a pile of junk—and trust me, there wasn't a lot of space. A cat screeched and jumped near my shoulder onto a stack of books, making me start, the books swaying a bit under her sudden weight, poofs of dust and dirt caught in the light.

It was impossible to enter the kitchen that lay straight ahead. Boxes full of everything and anything, loose clothes stacked floor to ceiling, with crap all over the countertops, stovetop, and fridge, blocking access to the back door. I shuffled to the right, down a hallway of sorts, squeezing past piles of clocks and broken records and CDs. His bedroom was down at that end, consisting of a single mattress on the floor in the doorway and stuff everywhere else. Some shirts, ties, and trousers hung from various lamps; other than that, nothing made sense. I took a peek at the bathroom and closed the door very quickly. The stench, the dirt.

"Nose blindness" is what they call it. When I finally commented on the eye-watering smell of urine, Marc looked surprised. He had lived with the stench for so long that he didn't notice it anymore.

Marc had 30 pairs of speakers that formed a row in the back of the basement toward the window. If you could call it a row. Actually, you couldn't really enter the basement, since there was just too much stuff in the way. And the backyard was a disaster zone. An old, rusted-out pickup truck leaned a bit onto two yellow fridges. There was a big blue tarp covering most of the piles on the lawn. To shield the crap from rain, or to try to keep the neighbours off his back, I didn't know.

After that first visit, we sat in his van again, me smoking, a little too stunned to speak. I opened a can of cider, chugging it down. "We will get through this," I said quietly. But underneath, I had my doubts. I wasn't really all that sure.

***

My family had been holidaying, on and off, in the Eastern Townships of Quebec for some years, first at a resort, then at several rented cottages along the lakes. And, finally, a farmhouse rental, big enough to hold all 12 of us at varying ages and stages.

That August, Marc came to stay over weekends, and he and I would wake early and climb in the car, heading to a Tim Hortons for coffee and Timbits. We would then just drive for miles, through villages and countrysides. We showed up back at the house around 10, where all was in swing, and we, I think, were a bit frowned on.

It was a wonderful time, but we had to get back to business and return home. I had been doing some research on hoarding and talked to a few people about help they could provide. A man named Richard was particularly promising. He ran a company that took on serious jobs—hoarding and crime scenes, other heavy-duty cleanups.

Richard and his partner Tina met us outside Marc's house. A next-door neighbour who was a friend and who knew about the situation joined us. I stayed outside, smoking and pacing, while the four of them took a tour, joining them in the backyard at the end. We agreed to meet at a local restaurant to discuss things over coffee.

"I think things are really serious here," Richard started off with, the five of us settled into a roadhouse booth. "You have a city deadline, and that's serious. I can make that go away, the city, the SPCA. Just let me know. But, I need to know: Can you part with 50 percent of your stuff?"

"No," Marc said. "No way."

"Twenty-five percent?" asked Richard.

"No," Marc answered.

"Could the two of us sort through your things together, and you give up 10 percent?" Richard said.

Marc shrugged. "Yes, maybe I could do that."

This was mind-blowing to me. I thought of all the junk that crowded his home. It *was* junk. How could anyone want to keep it? It didn't make sense.

Richard detailed everything that he and Tina could do. The whole process, with machines on site, workers wrapped up in protective gear, carting stuff away to be disposed of, loading it into trucks. And then an industrial clean. There would be interaction with the city, getting the authorities off his back. There would be counselling for Marc, a psychiatrist who specialized in hoarding, appointments all set up for him. It all sounded great, except the price tag.

"Marc, it's okay. You can find a way to pay it," I said. But, I knew right away that he wasn't going to sign on. I knew before the quote came in. That if Richard told Marc that *he* would give Marc the money, Marc would still say no.

After Richard and Tina left, over more coffee, his friend and I tried to talk Marc into it, to find the money. To me it seemed so simple; it could be taken care of in a week. Great, find the money.

In the end, Marc rented a couple of storage units, and decided to cart his stuff over. Would I help him? He hired two local women to come with a bucket and mop to clean. They were going to charge him two grand. I never found out what happened with them, but I don't think it worked out. He needed heavy-duty help, not a bucket and mop. Where would they even begin? No, that was not right.

***

What the hell was I doing? I was getting more and more confused. I had a mental illness, and so did Marc. I was cool with that. Or at least I thought I was. I mean, I supposedly had a big, open mind when it came to mental illness. I had my own and would look past any that a partner might have. I knew all too well what stigma was. But I started having a really tough time thinking about Marc and the issues that came with him.

A van so out of shape that its brakes suddenly stopped working, causing us to have a serious accident. Him pushing on to load up the storage spaces, which I did not support.

Pitou being signed over to me so that Marc wouldn't lose her to the SPCA. Being so out of touch with reality that it seemed to inhabit him. Not a psychotic thing—just an unawareness of the world around him, a trait that at first endeared him to me. It was becoming impossible to be in a relationship with him.

We were sitting in his van in my driveway, Pitou in the back. I knew what I had to do, but I hesitated. This was hard, harder than I thought it would be.

"You know, Marc, I wonder if I somehow make you worse off," I said. "Like, maybe helping you too much." So far, I hadn't figured it out, what exactly I wanted to say. "I think you need to do some of this stuff on your own. I think I get in the way."

"What's that?" Marc asked. "No, no, your help. . .I am really glad I have your help."

"But it's not going anywhere. You aren't taking your whole house thing seriously. You want to stop it all with band-aid solutions. But, that's not going to work," I said, "It's way too big for that."

Marc was avoiding my gaze, hands in his lap. "I just have to get it moved into the storage lockers. Then, I'll hire people to clean. That's what I have to do," he said.

"But that's not going to work," I said. "There is so much stuff! You need so much more help than that. And, you've closed off all the real solutions. I guess I'm wondering if maybe I should take myself out of this scenario. Maybe you need to deal with it on your own, in your own way. The city deadline is coming, I worry about Pitou, if you'll be allowed to keep her. And, I worry about you. But the truth is, I can't stand by and watch all of this unfold."

"Are you saying you want out of this, our relationship? No, I need you. You can't just leave." Marc was still staring at his hands.

"But I have to," I said gently. "I am not saying no to being with you. I am just saying that you have to fix all of these things on your own. I believe the whole storage idea is a bad one, but I guess I can tell you that until I am blue in the face."

How could I be rejecting him like this, when he was at his lowest?

"Do what you have to do, and then call me," I said. "I will be there for you, once you have fixed everything." Part of me knew that this wasn't true. He wouldn't fix things; I wouldn't wait for him.

"Are you really doing this?" he asked.

"Yes, I am." I opened my door. "I'm sorry, Marc. I just can't watch this happen to you. Call me when you have your house back, when everything is sorted out." I got out and leaned my head back in. "Goodbye, Pitou," I said, giving her a scratch under the chin. "Goodbye, Marc," I said to him. "I love you. I look forward to when you can call me." I shut the door.

And there it was, done.

I heard a few times from him over the next six months or so. Invitations to veterans' events, would my mum and I like to join him, and no, he still hadn't fixed anything. And then that was it.

What happened to Pitou? She wouldn't have made it in a shelter.

It was only a few months ago that I erased his contact information from my phone, so even if I did want to check in on him and see if he was okay, I can't.

Part Two

Chapter 21

My granny died in January of 2010. It was crisp and cold outside. She had made it well into her nineties, had lived a good life, and was dying a good death. She lay in her bed in the suite on Edison, and had many last visits with friends and family, with my aunts and uncles, many of my cousins making the trip up to Ottawa. On the morning of the day she died, my uncle and I went down to the liquor store, where we loaded up on wine and scotch and a small bottle of Grey Goose vodka for me. Later, we were joined by an aunt, and the three of us were in Granny's room with her when her breathing changed, my uncle saying softly, "We're here, it's okay," caressing her cheek. And she let go; she slipped away. It was gentle and easy, her death. A good death, the way people should exit this world. People came quickly to see her, and the rituals carried on.

The system had worked really well for Granny, especially as she had the money to take a step up in care. She was lucky. There was a nurse for about 12 hours each day, and personal support workers (PSWs) constantly getting things done for us so we could focus exclusively on Granny.

On one occasion, I went outside to the porch with two of my aunts, where we shared a cigarette or two. "You know," one of them said, "you could do that." She motioned indoors. "You would be great at it." She meant a PSW. At the time, I was broke and clueless about where to go. So, having no money or work, I was a bit intrigued. And, it turns out, my aunt was right.

***

The Herzing Institute was a small college in the basement of a shopping centre in the east end of the city. The PSW course was a six-month affair, half of the course being taught in the classroom and the other half working out in the real world. We were all a good bunch. I liked my classmates—there were about eight of us—and came to rely on them, especially in one of the long-term care homes where I spent six weeks fumbling around.

The coursework was super easy for me. And I am good with people, so that should have been great as well. But it wasn't until my practicum at the long-term care home that I reached a hard wall. We students fanned out through the wards, I was on one with Kim, my favourite colleague. I had to get 10 people, all with some form of dementia, ready and eating breakfast within 90 minutes. Bathed, dressed, diapers changed, groomed, all with a smile. But the max that I could turn out was two people; I was simply too slow and not particularly useful with my hands. The real nurses got impatient with me, and my days were horrible. I absolutely dreaded them and would go home in tears.

I got through the six weeks and made it out alive. I got the worst marks in the class. I was so ashamed that I couldn't add that extra bit of care to my charges. I was simply unable to do the diaper up without the other half falling down and so on. The two supervising nurses told my teacher that I showed little care for the clients, which was very untrue and genuinely hurtful.

Upon graduation in 2011, I was sent to an agency to apply for a position as a "travelling PSW." I was accepted right away, and after a few days of more training, including shadowing an experienced worker as he made his rounds, I was on my own.

I had my little white Mazda, I had supplies and paperwork, and I was given clients out across the west end. I went from home to home with great confidence, spending an hour or two doing whatever was needed. I could set the pace as I would like it, and I set it at slow but steady. Four clients a day, spread out, though I was meant to build up to a full-time schedule (I ignored this bit). I was reliable, kind, compassionate, and engaged. Every two weeks, I would drop off my completed paperwork at headquarters. I met many interesting people, mostly older adults, but a few younger ones. I did feel like I was making a difference, and that that was acknowledged. I can't tell you how much those last two points mean in the life of a PSW.

I worked part-time, unable to increase my caseload, trying to take care of my brain as I drove all around town visiting people. I made it through almost a full year when I hit a snag. In the late summer of 2012, my brain got sucked in by a particularly bad set of episodes, psychosis, and depression. I kept calling in sick over a period of about two months. The idea of getting out of bed and hitting the road to work for five hours became incomprehensible. I was exhausted and very, very down. When my call-ins became too much, when they were affecting the lives of colleagues (who had to quickly find my day's-worth of replacements), I was finally told to take a break. The bosses were very understanding, and we agreed I would take five weeks off, try going back in late October of 2012.

October rolled on, and I half-heartedly resumed my work. But I quickly fell back into the pattern of calling in sick every morning. It was decided—by me, my mum, my doctor—that I would step down and go on a disability pension. It was that bad, and it was that obvious.

I remember how poor I was at filling out the forms for CPP disability. My friend Jasmin was visiting me from Toronto for a few days and helped me punch up the application. I had to illustrate just how truly disabled I was, unable to work. I had to get it right the first time.

Dr. G. must have written a kick-ass physician portion, because I was accepted on my first try.

***

Today, my mum and I run most of our errands together and hang out with other people as a team. We have become regulars at so many places now: the bakery, the fish store, the liquor store, our friends. I think people must wonder about a 51-year-old doing everything with her seventy-five-year-old mother.

The reasons I moved here with my mum in 2016 were partly financial, my disability pension only paying so much. It was getting hard to take care of myself. I was still pretty much a wreck, my illness at its full force in those years. I made coffee successfully in the mornings, but making dinner for myself in the evenings was stressful. Going to a grocery store on my own to buy ingredients was hard. And now I wonder: Would I be able to take complete care of myself, without assistance from my mum, if I were on my own again, in my own place? (And, did I ever really, always needing a cash infusion from her? Have I ever truly lived independently?)

The difference is the anxiety that I feel, the panic attacks that started up when I had been on disability for a year or two. It is not schizoaffective disorder that creates the real disability anymore—over the past months, since the months of 2019, that has been easier on me, though not perfect. (I will write about 2019 later, as it was a real game changer for me. My illness is much different now, and in so many ways, my life has improved.) No, it is the panic and anxiety that cut my legs off today, and it gets even worse when I do have a change in mood or thinking. And I don't know what to do about it.

***

After I got on disability, I moved into a really cheap flat outside the downtown area. I fixed it up, painted it with bright colours, had curtains made. And I sat in my dad's red chair, smoking, listening to music, trying to manage my anxiety levels.

Buddy and Finny moved with me, of course, though it would be Buddy's last apartment. These two wonderful, dependable cats saw me through so much—almost all my apartments, New York City, through school and jobs. Through applying for disability, through all the smoking, which I now feel terrible about.

In 2014, Buddy died at age 18 and a half. I had him put down by a vet who made house calls. It was after terrible constipation plagued him for a while, with no treatment helping. Too many nights at vet emerg. It wasn't fair to him. I kept his ashes so I could mix them with Finny's when it was her turn.

***

I moved into my last independent apartment in 2015. It definitely was a step up in terms of niceness, but it was very much in the west end, and I couldn't really walk anywhere. But it was close to my mum's new place, now that she had left Edison, and I ended up hanging out with her a lot. We were still sorting things out, making sense out of the unfinished basement, looking at the order of rooms, the plumbing, the vents. We discussed tiling, colours, flooring, researching our options. My mum would cook up a wonderful meal, and then I would get into my little red Fiat and drive back to this quiet apartment.

And in the middle of the hallway, I would find Finny, mewing softly. I felt so badly about leaving her that I tried to spend as much time with her as possible during the day. But those evenings—every single one—I went to my mum's. I have a hard time forgiving myself, abandoning Finny at dinnertime, when she was so unhappy.

Finny would always cuddle with me and sleep beside me in bed. We had a little routine. It gradually dawned on me that she had arthritis and getting up on my bed was a major deal. So, one day I got rid of the box spring and made my bed just the mattress on the floor. Sure enough, Finny was able to just step up on the mattress and get comfortable.

She was clearly struggling, and I realized the time had come. On her nineteenth birthday, the travelling vet showed up. Finny and I had had a very special day. I wore my black dressing gown, soft and plushy, and I cradled her in my arms. From morning to the evening, I held her the whole time. When the vet came, I was ready.

Afterward, the vet took Finny's body, returning her ashes to me a few days later. I now had her ashes as well as Buddy's. The new owner of my childhood home on Edison agreed to let me spread their combined ashes in the backyard, which they used to love so much, even if just from the screened-in porch. I have not touched that black dressing gown since. It is in the deepest realms of my closet, never to be worn or washed again.

Finny's death was really hard, and the guilt was tremendous. It affected me profoundly. Several weeks after, at the end of May of 2016, I showed up at Dr. G.'s office in bad shape.

"You know, she's talking to me," I said to him. "My voices have moved over, stepped aside, and made room for her. She says hello to me." I banged my head with my right arm. "She says hello to you."

Dr. G. seemed a little confused. He leaned forward, searching my face. "It sounds like there have been some new thoughts since we last met. Tell me all about them."

"Finny tells me about the life she leads. She says it is just wonderful." I giggled a bit. "She says Buddy is there, and Mickey and Poppy." I stopped for a second, listening to more from my dead cat, taking in what she had to say to me. I contorted my mouth. "And she says my dad is there, and all of my grandparents. It is super nice. Always springtime." I suddenly felt very serious. "She tells me to go to her."

"What does that mean, go to her?"

"It's kind of simple. All I have to do is go to a bridge over the highway, and land in front of a car going 120 klicks. I won't feel a thing, and then I'll be there. With her, with all the others. I'm actually pretty psyched about it." I started to wave my hands around above my head, my thumbs turned up, excited.

Dr. G. rubbed his chin. "You know, I think it would be a good idea to call your mother in. Just hang on a sec." He flipped to the front of my file and picked up the phone.

And then, soon enough, my mother was there. Off to the hospital I went, this time clueless.

Chapter 22

From a birthday card dated 1995:

Jocy,

Try to get all that you can out of and enjoy being 26. It has at least one thing going for it—it isn't 30.

Love,

R.

Dear Ruby Tuesday,

Wow, that really blows my 51-year-old brain. How precocious we were! The folly of youth—how clueless we were back then, our lives stretched out ahead of us, waves of experiences, both good and bad, still waiting to surprise us as we aged. But here we are now, in middle age. We are rubbing our eyes and wondering how that ever happened, how the years got away from us. And we would do anything to go back and do it all again. Although this time, we are certain that we would get it right. I know you don't feel that way, but I do.

And for all this time, I have been older than you, you a child of the early days of 1970, a mere six months between us. You always rubbing it in, your youth, born as a new decade rolls ahead, with me planted firmly in the last months of an eventful decade, literally a child of the sixties. (Something which in later years became a source of pride for me, when "six months" meant nothing as we creaked toward middle age together.)

Now it is your turn to be the older one, the wiser one, the one with experience, guiding me through menopause, the aging process as it turns me into a shadow, something invisible, no attention needed. A woman in her 50s. Except you have a husband, you have kids, you have the things that make aging worth it, a badge of some sort. Well done, well earned. I have no such things, unless you count actually making it to my fifties alive.

Now I turn to you for advice, for relief. I just turned 51—come on, really, time for loose skin below my chin already? You tell me crepe-like skin is part of the deal. Changing hair texture, hot flashes, small brown spots, laugh lines hardening to wrinkles. A brain like mush, and with it, the ability to remember things sliding away.

***

I woke up at 3:00 a.m. in the dark, a vague feeling of needing to pee. It can wait until I get up later, I told myself. But then I decided to go ahead to the bathroom, that it would give me the opportunity to sleep in later. Unfortunately, I slid on to the floor as I was turning off my mattress and landed in a lump. I went to haul myself to standing, but a sudden leek of pee was on me, sending me back into that lump. That's strange, I thought, let's try that again. Sure enough, with the exertion of hauling myself up, I peed a bit again. It was dark, I was half awake, and I was a little bit scared. I realized this exertion thing wasn't going to happen. So, I got on all fours, my knees on the hard wooden floor, and I crawled out of my bedroom, down the hall to the bathroom, into it—still completely in the dark—and over to the toilet. I can pee in here if I have to, on the cold tiled floor, I thought. Hauled myself up and sat down on the toilet, just in time for whoosh!

Ruby, you didn't prepare me for that!

***

I have worn many hats in my life. Girl, woman, daughter, sister, friend. Woman with mental illness. American. Canadian. And those are just the basics. There are so many other hats I have worn, or at least tried on. I tried, as I became older, to navigate all these hats in my life. Through my childhood, my teenage years, young adult years, and now my middle years, I have taken those hats off and on again and again, trying to make sense of each rite of passage.

Now, take all those hats, and live them with a serious mental illness. An up-down mental illness. A psychotic illness that twists every experience in its path. Every one of those hats is bruised by it, is informed by it. My mental illness made it really hard to establish an identity, to really wear a hat. This especially when I was so obsessed with appearing normal. Normal Woman hat, if there is even such a thing.

Bipolar disorder can lead to a lot of trouble. And not just the numbing low of depression. There is the sweet seduction of mania, so pleasant at first (before the psychosis and the darkness hit). It can often feel so glorious and liberating. It can bring with it the need to spend money, to shop in a frenzy for so many things, big and small. This is something the depressed me understands little about, except in the form of regrets and maxed-out credit cards.

Is the "normal" me when I am depressed, lost, down and out? Is that my baseline? I have lost track over the years. Maybe take some pills, achieve a state that appears to be of normalcy, a state where I am better. Is that the real me? Am I walking around with a normal mood that is only such thanks to medication? And mania! The me that laughs and talks loudly, sees things golden and pure, fast and efficient. Surely that is me, the real me. Take more Seroquel, Zyprexa, Haldol, more Thorazine. Beat it back, like a small fire, beat it back to normalcy. Whatever that is. Some tell me that rather than creating a new personality, the drugs just peel back the sick layers and reveal the real me. I don't buy it—we haven't seen the "real" me in decades.

With all of this going on, it is hard to work out just how the concept of disability shapes my life. There is a disabled me, that's for sure, a disabled hat. Although I try not to incorporate it too much into my identity, I cannot dismiss it entirely. But I am not just a manic depressive, a schizophrenic, a drunk, a nervous wreck. I have a mental illness, but it does not define me. It may shade all my selves, all my hats. It may create disability. But it is not the first thing out of the gate.

Sometimes I see that my illness is with me, everywhere I turn. And, sometimes I think that is not such a bad thing. I ask what I would have been like without it, without my illness. But, what am I because of it? Surely, I can find positives out of it. I am more compassionate, more sensitive, more forgiving than I would have been without my illness. When I experience true happiness, I am more thankful than I might have been. When I see a person who is obviously struggling on the street, I am more connected, I am not afraid.

***

Another thing I stumble over when I begin to ask questions about myself, about who I really am, is what kind of impact my sexuality has. Sex itself is something that I don't hold as steadily in hand as I wish I did. I have a fractured path with it, from when I was six years old, and never really got off on the right foot after that.

My brothers and I were not raised in a very open family when it came to this topic, and this was, I think, due to my father and his upbringing. I did get one book when I was 12: *What's Happening to Me?* And another one a little later, *Our Bodies, Ourselves,* something my dad snorted at when the daughter of family friends handed this jewel over to me. I am sure that this is evidence of the environment I was in.

So, um, yes, sex itself—an uncomfortable hat, and not a totally relaxed topic, unless I am in one of two mind frames. And this includes both being with lovers (you see, it was hard to write that word), as well as just discussing it in everyday settings with friends. I need to be either drunk or high. (I mean high as in a mood swing high. I have never been seduced by recreational drugs.)

When I lost my virginity, I was manic. When I first slept with Stagger Lee, I was mildly, happily drunk, and a tad manic. Most of my time in bed with him and others over the years was either when I was drunk or hypomanic. When I am drunk or high, I don't mind saying the word "lover."

On two occasions of my many manias, I experienced a round of hypersexuality, which can easily happen in this illness. (This basically means that I wanted to have a lot of sex, as opposed to my usual hyposexuality, lack of sex drive.) The first time was in Ireland—this was the beginning of my highs and the beginning of my sex life. I smiled, laughed, flirted, and slept with quite a few people. And then, again, about 20 years later, when I got mixed up with some men on a dating site. It proved to be very scary, how suddenly I could turn.

***

Although I live in Canada and consider myself to be a Canadian, I have to acknowledge that I was born in the US to an American father, and that when I die, there will be no Pattens left in Canada. It will have just been a blip, starting with my dad following a psychoanalyst up here, and ending with my brothers chasing dreams back in the US again.

I have issues with the American me. Lots of people seem to. Once they know my heritage, once I reveal my birthplace, I am immediately placed under suspicion. How can an American be a real Canadian? It has been said that one part of the definition of being Canadian is in fact to not be American. I am at the losing end of it, and there isn't anything I can do about it. I don't struggle with the European immigrants my mother's family gave me. But I will always have to answer questions about my birth. But maybe that is not that big of a deal. A luxury, perhaps—which white Western country was I actually born in? So many immigrants have far more legitimate grounds for an identity crisis. I should keep my mouth shut.

***

My mother's side of the family lived through interesting times and made many choices along the way that had a huge impact on her and her siblings. By the time they settled in Canada in 1949, the lore was already being spun. Nazis, hidden Jews, the Resistance, London during the Blitz. There were great stories to be told there. Even the dark ones, about the few who really were Nazis.

My father gave me hearty New Englanders and wealthy Southerners. The real deal, going back centuries. My dad used to work on his family's genealogy and found stories of plantation owners who took their lemonade on the veranda while their slaves did punishing work out in the fields.

What does my family's past mean for me now? It is a big load to carry, though everybody has dark spots in their story. (Dark spots like my grandfather's family in New England, with the Salem, Massachusetts judge.) However, Nazis and plantation owners go well beyond those ordinary dark spots.

Perhaps my role today is to reflect on my family's legacy, think of all the horrors that come with it. I can't change the past. But, as I go forward, I can be more mindful of others around me: who sews the clothes I wear, who picks my fruit, who bags my groceries. I need to challenge myself at every crossroad, with eyes wide open, with actions that bring light into the darker chapters of my family history.

***

"Yank, Yank, go home! Yank, Yank, go home!" This during recess in elementary school, before I had made little friendships with other stragglers. It is amazing to me that I have lived the life of an outcast this whole time. It started there in school, with my patched eye and lack of friends. It would roll farther in the snow, picking up speed with "Loser," "Fattie," and "Psycho" being added as I rolled along. The negative hats, the painful hats. They have played a role in who I am as well, and I will never forget that.

I have been sifting through myself over the last few pages, looking at some of the things that come together to make up me. It is a challenge, but one that I think everybody goes through. And, it is ongoing. What I did yesterday, what I plan for tomorrow and the future, all continue to add to my sense of identity. I believe that I will continue to build and grow, change, until the day I die, just as others do. I do not know what lies ahead for me, but whatever there is, it will make a difference to who I am. I still have more hats to try on.

Chapter 23

I live with my mother. I am 51, and people think I am off simply by that fact. And they're right. That is one sign that all is not right in me. One sign, for me. Others who stay on in the family home may not have mental illness, of course. There are many reasons involved in taking this path. But for me, living with my mum is a sign that I am a bit off.

This is my fourth attempt at writing the chapter on Stagger Lee. He was with me from the winter of 1993 to the fall of 2007. There was a lot of living and growing in there. There were dreams of wellness, friendships, sex, marriage, children, careers. It was all that and still more. He held out hope and love and security, and I brushed him off.

So, here is my fourth attempt at this chapter. The first three sent me into tailspins of self-doubt and depression. Out of the entire book, there is none like it. It is a chapter of pain and regret, of shaking the window into the past, rattling it with ferocity, with desperation. No, no, I want to do it again, I want to make different decisions, I will cry. But of course, there is nothing to be done about it, no second chances. Years ago, I made decisions that have left me living in my mother's downstairs at the age of 51, today.

This is not whinging. This is anger at myself.

In daydreams, I named our children. Planned a wedding. Found the perfect house to live in, with our growing family.

But there are no children. And, how I wanted them! I fucked it up, and here I am with my mum, who could have been grandma to kids living nearby, in that joyous role. I feel I have robbed her of that. She stays in close contact with the kids south of the border, visiting with them as often as possible. But I know she notices it too, the empty chairs. Many of her close friends and family have grandchildren around them, and after talking to them, I know she is a little saddened.

The months around my fiftieth birthday in 2019 were difficult, especially since I had just come out of hospital. Twenty-five was a hard one, 30 maybe not as bad. I was not prepared for age 40, and now this. Fifty. Actually, 51. Solidly middle-aged. I have met my stale date, and now I must go about laying to rest any dream I ever had for myself.

I wonder if that day has come for me, that day when dreaming ends. I have no more to lean in on, no backup plans. I should have been prepared. But it turns out I wasn't, and now I live life day-to-day, not much variation, with my fifties and sixties stretched out in front of me, the plague of sameness slowly smouldering in my heart and head.

I am being hard on myself, I know. Overly dramatic. Lots could happen in the coming years. My mind is clearer than it has been in a long while, for months now. Maybe I can reverse that plague of sameness, take on something new, work on this book, write those difficult chapters, including the one on Stagger Lee.

I remember when I was a kid, thinking about how old I would be when we reached the year 2000. Thirty, which seemed so old. But that never mattered. I would be slim, I would be happy, I would have kids and an adoring man, and I would be a brilliant writer–musician–filmmaker–similar. I would have it all.

I have to say, it seems to me that up to now, I have achieved very little in my life. I guess that is what can happen when you spend most of your adulthood being knocked about by an illness, especially of a psychiatric nature. An illness that robs you of your ability to play out your dreams, and to create the groundwork on which to build. An illness that at other times spins you out of control, everything coming at you fast and furious. An illness that can cause your thinking to do somersaults through logic, landing in a place where it settles into a loss of reality.

***

I love you. I had heard these words once, I had true love, and I let it slip between my fingers. I was playing and didn't think it was a serious choice I had to make. I was wrong. And the pain of mental illness—it felt like it was something to live for. That going through it would give me a badge and an ability to reach for the top. That, when I conquered it, I would use that pain to be like the others. The others who had learned to live with their demons, to use them to stoke creativity, and become film directors, authors, poets, composers. A *Touched with Fire* sort of thing.

So, I gave in to it a bit, I became fully ill, my life became one of disability. And that suddenly was all that it was about. And I didn't fully appreciate how the years were being ticked off, so fast, like months, really, not years. And that magic age—I still do not know precisely what that age was—came and was passed. And now, suddenly, the magic lives in the past. Always dreaming about the future, and suddenly I am now forced to look back to when it was good, my face smushed up against a window, a window into my past. Because there were times when it really was good. And I never really lived for it. I only dreamed.

***

Upon arriving home from work back in the late nineties, I would take my meds right away so that the timing was just right. Just right, so that I could get my daily fill of *M*A*S*H* reruns and then pass out on my bed. My head would be filled with visions of mad, intense love with a sexy, sensitive doctor, these visions sinking away with me as I drifted off to sleep.

Through much of my adulthood, I had found it best to love men who were not real. My daydreams and fantasies were populated with men like Hawkeye Pierce. For these men, I would be the one woman that would matter most in their lives. I would be so spectacular as to cause them to fall off their seats. Sometimes, my head would get so lost in these stories, I would get a sense of how truly sick and disturbed I was. It became clear that other people didn't daydream these things, or not to the extent that I did. I felt embarrassed. I never really fessed up to Dr. G. Yes, many of those around me knew I lived with mental illness, that I got sick with it every now and then, and it could turn into insanity. But these people did not understand the true nature of my insanity. They did not know that it informed my every day, that it wasn't there just for hospitalizations. That it crept into my thoughts as a desperate plea for love.

***

I wonder if I would have taken to school, studied my way into an interesting and worthwhile career. Or, would I have taken the creative route, followed my dream into film? Maybe I would have done nothing, found nothing, worked at nothing. No real job, few friends, overweight. Even without an illness, I wonder about that.

"What do you want to be when you grow up?" As a child, I loved playing that game, entertaining that essential question. I am good at talking about careers that I could have enjoyed. I have lots of experience with it. There were many things I wanted to be when I grew up. I wanted to be a veterinarian, a marine biologist, a zoologist. Yes, it would be something with many degrees attached to it, but it would be with animals, whether from the little examination table to the Jeep quietly tracking a large male lion.

I had a future, whether it was zoology or teaching piano. I could have been a music editor in film, something I now know would have been the best job ever. I had all the tools with me, in myself. I was smart and able to attack anything at all. It was all straight ahead for me. At least, until I got sick. When I couldn't focus, couldn't get out of bed, couldn't stick with anything.

Total systems shutdown.

There are so many could-haves. Everybody has lists of could-haves in their back pocket. Few of us reach the could-have goal, made it in reality, as opposed to somewhere where the brain stores dreams and wishes.

Two of those people, the kind that do what they want to when they grow up, are my brothers. One is the chair of politics at an Ivy League school, the other a lawyer turned wine merchant in New York City, his career made on a big wish and a lot of work. Not easy, but fun in the doing.

I could have tackled almost any of my dreams. I should have. But, Dr. G. tells me it is not so cut-and-dry. Everybody struggles, those with mental illness especially. I have reason to be jealous, to be sad, to be angry. There was a reason I didn't meet all those goals along the way. Not my dream job, not even a job that was close.

But take it easy! The fact that both my siblings hit the nail on the head should not be reason for such self-pity. I should dust myself off and roll up my sleeves. Brush off that keyboard, see what I can do. I am not talking about bootstraps—I hate anything that has to do with bootstraps. I am just trying to be a little forgiving of myself. Give myself permission to go easy, and use my improved mood and mind to play. Who knows what will come of it? I have begun right here on these pages, and I will see where it takes me. A hat for a writer, maybe?

Chapter 24

Sometimes I will let myself go there, back in my past. Sometimes I imagine how it could have been. It goes something like this:

I am 26. I take my green bike and ride lazily down the Dovercourt hill, heading for the Boots at the mall below. Not sure which one is the best, I buy all three kinds of pregnancy tests available to me. The ride back is harder; not only is it uphill, but the tests are very heavy themselves, psychologically, burrowing down in my knapsack on my back. I had heard that cyclists shouldn't use backpacks—it changes their centre of gravity and makes it easier to get knocked off. I ride too slowly for that to be an issue, and anyway, wouldn't a fall at this point in my life be a good thing? Nothing invested yet.

Only when I test positive on all three tests do I try to reach Stagger Lee. He should come over after work. I would say we have a lot to talk about.

***

The snow is so white and the sun so bright that I squint down to the little bundle in an orange snowsuit playing around my legs. I smile, and the bundle giggles, looking up at me with blonde curls and dark eyes, my daughter. I realize that I am always taken aback by the fairness of her hair—I had never thought that any child of mine would be anything but dark. But as I always come to remember, Stagger Lee is blond, or was until grey hair started showing up in his beard, his sideburns, the thick mop on his scalp.

"Soph," I say. "Do you see him yet?" She stands straight and covers her eyes as she gazes at all the kids streaming out of the school door, like she is a sailor and is on the front deck, checking the small island out, the one that her boat was about to meet.

As usual, Julian comes at us from the left side, the one opposite our sight line. "Hey, sweetie, how was your day?" I call this out to the seven-year-old in a green winter jacket who has unceremoniously dropped his backpack on the ground beside me. A grade two mum beside me looks at me and rolls her eyes as she laughs at our two. They are both slamming their bodies on the top of the hill, sliding down on the track, landing at the bottom in a pile of boots and snow pants.

"Come on, Julian," I call out. "Today is Grandma!" He comes running at that. My two love their time at my mum's house. Hot chocolate, baking cookies, listening to Joni Mitchell as the winter sun sets at 4:00 p.m. It feels good to leave them there, memories of my own childhood stirred up.

Once alone, I drop the dog back home and head toward the community centre and the pottery room there. I look at my items in the window, fired up with blues and greens, mugs and vases, dinner plates and fruit bowls. Nothing super outrageous, nice enough to adorn a shelf but basic. Enough to contribute a little money to running our household as I sell them on Etsy and at craft markets. But today, I am only there to pick up some papers. I really have to be at the library, my real job.

Stagger Lee and I manage, just. With another one on the

way I remember as I put my hand on my belly, rubbing the baby bump fondly with my right hand. Stagger Lee is definitely getting snipped after this. Two were a stretch, three will be challenging. And it has to stop there.

I see my mum and my kids later in the afternoon. They have come to the library to load up. I have to shush them down when they call out to me, behind a computer and desk. They always forget that, when they see me at work, they have to use their quiet voice. Or, as my mum says, their museum voice.

I see them going out a little while later, all three of them loaded down with books, smiling at me, knowing I won't be home till after seven, near their bedtime. My mum will get supper going—broccoli pasta, which the children adore, oblivious to the fact that a whole can of anchovies is melted into the sauce. Stagger Lee will be home at 6:15 p.m., as usual, the bus dropping him about two blocks from our little river home with the slanted second floor where the bedrooms are. It is by foot, bike, or bus for us, maybe an Uber, since we can't afford a car.

He will position himself in his little office, playing music, something grunting and growling. Tom Waits on a bad trip, in a bad mood. He will finish up on that report that just didn't get done at work earlier in the day. Too much time horsing around with his work mates. Survival, necessary in his line of work, collecting taxes from ordinary Canadians. I know how much he hates it; it is completely antithetical to his sunny ways. But he needs the money. We need the money. My mum has offered us some so that he can go back to school, find something he really wants to do, like animation. But he refuses the offers. Too proud, I can understand. So, the taxman he is. Reviled. How could Stagger Lee be in any way reviled?

I love being pregnant, even though there are risks. I refuse to take my psych meds, and I bump around between Stagger Lee, my mum, and Dr. G. I guess I am protected by their support, as well as the hormones, as I experience no major downs, no major ups, and no paranoia. And now this third one, another little one coming along, populating my life with its wonky old house, a loving husband, kids, dog, cats, fence. And so it is.

Part Three

Chapter 25

If it hadn't been for Jasmin, I never would have known. If she hadn't encouraged me to check my Visa statements, all would have remained buried. Maybe it was better before I knew about it, before I examined those bank documents. It's not as if it has been useful, knowing about those lost months. But I do know now, and now they sit there, taunting me from the table beside my desk, asking me to figure them out. And so, I will try. With help from people in my life and their memories, from Dr. G.'s recollections and notes, and from my bank statements that cover that time, I can pretty well reconstruct that part of my life. I even have fuzzy memories of some of the events I have found along the way.

I am going to begin with what I do remember, without prompting from my credit card. It was after Marc and I had broken up. Marc wasn't around in the year 2019. He missed the fuss and the muss, the near hits and near misses and the tremendous relief once it was all over. 2019 was the year of my fiftieth birthday, and it was hell in waves. Just when it seemed that things were righting themselves, another force would knock me over, rendering me flat out, unable to get up. Though I am now finally standing again, it took a lot of work, support, and courage to get me here. It was courage that I didn't know I had at the time.

***

It started with a manic episode in January 2019. It was a bit unusual for me to have a manic episode in the middle of January. Most Januarys are spent tainted by depression and psychosis, remnants of the incredible sadness and jealousy I can feel when I visit my brothers and their families over the holidays. Getting high, getting manic, starts around March or April for me (as it does for so many with bipolar disorder). So, right off the bat, January was unusual.

I was still with Charles and Elizabeth, the lovely couple I had been helping out for a couple of years, and I am not sure how I managed to contain myself while around them. I was chattier, faster, accomplishing many tasks at the same time, over a shorter period of time. Elizabeth knew something was up; she must have. I was getting a lot done and had more to talk about with Charles. I was charming with their friends, gregarious and outgoing.

However, while I was with Elizabeth and Charles, another side of my mania played itself out. I wasn't sleeping very well, if at all. I lost weight, a welcome relief after the months of November and December, the annual weight-gaining frenzy. I was looser with my friends and family, though fortunately not too loose.

For reasons that mystify me and must have made sense only during the mania, I bought a car. The car that I had, a white Honda Fit, was perfectly fine, more than fine, even. What possessed me to show up at my local Honda dealer and ask for a new one, I will never remember.

James, the salesman who helped me, was quick, smart, and totally happy to take me on as a potential client. We negotiated, talked about what monthly payments I could handle, and had my car assessed for trade-in value. I claimed to him that it was between a new Fit and a Mini Cooper. I was going to the next dealer if he didn't offer me a good deal. Several times, James would excuse himself to see if his boss would "allow" him to sell the car to me at such a "low price." After a bit more back-and-forth, I suddenly said, "Okay, that sounds great, let's do it!" I think James was a little surprised by my sudden decision but hardly missed a beat, pulling out documents that we were to fill out.

And I walked out with a shiny new car, a black Honda Fit, with monthly payments I couldn't afford. I hadn't been manic in a year or two, but I totally made up for it with this sudden episode and buying a car (an act I had read about in textbooks, always thinking that it would never happen to me). Fortunately, the mania didn't last very long. Little did I know that this craziness was just the beginning of months of pain and hurt that would only be clear to me after it was all over.

The year 2019 was off to an interesting start. I am reminded of this whenever I drive my car, and sometimes even when I just look at it.

***

Then there was the second period of destabilization. This period started at the end of January and lasted for about four weeks. According to Dr. G., my mania was followed by a depression and then a period of psychosis. Seismic shifts between depression, hypomania, and psychosis rumbled through the month, finally letting up one week before the month of March. That fourth week in February, before I changed the face of everything in my life, was calm. That one week, nothing is recorded as being negative. Dr. G. found me to be free of anything worrying. Clean slate.

But it wasn't all that clean after all. Ruby tells me that on the twenty-third of February, five days before I fucked everything up, I called her to tell her I couldn't handle watching the Oscars with her and her mum. Something that usually played a fun role in my life was dropped off the calendar, with, apparently, little to no explanation.

***

Should I have poked the memory beast? Does it really matter if I remember, or learn, the events in the middle of 2019? Doing so brought me into a recent depression, which is not surprising—understanding what actually happened that year is shocking to me. By gathering information from various sources but still not being able to place those events firmly in my brain—is this really recalling memories, or am I just painting new pictures out of other people's stories? Will I never really be able to recall what I went through and own that recollection?

I think I will always be on the wrong side of the window, my face smushed against the glass, my memories on the other side, untouchable. Almost there, almost have it, but not quite. And does it matter? I have many of the facts, and they all paint a horrific few months. Why would I want to feel that again, feel the searing pain of the month of May, the craziness of the month of April? I think, better let it sleep, that memory beast, but it is too late. It is awake and trying to break that glass pane.

***

On February twenty-eighth, I walked into Dr. G.'s office, my purse and a bottle of water held tightly. I was fully engaged with my voices, they were loud and intrusive, and I half spoke to my doctor, and half to them.

"Wow," I barked, "I gotta keep you all straight!" I waved my fingers and hands in the air, a strange giggle coming out of my chest.

Dr. G. looked straight at me. "Okay, so it seems like you've got a lot going on," he said. "Tell me."

I started to pace. "This is it," I said. "This is the day that I finally get it done. Whoa. Oh my, God. Yes, today, today, today." I started singing in a little girl's voice. "I'm gonna die, I'm gonna die. . ." Did a few twirls, sat back in the chair.

"Hello!" I said to him. "How are you?" I was pretending to be all serious. Before he could say anything, I reached into my bag and pulled out a big pill bottle. "These are going to make my day!" I waved the bottle around, the pills inside loud like a maraca. "Shake, shake, shake your booty!" I sang out.

"What's in the bottle?" Dr. G. asked me, so calm, as he always is.

Before I could answer, my voices came in for a swoop, a deep dive. *You know what to do. Do it! Never mind him. It's time! Do it! Soon you will be here!*

"Okay," I said out loud to the room. "Here's what's going to happen. Off with the lid!" I popped the top off the pill bottle and tipped it over into my hand, pouring out seven or eight capsules. I washed them down with my water. "This is what's going to happen."

"Jocelyn, what's going to happen? What do you mean?" Dr. G. asked. He was leaning forward. "I think you need to go to the hospital. Jocelyn. Jocelyn, focus on me. You need to be in hospital."

This was the funniest thing I had heard in a while. My voices laughed with me. *There is nothing wrong, he's trying to make you lose your focus!* I measured out 10 capsules, counting like the Count on *Sesame Street*. "One pill, ah, ah, ah! Two pills, ah, ah, ah!" I shoved them into my mouth. *You are almost there. That's a girl. Keep going.*

"What the fuck," I said, giving up on the counting. I started cramming pills into my mouth. I felt frantic, I got up again, pacing the small office, singing, "I'm gonna die!"

Over my singing, I could hear Dr. G. talking. "I don't know what she's taken, but it's a lot," he was saying into the phone. He took the empty bottle from me. "It looks like she has taken nortriptyline, though there might have been other pills. This is very, very serious, this could do a lot of damage to her heart."

He was still on the phone, talking and talking. I stopped listening. I started singing again. "I'm gonna die! I'm gonna die!" The voices chimed in, singing along with me.

Why the fuck was he so calm? *Sing it aloud! You are there! Sing it!* "I'm gonna die, I'm gonna die," I sang. I started clapping my hands in rhythm. I wasn't paying my doctor attention anymore. My voices were too loud, my doctor grew smaller right in front of me.

There was someone else in the room with us. He was talking to my doctor. "They're behind me, 30 seconds," I heard this new person say. And then there were more, beeps and whistles and staccato voices coming over radios. A woman was there, speaking into hers, making my voices alarmed. *She's got it all wrong! Listen to her! What crap!*

I was starting to feel funny. My head wasn't right. "I'm a little dizzy!" I said.

"That's okay," the woman said. "Just have a seat here." She motioned to a stretcher that was crowding the hallway. "Have a rest. It's okay."

And so I sat down, the spinning in my head getting worse. I lay back, and immediately I was covered with blankets and straps. *It's too late! They have you now, you fool!*

Dr. G. was standing up, he was thanking these people, saying goodbye to them. I was moving, I was looking up at people, at their chins, and I was moving. *Get off! Get off now!* "But I can't!" I said out loud.

We were out of the office now, and I was watching the ceiling as we made our way down the corridor. Over to the elevator, and then in it, waiting to go downstairs. When we came out, we went past the pharmacy. *They know you! They are all laughing at you!* The voices were beginning to babble incoherently, sloshing around in my brain.

They wheeled me out front, where there was an ambulance with the back doors wide open. The last thing I remember is those doors shutting on me. Then, all is black.

***

The voice is very far away, very faint. A second voice, too, deeper, off in the distance. She said, "You might need a second person to help move her; she is really heavy."

I tried to say, "Hey, I can hear you!" but I couldn't speak. There was something in my throat, something in my mouth, something covering my face. I fell back under the storm clouds, oblivious to the sounds of the ICU around me.

The second day—was it a day?—it was the same thing. I started ripping at things, trying to pull the mask off my face, trying to get at whatever was in my throat. "Calm down, calm down," a gentle voice said. "You will rip out your breathing tube. Just lie still. Your mother is here, she wants to say hi."

I could see my mother seated to my right. She was a bit

blurry, her voice a little distorted. I wondered what was wrong with her. I tried to ask her where I was, what was happening. I couldn't do it. She gave me a sheet of paper and a pencil. I scribbled down questions, letters. But I couldn't control the pencil, couldn't hold the piece of paper still. I made lines and twirls, large capital letters followed by bumps in a line. Aside from the cats, I probably wanted to know several other things: where was I, what had happened, why couldn't I talk, how long had I been out for? But I simply could not communicate. I fell back and retreated into darkness.

The next time I woke up, my mother wasn't there. I still had tubes and a mask. I started trying to remove these foreign invaders, frantically pulling at them all. A nurse rushed over and pulled back my hands. "You're okay," she said. "You're okay. Your mother just went to get a coffee. Don't pull at anything, okay? We'll be taking you off your mask soon."

I was moved out of ICU. As promised, my mask was off, the various tubes removed (not the loveliest experience)—all I had on was a small, discreet, two-pronged nasal oxygen tube. I was wheeled to a regular ward. I had begged them not to take me to the psych ward; they told me that decision would be made later since they still had medical concerns that needed addressing.

I continued to need oxygen and was still poked and prodded for regular blood draws. Still given my meds, nortriptyline conspicuously absent. Some new ones that were temporary, they told me. And I grew stronger, accepting treats from the coffee shop, taking a few walks in my shared room. My roommate was an elderly man, his older children keeping vigil at his bedside, talking quietly.

Amazed by this hospital room that had lockable bathroom

doors and a private shower, I decided to clean myself up, get washed, do my hair. Grabbing the pile of clothes that were mine, I must have been singing in that shower, I was so relieved and happy. I dried off and pulled on my jeans, straightening them out. Great to be in something other than hospital pyjamas. I then grabbed my bra and tried to put it on. However, it wouldn't work, I couldn't fasten it. They had cut it down the front, right down the middle. So too my shirt (a purple shirt that had long been one of my favourites). Cut down the front, quick work done by the nurses and doctors who had to get access to my chest and heart as quickly as possible.

I think if anything has stayed with me as a shock from that episode, it is not the ambulance or life support, but the cutting of clothes in the emergency room. Doesn't that only happen on TV?

Chapter 26

Once my body had mended, the doctors needed reassurance that I would not simply go home and try it all over again. Maybe not pills; maybe something different the next time. My behaviour had been bizarre, a sudden emergency, and they wanted to clear it with psychiatry before letting me go home.

The psychiatrist was young, warm, and empathetic. We spent some time chatting—she wanted to rule out psychosis, depression, mania. She wanted an explanation as to why I had taken such a large number of pills. That was what everyone wanted: an explanation. And I couldn't help them out. I was clueless as well. I'd heard the voices, but they were just along for the ride, agreeing with whatever my brain wanted. Unlike every other one of my hospitalizations, trying to understand what lay at the core of this episode was proving difficult. But the psychiatrist seemed satisfied with my mental health and cleared me for checkout. I would not have to transfer to the psychiatry ward.

I was released to the care of my mum and was to see Dr. G. twice a week. I had let down my mother, in particular, but also Dr. G.—it couldn't have been that pleasant for him either. He has told me since that he was very, very worried about me and that he did not feel calm on the phone, despite seeming so. I did not know how to apologize to him for something that was almost cruel. He has insisted that I need not apologize, but the guilt is still there.

Letting down my mother was very different, a whole new ballgame. This definitely was not the first time, however. I can think of many instances in the past where my mother was hurt by my words and actions. Spouting psychotic jingles on the living room couch; getting angry with her for her "intrusive" behaviour; those early overdoses and alcohol use. And I broke all the rules, in very sad ways, the rules of acting like a decent, honest human being. At the time of my overdose, my mum, like everyone else, thought that I was finally in a good place, that the wobbling in January and February was just that, a wobbling. Nothing more. I didn't know what was to come, so how could she?

Reestablishment of trust was a hurdle to get over, at least between me and my mum, and building it back up again was a difficult thing. If I can make a suicide attempt out of the blue, what was stopping me from trying again? It was a bit like a dance of give-and-take, a slow buildup of believing each other, letting loose a little bit. My mum and I are very close, which made it easier, while at the same time making it harder.

Dr. G. is a psychiatrist—it's his job to deal with behaviours like mine. However, six months later, he hesitated when I asked if I could go back on nortriptyline.

"I'm not sure if that's a good idea. But, it sounds like this has been on your mind. Tell me a little bit about what you are thinking," he said.

"I just think nortriptyline is a very good antidepressant for me. I think maybe I need it now. I know I really fucked things up in the spring—we still haven't finished with that. But, now that I am not on it anymore, I really see what role it played for me. I think I need it back." I had been feeling somewhat depressed, and there wasn't anything to pierce through that. I had hope with nortriptyline.

"Do you think you'll be back in danger if you started taking it again?" he asked.

"Well, I think I could put myself in danger with lots of things. I have a lot of propranolol at home, and I know taking all of it would pretty much stop my heart. There are other drugs that I am on that could do the job, let alone over the counter stuff. Let's see, what else. . ."

I was speaking kind of loudly, trying to sell it to him, the routes to suicide that didn't involve nortriptyline. "There are the standard ways, ones that don't involve pills. I don't want to talk about those, I don't want to make light of them. So, pills, yes. Pills would still be my choice, and I have plenty on hand that don't include nortriptyline." I realized what I was saying, that it sounded like a threat or a plan. I needed to clear that up. "I am not planning anything. You have to believe me when I say that I am not having thoughts about suicide. I'm just in need of something different. And I know what has worked in the past."

Was I bullying him into prescribing a drug that I had overdosed on in front of him the previous spring? Don't worry, doc! There are so many ways to off myself! I'll be fine.

What a ridiculous conversation this was.

***

Today, when I look back on my actions at the end of February in 2019, when I try to understand why things got so bad so quickly, I draw a blank. I feel sickened by the memory of that day. The silliness of overdosing in front of my doctor while giggling like a schoolgirl. Now, I am thankful that I did try it in front of him. He saved my life. It was so very, very close.

Dr. G. later told me that what had happened in his office on that day was the most profound case of ambivalence he had ever witnessed.

And when an ambulance goes by with its sirens on full tilt, my eyes fill up a little bit, and I feel a slight punch to my gut. What had happened was a stunning shock, a reminder that life could change in an instant.

Chapter 27

My overdose and subsequent hospitalization are really the last things I can remember clearly on my own, though much of it too is lost in fog. Those four months, mid-February to mid-June, are basically a blank to me, with spikes here and there where I have memory, albeit patchy. I did so many crazy things during the spring of 2019. I need to know—was I a jerk, was I an asshole to others? Did I make a fool of myself, should I be embarrassed? For the most part, I can only imagine. And that has to be okay.

***

The first weeks out of the hospital were not unusual. After apologies, I was back with Elizabeth and Charles. I kept up the same routine as before hospitalization. Left at the same time each morning, picked up a coffee on the way. Found parking spots along the same streets. Took the old elevator up; for some reason I preferred it to the regular one.

This is where things fade, where my brain stops recording, where I have to rely on outside sources to fill in the parts where my memory got erased. A study of my Visa statement for the month of March shows some bumpy action. The first week out of the hospital seems to be fine, the usual automatic payments on things like newspapers, Netflix, cell phone, other little things here and there. But then I start seeing some other transactions I do not recall fully. Two villa rentals, two airplane tickets, airline insurance, and an Auto Europe booking. All for a two-week holiday on the island of Martinique, done in style.

Martinique does sound beautiful. It sounds like the northern half is very different from the southern. Apparently, I solved that problem by booking two villas, one in the north, one in the south. Add on a few days in the capital, Fort-de-France, and it was seemingly going to be a top trip of my life. Climbing Mt. Pelée, snorkelling in the clear waters of the Caribbean, taking walks through jungles. Pretty perfect.

Ten days later, it seems that I changed my mind about the trip and decided to cancel as much as I could. Some of those charges got reversed, and most of my money was returned to me. The plane tickets were a loss since I was truly screwed by the so-called insurance I had purchased. But the villa bookings and the car rental were refunded to me. I must have been relieved, I can only imagine, though those airline tickets must have hurt.

Then it seems I started booking for a tour up the Gaspésie region of Quebec. My mum and I were to drive to Quebec City—only five hours away. There would be a three-day stay in this gorgeous gem of a city before getting back in our car again. We were to tour along the coast, driving to the tip, where it fell off into the Gulf of St. Lawrence, before taking a different route home.

I had booked a lot of Airbnb accommodations, and when I went to cancel a week later, my down payments were lost.

What was my problem? I don't understand why I would book Martinique with such detail, and let the charges go through. Give up all that, and then create a new trip in Quebec. I never made it for that trip either. I haven't left

North America since 2012 when I went to Russia. And now I am flat-out broke, so things aren't looking up in the travel department.

***

The dog story is the most bizarre, easily beating out lost travel arrangements. I decided in April that I would adopt a dog, so I started checking out resources. A dog! Another "What the hell was I thinking?"

Dr. G., looking at his notes, tells me that I was really down one day in early April since I had not been approved by Dog Tales, a world-famous dog rescue and adoption organization. Checking now, I see that they have many wonderful dogs for adoption. I must have submitted an application, and it was probably bat-shit crazy. There I was, a woman on her own, not much income, no experience with dogs, and a bizarre application. No wonder I was turned down. But all I saw was rejection and dismissal and must have talked about that with Dr. G.

One of my true wishes, aside from living in the country, is to have a dog companion. Like so many things, however, this will not come to fruition. Things happen, life happens. You get used to it. Sort of.

***

There were the other charges to my Visa. One was $880 from the SPCA just over the border in western Quebec, and the second was $350 spent at a local pet supply store. This did bring out a slight memory when I witnessed these charges. I have Ruby to confirm them and to expand on them. So, I pretty well have this one figured out.

Izzy, my name for her, was an Australian Shepherd I fell in love with. I took her out on a walk around the building where she was housed, checking her out, her checking me out. I decided that she was the one for me but worried that I would be turned down by the SPCA. However, they were pleased that I wanted to adopt her, and we started the process, all the paperwork.

I was thoroughly unprepared for a dog to live in our house. So, we decided that Izzy would remain at the SPCA for a while, a boarding fee charged to my account, while I got things set up at home. Ruby tells me that I shared photos of Izzy with her and was genuinely thrilled to have a dog to bring into my home. Never mind that Izzy's breed doesn't mix well with cats, two of whom I already had. And who knows where my mother was in all of this.

The next day, I decided to pay Izzy a visit as I prepared for her arrival. I stopped off at the pet shop near the SPCA and spent some money on dog supplies. I don't know most of what I purchased, but I did have a bed and blanket for Izzy to get cozy with. I again paid a boarding fee.

And then I finally cracked and ended up in hospital and had to give up on my new friend Izzy.

Chapter 28

"Let's see, well, I have some concerns. . ." I was in Dr. G.'s office, and I was trying to skirt the issue. But, I pressed on. "I, uh, well. I lie in my bed at night with no sleep, and I think about this. I think about this all the time now." I paused. How do you speak about this, the unspeakable? "I think about killing my mother. I think of her in her bed upstairs, and I know that I can't leave her alone. When I die, well, when I die, I will ruin her life. So, I would smother her with a pillow. I would kill the cats. I don't know how, but I would have to. They have to stay together, with me. And then myself. I was going to do it last night, but I have to leave a note and an explanation, an apology. And I wasn't up to it." I closed my eyes, waited for him to get the police on the line.

"You know, what you describe does not make you a horrible person," Dr. G. said gently. "These are obsessive thoughts that you are having. But they are not a plan. You will not kill anybody. You simply are not the profile. But, I am concerned about you and your thoughts of harming yourself."

His answer confused me. I felt horrible, I felt evil. But Dr. G. was telling me it was all fine. That thinking about strangling the cats, and heading up to my mother's room, quiet as a mouse, to kill her too, well, thinking this was just fine. A-okay.

But they weren't okay, these obsessive thoughts. There have been very few times that I have asked to go to the hospital. I was genuinely frightened. It was a few days later, on a mid-April Sunday, that my mum and I decided that I needed to be in hospital. Obviously, I don't remember all of the details, but my mum and I have glued them back together so I can "remember." Dr. G. called us back on Monday morning. He had made arrangements for me to go to the Montfort, a hospital way across town. There were no beds closer.

Apparently, I told the emerg doc there what I planned. What I planned every night down there in bed, each night deciding that all four of us had another day to live, a reprieve, a stay of execution, because I couldn't get it together.

I had been on a form 1 (a 72-hour hold) many times during prior hospitalizations. Always "danger to self" box checked. This time was the first time that I had two boxes checked, the second one being "danger to others."

I stayed at the Montfort for exactly two weeks. I don't remember much of it at all. The corridors of my memory reveal black and greyness, and much quiet. It was a large ward with many people on it, people who mostly stayed in their rooms. There was the kitchen area, where I got my crackers and peanut butter, and weak tea, my standard in-patient meal, ignoring the horrid vegetarian meal that was available especially for me.

There was a computer room where I would spend hours every day, emailing obsessively with two friends who lived in the US. According to them, I was writing confused, mixed up, bizarre letters with tons of typos, very unlike me. I remember arguing with other patients for screen time, since there were only two computers. I would sit in the room on a vinyl sofa, watching who got in line, who was waiting, and where I was in the queue.

My psychiatrist at the Montfort was kind and compassionate and visited me every day without fail. She kept me on the drugs that Dr. G. had phoned in, tweaking one here, substituting another there. Increasing several. Her feeling was that I should take a stab at being transferred to the Royal Ottawa Hospital, the psychiatric facility where my dad had worked so long ago. She told me she was going to put in an application, but to beware since it took a while. However, 10 days later I had pulled out of the psychosis and depression. We held a family meeting; a space had in fact opened up at the ROH. My stay there would be long-term, at least six months.

I didn't feel sick at the time of the meeting, certainly not sick enough to take one of the spots open at the ROH. So, I declined. Doing as well as I was doing, my psychiatrist couldn't hold me anymore, so I was released.

I got out of the Montfort at the end of April; we were starting to get some warm temperatures. I had a meeting with Elizabeth. She wanted me to work Monday and Tuesday mornings only, in order to drive Charles to his music sessions, which I thoroughly enjoyed. (I learned so many golden oldies; "Moon River. . .") According to Dr. G.'s notes, I took this news hard; it pulled me down into the murky water of depression and self-doubt.

I was basically out of work. I had loved working with Elizabeth and Charles, and I was sad never to have that again.

Chapter 29

The first piece of art I ever acquired on my own came from Granny. A tiny landscape, it was the first painting that she had bought on her own. She was very proud. I now treasure it. If only it had stayed that way. Art that meant something. Not greedily grabbed at, torn off the walls of galleries. I'll take this one, and this one, and that one. No sense, nonsense.

When I had first moved out with Ruby Tuesday back in 1994, I had a Braque poster and my framed Connemara map. I had some pictures of people who were important to me. I had framed a couple of pieces that I had done in high school art class. Still life with artichokes; a dream sequence with a paper man on a golden rooftop, very much in the style of Chagall; a close-up of a frog. It wasn't bad.

It wasn't until Stagger Lee picked up a few prints at Art in the Park for a gift of some kind, Christmas, birthday, housewarming, any time, that I first got interested in collecting art. From making my home richer, happier, more colourful, and interesting, there were many things I liked about collecting pieces and checking out art galleries.

One serious evening several years before the mass collection of 2019, I purchased three pieces on my own. It was at a show put on by Stagger Lee's collective, and I helped him set up and watch his corner. He had a painting halfway done on a big easel, yes, how very artsy! There were six or seven other artists in the collective who had works for sale. I would wander up and down the hallway, checking in with others to see how they were doing, what they had for sale. I was dizzy with desire. I wanted to buy, but I loved so many pieces that I could only, finally, narrow it down to three. Add some nice framing work, and I was set up to be a collector of art.

I also acquired many paintings by Stagger Lee, which I still have, much adored. I feel happy that I can have some of his crazy renderings on the walls of my apartment.

And then it stopped. For the longest time, I acquired nothing. I think through illness, through my ended relationship with Stagger, I just didn't have it in me to continue collecting.

And then it was 2019. Everything was different about this year. Sort of up, sort of down, a few pills, what now? Maybe sort of up again, at least as far as my credit card was concerned.

I had learned about Eduardo Guerra on a trip to Havana, where I had bought one of his pieces. It was in a covered art market where a woman ran a stall, gorgeous drawings and etchings by Guerra. I fell in love with one of his etchings in particular. The price was a steal, but I am forever embarrassed and ashamed that I haggled with this woman in the market. I was a rich white Canadian tourist trying to beat that price down, a price that was not high to begin with. I am not proud. They tell me it was part of any deal in that market, the haggling. But, I still cringe.

So, that spring of 2019, I got online, and found a dealer out of Toronto with some of Guerra's prints. I looked around my downstairs apartment—nobody seemed to care what I was doing on my computer. I went through all his works on the website and chose two that were already framed. And then chose two more. I used my credit card, purchased the art, and had it all shipped to Ruby's home.

It was her home, or at least the town she lived in, that proved to be a dangerous place, located close to General Fine Crafts in Almonte. It was not what you expected a small-town store to be. No candy by the cash, no board with locally themed magnets, no just-made-up-the-street ice cream and fudge. No racks of cards with fall foliage greetings.

General Fine Crafts showcased the works of Eastern Ontario artists: ceramics, sculptures, prints, paintings, works of collage, hand-blown glass, and the grooviest small lithographs. In other words, my heaven. I decided to shop there while I was waiting for Ruby, who was over at the bookstore across the street on business. I started picking up various pieces of pottery, bringing them up to the cash. My mum had her birthday in less than two months, and I wanted to make it special for her, knowing how much she loved works of ceramic.

Gradually, I fell into the Zone. The Zone where my credit card starts to melt a little, its balance growing less important with every passing minute; where I became a bit lightheaded, a bit dizzy, knowing that I am going to let it all fall away, all the rather important things in my life like budgets, money, and bank accounts. The Zone where I upped my game and really started spending.

I started looking at the walls of the shop, my mother's gifts already wrapped at the cash, ready for me to pay.

"Okay, so I am not done yet!" I exclaimed. "I think I need some help with the art." On the walls were paintings that took on a glowing beauty, myriad colours, lines of expression, dashes of black, circle, triangle. I started singling pieces out, asking Richard, who ran the place, questions about each piece and the artist who created it. "What was used on this one?" I asked. "The texture is fascinating. You know, take that one down, put it with my stuff." Over the walls I hunted, up, down, over, to the second room at the back of the store, choosing things as I went. I flipped through the prints, pulling out several of them. "I need some help here," I joked. "That's the same artist who did the painting with the wine goblet, isn't it? You can put it with my stuff, and this one too." I handed Richard two large prints.

The biggest, costliest piece was a painting by the Japanese–Canadian artist Norman Takeuchi, whose exploration of citizenship, alienation, and identity all appealed to me. There were several of his that I loved, but even I knew that I could only afford one, at least on that particular spree.

Ruby entered the shop, her work at the bookstore complete. (I had declined an invitation to the bookstore, since we agreed I was safer in General Fine Crafts. I might go crazy in the bookstore with all those books around me, prompting a frenzy of buying and ordering. Oh, how I wish that were the case!) She was not impressed by what was going on, paintings being taken off the walls, cleaned gently, and wrapped in newsprint.

"What's happening here?" she asked me. "You're not taking all that stuff, are you?" She looked concerned and a bit exasperated.

"Well, not today, I'm not," I said. I turned to Richard. "I'll pay now, but can you keep everything for me for a couple of days? I don't have the room in my car right now," I told him. Richard agreed to keep my items snug in a few boxes, waiting for me.

I picked them up several days later, purchasing a few

other things when I popped in. I drove back to Ottawa and squirrelled the boxes into my apartment, out of the way. I don't remember this, but I have Ruby's recounting, and a whole lot of beautiful things in my apartment.

I went online two nights later, combing the Internet for pieces by Takeuchi that caught my eye. There was a gorgeous one housed at Studio 22 in the town of Kingston, only two hours from where I sat at my desk. I purchased it on the spot.

I told my mum that I was going to drive to Kingston to pick up a painting, and she insisted that she was to do the driving, accompanying me on my mission. I made a reservation at Chez Piggy, a lovely, well-known restaurant in the downtown part of Kingston, and after walking along the waterfront, we headed there for lunch.

My mum decided to have another coffee after we had eaten, and I headed over to the gallery on my own. Dangerous move—I felt my credit card in my bag do a little jump. Walking in, I was greeted by a woman named Ally, one of the heads of the gallery. She went to retrieve the Takeuchi piece while I began to study the paintings on the walls. When Ally returned, after showing me the piece I had purchased, I began to ask her about other beautiful things hanging in the studio.

I pointed at one large one, all neck, beak, and an eye. We checked out one with three groovy trees that I fell in love with. I went around the room, pointing and purchasing, all in under 10 minutes. Aware that my mum was waiting for me back at the restaurant, I gave Ally my credit card number and told her I would be in touch to organize shipping. I walked out of the gallery with the original Takeuchi in my hands. I was on a high but had to contain it when in the presence of my mum.

It seems that my mother and Dr. G. had already identified me as being full-blown manic anyway, so I obviously had not been successful in keeping it all together. And I thought my last mania ever had been the one in January, when I had purchased my car. But no, there is a mania there that I know nothing about, not even a flicker of memory bringing it back. The mania, which was sort of evident on that day in Kingston—when I marched through the gallery, pointing and saying, "I'll take this one, and this one, and that one," rapid-fire—was at its height.

Dr. G's notes make a clear case for my being very high. They include a description that I find hilarious: "Patient is jocular and tangential." What sort of word is that, "jocular"? And aren't I always a bit "tangential"? Hmmm.

Although my mania was short-lived, my painting-buying spree still held up. I visited General Fine Crafts again. I bought some prints and a small collage and fell in love with a large Takeuchi but left it there, hanging. I went on Studio 22's website and purchased more, to be delivered to Ruby's address.

The final art blow happened when I was with Jasmin in her Toronto apartment over the May long weekend. I actually remember three things from that visit. We went north in the city, to the biggest Asian mall in North America. I remember we ate Korean food, and I purchased $300 dollars' worth of good luck kitty figurines (still unwrapped in my closet). The second slightly fuzzy event for me was seeing a film about the life of Aretha Franklin as part of a documentary series. Very fuzzy there. My final memory is of lying on Jasmin's Uncle Charlie (a good friend of Jasmin's had her chaise/sofa christened Uncle Charlie). Jasmin was making coffee, and I was waiting for General Fine Crafts back in Almonte to open.

When it did, I phoned them, swooping in, and spent four thousand dollars on that big, beautiful, gorgeous Takeuchi. Jasmin, though I am sure she was not surprised, probably rolled her eyes at my extravagance.

But it was Ruby who pulled me up by my collar. She sent me a picture of some boxes in her foyer, large thick ones piled on her carpet, with slender boxes slotted in between.

"I can't do this anymore," she said over the phone, an edge to her voice. "I am going to bring all of this stuff to you, and I am going to tell your mother what you've been up to. This is just nuts." Her voice softened. "You've got a real problem, Joc."

"Okay, okay, I know," I said. "I don't know what to do. You're right, I have to fess up to my mum. I have no money left, and I have my bloody computer just sitting there late at night, downstairs, where only the cats will find me. It is so fucking tempting. But, I know, this has to stop." I was sounding desperate. The idea of having a conversation with my mother about the whole thing was almost unthinkable. Maybe I could work it so she never had to find out? But I had zero clue as to how to make that happen.

"Are you manic, Joc?" Ruby asked, gently. "You seem to be bouncing around quite a bit. What does your doctor think?"

That was a good question. What had I been telling him? Was I downplaying my spending to him, not letting it seem as extreme as it was? "Maybe tell him first, I think," I said. "I don't know, give me a day to figure it out."

We got off the phone, and I sat in my armchair, almost crying, yet too far gone for crying. The sound I was making was more like a loud humming, vibrating in my throat, hurting. "Fuck it," I said out loud, to no one. "Let's do it." I got up and walked up the stairs to my mum.

I found her in the kitchen, stir-frying peppers. I started walking toward her, bringing my face up close to hers. And then I lost it. I started sobbing uncontrollably. "I have done something terrible," I managed to get out.

"It's okay, it's okay," she said, dropping her spoon and throwing her arms around me. She held me tightly. "What's going on?"

"I have to tell you, but I can't." I took a step backward. "God, I have just screwed everything up. My money. . .my money is all gone."

"Come on, it isn't really. What happened? Tell me." Her face was so serious, I knew I couldn't tell her the whole story.

But I straightened myself out a little. "Remember that painting I bought in Kingston a few weeks ago?" I asked. "Well, that was just the beginning. I have bought many, many more paintings. I ordered more from Kingston, I bought lots in Almonte, I bought so much, I couldn't even tell you what I have now."

"Okay," she said quietly, "go on."

I fought back tears, my voice shaky. "I have spent all my money." She gave me a funny look. "All of it. I have $500 left on my Visa. Oh, God, it's so bad. I don't know what to do." I was covering my face with my hands, groaning.

"What is your credit card limit?" she asked.

"Thirty thousand dollars." I just let it out, knowing that it was all going to come out soon anyway. And, there it was.

"Jocy!" She gasped. "That can't be! How did this happen?! What have you been doing?!" She was getting upset, the two of us standing there in the kitchen, full of rising voices and wild gesticulations. "Where are they? You have to return them all, immediately, get your money back! This can't be!"

"No," I said, backing away, "I can't. I absolutely cannot. They won't take them back." I was pretty certain about this. The artists would have already been paid. I could not face Ally or Richard with this. There had to be another way. "I will find a way to sell them online." I didn't have a clue about anything anymore. I was losing it again.

"Okay, okay," she said, holding her arms out. "We will figure it out, we will figure it all out. You can sell them online, yes, that would be possible, I'm sure."

Did she sound sure? It was hard to tell. But she wasn't angry anymore, which was a huge relief. I knew then that all would be okay. She was ambitious, she was capable of making the problem go away. I was in her hands now, and I felt better than I had for days.

What the fuck had I done? Not only were the art pieces a final sale, but the actual idea of returning them to General Fine Crafts or Studio 22 was impossible to me. Over four weeks, I had collected lovely pieces and had so many dealings with Richard and Ally, and I would have felt embarrassed and humiliated if I were to turn around and take all those pieces back. I was a fake, a fraud, a little girl out of control. I had just been playing a game.

The next day, Ruby delivered the boxes to me, and as I cut them open, I remembered exactly what each and every work of art was. I was immediately filled with a need to look at more, excited by it. But, I kept those feelings in check. I was at the end of the road.

I leaned each painting up against a wall downstairs, gently using bubble wrap to make sure they didn't get damaged. After I had three or four of them settled, I moved over to the other side of the wall, arranging more paintings there. I had no clue what to do with them. They overwhelmed my apartment. They took up so much space.

Eventually, over the coming days, I made an effort to sell some of the paintings on Kijiji. But I had zero success. I contacted a couple of galleries in the city, but none of them would buy the paintings off me. I didn't know what to do. And so I did nothing.

Today, I wonder if something online was possible, a couple of different websites having looked promising. But, at the time, my brain was not equipped to do more than make a few phone calls. It was suddenly muddled, the streak of fire having burnt itself out.

The artwork now hangs in the upstairs TV room and across my apartment walls. My mum says that she can't look at it without a twinge of sadness. I had somehow gotten out of my financial crisis, how I don't remember. And, I had made peace with the paintings. I now even enjoy looking at them. It feels like it happened decades ago. It was far, far away in the past, and I don't have to worry anymore.

***

Aside from art purchasing, trip planning, and dog adoption, those months held many surprises for me when going over Dr. G.'s notes and reading my Visa statements.

- $1,000 dropped at Pier One Imports. I seem to have an excess of throw cushions and more glassware than I did before this time period.
- $800 on an abrupt move from iPhone to Samsung, just because I was curious.
- $1,000 for an online purchase at Addition Elle, a plus-size clothing store where much of my wardrobe comes from. However, when I sweep my closet and open all

the drawers in my bureau, I cannot find a single thing from that experience. Just the same old sets of clothes. Where did it all go?

- $2,000 on cash advances, and I don't have a single, solitary clue why. But today I am still paying interest on them.
- $1,200 at Anthropologie for quilts and blankets. They match my new throw cushions.

And, when all was said and done, I'd spent at least $14,000 on art alone in the month of May 2019.

***

Aside from my shopping frenzy, May was a pretty terrible month. I didn't go back to work, just lived weeks of depression, psychosis, and, apparently, this full-blown mania. The first week was about my layoff. The second I was psychotic, and the third week I finished setting up my art collection, with my trip to Toronto being the highlight of the month. Good old Uncle Charlie.

But I was very fragile, and realizing that my money was shot, I fell into a profound depression. Dr. G.'s notes reveal that I saw him 8 times in 14 days in the second half of May. Every second day, basically.

During the final visit, I was apparently acutely psychotic with command voices telling me to kill myself. Dr. G. called my mother to have her come and take me to the Civic Hospital. I imagine that I didn't argue or try any stunts like before. I just accepted my fate and hoped the evilness that I had been experiencing would go away quickly.

Chapter 30

After a long night in the psychiatric emergency department, a night of pacing and twisted thoughts, I was taken up to the ward. (Psychiatry was no longer on the main floor, with the kilometre circuit. It was now on the sixth floor, where I had been taken for the past two or three hospitalizations.) I was pretty tired and groggy, and looked forward to passing out on my bed in whichever room they gave me.

It turned out I was in the last room down the hall, away from the nursing station. It was a room with two beds but there was no sign of a roommate. A nurse came down with a computer pad. She was going to do intake. We went through a million questions. "So, how are you feeling right now?" she asked me. She was a bit brittle. I remember our conversation and its sequelae very clearly. Somehow, the memory stayed close to the front of my brain, where I can retrieve it any time.

"Yeah, I'm okay. The voices are bothering me, but right now, well, they're okay. Maybe I should just sleep. I am pretty sure I can now."

"Do you want some Haldol?" she asked me.

"I think I had a lot overnight. I really don't think I need it; I just want to sleep. I know I will."

She asked me again, or rather, suggested, "Don't you think you need some Haldol?"

I was starting to pull the covers up over me. "I think I'm okay."

The nurse left, and I turned over to go to sleep. But 10 minutes later, she returned, accompanied by 7 or 8 nurses and orderlies. The group surrounded my bed, and the nurse pulled out a syringe. "This, obviously, is the only way, as you are not co-operating." Somebody pulled my pyjama bottoms down to expose my hip and upper thigh. Jam, in went the needle. I whimpered, and then they were gone. I lay there frozen after they all left, humiliated. I knew we would all have different versions of this event, but I never felt friendly to that nurse ever again. I don't know, let's call her Nurse Ratched. She was, thankfully, an exception within the nursing group.

Then, because I obviously was not conforming to the rules, they moved me to a room across from the nursing station. When I finally was settled in that room, I was front and centre, with a guard 24/7 and a bed exposed to all. I had been quiet in my first bed, definitely after the Haldol shot. Why move me? My only sin was that I had disagreed with Nurse Ratched. It was a power play.

One evening, I tried to slide down my bed from a sitting position to a sleeping position. But my pyjama gown got caught around my neck and wouldn't move any farther. I was choking on my top, pulling at it with my fingers, trying to pull it down, off from around my neck. The orderly watching me came forward and asked me what I was doing. He helped me with the top, and I thanked him.

It seemed pretty straightforward to me. However, that got whispered about from orderly to nurse, and from nurse to nurse, right in front of me. Hello, I can hear you!

Watch her carefully. She tried to choke herself.

But yes, they were just doing their jobs to keep me safe.

***

I only remember bits and pieces of this particular hospitalization. I've been told that I stayed in that bed in front of the nursing station for seven days. My mother was livid. In meetings with my new psychiatrist (Dr. S., my old hospital doc, had sadly retired), my mum would argue that there was no reason to keep me under such surveillance, that it had gone on too long. I was obviously not a threat to anybody, I just shuffled around with no interest in anything. My doctor snapped back, "Well, I have to be careful with all my suicidal patients! Do you not want her to receive my care?"

My mum complained to the nurses and doctor many times; I'm sure she was seen as a bitch, but to me she was a mother who wanted the very best care for her daughter.

It took a senior nurse to come by my bed and ask me what I was still doing there, as if it were up to me to make the rules and execute the orders. I was moved to a regular room shortly after.

My doctor organized a meeting for me and my mum. Her resident sat in. We were there to figure out how to deal with this treatment-resistant episode of depression I was experiencing. They talked drugs, back and forth, the words piling on top of me. "We could try that..." My psychiatrist sounded doubtful. "We could try Clozapine again."

I was sliding backward, sinking into my head, so discouraged.

"Well, there is always ECT," said the resident. That sort of hung there for a bit.

My doctor grabbed it out of the air, holding it up. "Yes,

there is ECT. I was thinking the same thing. Jocelyn," she said, turning to me, "what do you think of that treatment?"

I bent my face up to her. "I have no clue," I said. "I really have no clue. But, I feel so exhausted. I am tired of my brain, I am tired of all the drugs. I need to move forward, but I'm stuck. Stuck in a big, fat lump." ECT was Electroconvulsive Therapy; she was talking heavy-duty. It was something that I never thought I would be up against; it was something I was completely surprised by.

"Well, maybe we have finally found the way to get you back on your feet." She seemed to be getting excited. "Today, ECT is totally safe. It is not the same procedure that was done decades ago or shown in movies." She was watching my face for a reaction, any reaction. "I know that inducing seizures sounds like an unlikely way to treat depression, but it is actually highly effective."

"Okay, I'm listening." I was beginning to get a buzz in my head, like my own private mini seizure, shocking me forward.

"The procedure is done 3 times a week, for a total of 9 to 12 treatments. It has very few side effects, a headache maybe. We would keep you in the hospital the whole time." She continued to watch my face. "Right now, we don't carry out ECT here in this hospital. We would have to transfer you to the General."

"I am not going anywhere," I said. "I am not going way out to the General. That's crazy."

"Jocy, the General is not that far. I think this is something we should explore," my mum said. She was clearly siding with the doctor on this one. "Just think, if it worked, how you could get your life back. Maybe this is the magic bullet."

I didn't know what to say, what to think. "I need time. I

need to know more about it," I said. I had in my head what Sylvia Plath had written about her own ECT. I remember feeling horrified by what they had done to her. But that wasn't being fair. That was 70 years ago. Maybe my doctor was right—just a headache. "Okay," I said, "What do they do? What happens?" I was starting to feel overwhelmed.

At this point, my psychiatrist was in sales-pitch mode. "Well, in the morning, you are taken to the procedure room on a gurney. The doctors and nurses will hook you up to monitors so that you are totally safe. You are briefly under a general anesthetic during which time they induce a seizure. And that's it, then you wake up in recovery. Like I said, you might have a headache, but really it is such a simple treatment. It is amazing what it can do. I can't wait for you to feel the benefits of it. This is very exciting." She gave me a big smile. "I think you are the perfect candidate for ECT."

"Well, we have a lot to explore, there are conversations to be had," my mum said. "Right, Joc?" I was holding steady, still in a lump, but my head turned up. I nodded.

But, when the doctors left us in the conference room, I started to cry. "I don't want to go somewhere else," I told my mother. "I can't move to the General. I can't deal with a new doctor, or a new psych ward. I won't know anything or anyone. Everything will be too different." I struggled to regain control of myself. "Maybe I should just go home instead. I am okay enough for that now. This is all good now." I wiped my face. I knew that I was still so very breakable.

"Please don't go down that road again," my mother said, her voice betraying only a bit of panic and a note of resolve. I knew then that I would be doing ECT. We would talk about it, we would research it, but I was going to do it. That was what was in her voice, and I was too tired to argue. And, anyway, they finally had my attention.

From the Mayo Clinic web page on electroconvulsive therapy:

"Electroconvulsive therapy (ECT) is a procedure, done under general anesthesia, in which small electric currents are passed through the brain, intentionally triggering a brief seizure. ECT seems to cause changes in brain chemistry that can quickly reverse symptoms of certain mental health conditions.

"ECT often works when other treatments are unsuccessful and when the full course of treatment is completed, but it may not work for everyone." (www.mayoclinic.org)

I really didn't know about the General, that decision was really stressful. Like the Montfort, it was a long way for my mum to commute. And this meant I had to get used to a whole new hospital, with a new ward, its own lifestyle and rhythm, new nurses and a new doctor. It would be a pretty big adjustment. I was still so fragile. I didn't know if I could do it.

My mum researched and read everything about ECT that she could get her hands on. And I watched a few YouTube videos about it on my iPad. It was all very sudden and intense.

We met as a group—this time joined by one of my aunts—with a different doctor, one who, splitting his time between the Civic and the General, helped coordinate the

ECT treatments done at the latter. He went into a few extra details about the logistics of a treatment, explaining the early hour, the anesthetic, the seizure, and the side effects. I had always known that it could cause memory loss, and he agreed with that. It might include some memory problems around the time of treatment, an hour lost here, a half-day there.

He too felt I was a good candidate for ECT. We would have to decrease my clonazepam for a bit before we could start, to make sure its anticonvulsive properties didn't interfere with the seizure. But otherwise, it was full steam ahead.

Or so it felt, for a while. Waiting for a bed at the General took days. I was getting increasingly anxious about what lay ahead. And, once at the General, the wait would continue.

Chapter 31

Terrified that I would forget everything around the time of my treatments, I asked my mum to bring in a blank notebook and a good pen. I started my new journal right away, with my first entry while still at the Civic.

The first one reads as this:

Today had my first outing since I arrived here, 13 days ago, on the 30th of May. Mum picked me up at 4:20, and we went home to Maggie and Birdy, and a glass of wine on the back porch. I found that my mood began to drop after only a few hours, and we made the decision at 7:45 to take me back to the ward. Arrived back here, lay down on my bed, and burst into tears. I explained to Kim that if I had been doubting my decision to do ECT, I certainly wasn't anymore. I realized that I wouldn't last a week alive out there.

Tomorrow or Thursday, I make the transfer over to the General in time for my first treatment on Friday. It is becoming a reality.

And then:

At the General now. Mum ended up bringing me here, they couldn't get the transportation sorted out. It was a long wait, and I had to take meds to calm me and my anxiety down. Took Haldol/Ativan mix. (See, I know when I need it!)

Very nice unit here, way nicer than the Civic. Am in a room with two other women—I don't know their stories yet. Met my new psychiatrist, Dr. A. Really, really like her. Won't do ECT until I have an echo to check out my aortic health. If that is done tomorrow, then treatment begins next Wednesday. The waiting for it—it is really shitty, but I appreciate her caution. Over the next week, she plans some med changes, with the possibility of trying Clozapine for a third time.

Mood v.v. low. Have back-to-back passes for the weekend. We will see how I get on.

And then:

4:30 a.m. Been awake since 3:00. I definitely find my roommates intimidating. They seem very 'cool' and 'hip.' Really want to start Remeron for all its sleepiness. Will pace some more now.

And then:

Two day passes over the weekend. Serious anxiety attacks on both days. Had to take Haldol. Back now. Just got off the phone with my mum, in tears. She seems very stressed by the whole thing. I don't want to do ECT. Anxiety level through the roof. She is coming tomorrow for a meeting with the doc and me at 11. I can only pace, which actually makes me even more anxious. Mood low, low, low. Have to do ECT—won't survive out there. That's all I got for now.

And then:

Finally had echo. Very soon they came up to tell me the good news: all is excellent with my aorta! There was delay after delay in getting the test, but they wouldn't shock my brain until they knew everything was in the clear. So now, we are ready to go—I feel a mixture of excitement and dread. Two days to go.

And then:

My mum loves Dr. A. She said the doc was the best psychiatrist I've ever been treated by, bar none. I really like her too. She is soft-spoken and calm. She comes for me every day, and she answers all my questions. We talk about the anxiety a lot. She wonders if it is partly because we did a fairly big decrease in the clonazepam. And I think I am pretty anxious about ECT. Of course, I am.

And then:

So, I have found out a little about the woman next to me. She says she has borderline personality disorder and depression, but she wonders if she has bipolar disorder. She is actually here for ECT, something she said worked perfectly for her last time with no side effects. Thankfully, she didn't ask anything about me, for which I am grateful.

And then:

So, I missed the NBA championship. Apparently, Toronto won, the Raptors won. Everything is the same here, untouched by the news. I stand in front of the TV, watching the crowds in Toronto as the team parades through them. They look happy, everybody does. The woman standing beside me shifts her weight from foot to foot. Up, back, down. I am certain she has akathisia, an inner restlessness often triggered by antipsychotics, something that I am very familiar with.

The ward is bigger than the Civic. It is more drugged than the Civic. I am incapable of guessing what other patients have, with an exception here and there. I wonder if this is because my anxiety is so high. I know I have my head up my ass. I am here for me, to get me better. Feels weird. Good night.

And then:

So, my roommate will be going downstairs for treatment alongside me. I asked her a million questions about ECT. She said it is really simple, that I shouldn't worry about it. I should try and sleep the night before, but I don't know how that will go for me.

I said goodbye to my mother like I will never see her again. If I make it through the ECT, and remember who she is, then that will be a miracle. At least they will have this notebook in the side table beside my bed. They will know how I felt before the big day.

And then:

So, it is bedtime, the night before my first treatment. They already gave me my meds. (They left clonazepam out of the mixture, which sucks for sleep.) And now, it is just me and the night. People outside, not too many. I don't know how I will sleep. Keyed up. Apparently, they will wake me up at 6, get me all sorted out before I leave my room. My roommate snores beside me. This seems like nothing to her. And maybe it will be for me too, after tomorrow. I will lie in my bed, close my eyes, and hope.

And then:

So, I read through this journal and remember everything that I wrote about. I remember ECT, earlier, and I have so far remembered today.

So, how it all happened. I am not sure I can explain everything here, today, but I will try. I can always write more here tomorrow.

So, they woke me up at 6 (I guess I finally slept). I changed into a gown and waited. It is unclear why they had to have me up so early. We did a lot of waiting (roommate too). Finally, a couple of gurneys appeared around 7:15. I lay down on one and was covered with blankets. The guy steering me was nice—he told me not to worry, that this 'acts routine' (something he said). He always does this, bringing people for the 'procedure.' He might be the one to take me up to the ward again, after everything is over.

It seems like we went up and down, in the freight elevator, maybe down to a basement section? I am not sure. My roommate went first, and I could see her in the section beside me, where I was parked. We both waited.

Eventually, after a couple of people went past us, they came and got her. I saw a bit—they wheeled her up into the sectioned-off 'room,' where there appeared to be four or five people in gowns. And then they pulled the curtains closed, and that's all I got to see. She rolled passed me about 20 minutes later, her eyes were closed, asleep? And she was taken to my right, the same as the others. Probably where they wake up and come back to life? I couldn't see.

And then they came for me. My heart turned over a couple of times in what felt like my abdomen. I was positioned in the middle of the room that was sectioned off by curtains. I only recognized the ECT doc and a nurse from the ward upstairs. They started talking to me, saying hello, how was I feeling, basic stuff like that. And then they explained everything that would be happening to me. As they did this, others were busy with other things, like placing the electrodes on my forehead and tending to a computer. Then, they told me that they were going to start the anesthetic and get things under way. I saw the mask as it neared my face, felt it gently surround my mouth and nose.

And then a bit of a blip, and I continued to lie there, watching everybody still working with tubes and computers. I said out loud (it was hard with the mask on) that I was waiting to go under, what was happening? They were joking with me that the procedure had already taken place! I laughed, but it felt kind of surreal at the same time. What was I doing, lying there in the middle of all these people? Had I just had a seizure? Was this the year 2019, where they are still making people have seizures to get 'better'? It all of a sudden felt somewhat absurd.

The main doctor told me my seizure lasted 43 seconds—43 seconds. What noise did I make while it happened? Was I grunting in one locked-down hum? Was I contorting myself slightly off the bed, muscles clenched too tight together, back arched, snapping my mouth closed? Had they given me a guard for my tongue? 43 seconds is a long time. A long time for my jolted seizure to last. For them to stand and watch.

The nurse from the ward asked me if my left arm hurt. Apparently, it was flailing around for 43 seconds. They are not allowed to touch me during the seizure, so that flailing arm was watched by everybody. I was allowed to ask for extra painkillers in recovery, if I needed them. That would be marked on my chart. But I felt nothing. I thanked everybody before I was wheeled out, as if they were acknowledging the great performance I had just given.

Recovery was full of people lying around, in and out of sleep. I was wide awake. I was positioned in with my head up against the back of the room, in a row of people who were coming out of day surgeries (I asked). The kind where you could go home a little while later. I could go home after an hour or so. But sadly, I was going back upstairs. . .

Which is where I am right now, in my room, leaning up against the headboard of my bed, the best place to write out my thoughts. My mum comes soon, and I am tired of writing, both physically and mentally. My left arm feels fine.

And then:

More to record tonight. I worry that when I lose my memory, all of this will be a blank. All I will need to do is consult this book. I was able to give my mum and my uncle a good recounting of the ECT treatment, they seemed to find it pretty interesting. Curious, eh?

Anyway, after arriving in recovery, I was hooked up to a couple of things: blood pressure, heart rhythm, oxygen. I was doing well with all of those, and suddenly I felt a real anxiety about lying there, not allowed to get out of my bed. I wanted them to call an orderly immediately so I could get upstairs. I kept asking, and they kept saying they had ordered for one, but things were slow, backed up. I was so frustrated. I don't know why I was so anxious: the procedure was over and apparently had gone well. I just had to ride out another half-hour or so to leave this big room. And a guy finally came and brought me up here. I didn't need pain medications, though a dose of Haldol and Ativan was well timed.

This afternoon, Dr. A. came by to see how I was doing. She seemed thrilled that things went as smoothly as was reported to her, informed by others, I suppose. But she wanted to get my take on the whole event. What a lovely doctor!

***

I am not sure what went wrong after that. My entries trail off there. I guess I realized that I could remember things and was totally cool with it, so I no longer needed to record my experiences. And I do remember pretty much everything around the time of the ECTs.

I was a quick study, going through each of my treatments with relative ease. Dr. A. sat with me, my mum, and my uncle, and talked about maintenance ECT and how it could benefit me. Maintenance ECT meant that I would just show up for day surgery and have a seizure twice a month or so. But the bureaucracy and the red tape made it difficult, and frankly, I was relieved. I didn't think I was acing it anymore, though after my fourth time, the doctor came into the recovery room and told me that I was the "poster child" for ECT.

But after the second time, I remember being suddenly very negative about the whole thing. I dreaded the next treatment. I did not share that with Dr. A. or my family. I felt I would be letting them all down. And, in all honesty, I was feeling a lot better.

***

My third treatment was a bit of a disaster, as far as I was concerned. I went under, and then, suddenly, I was awake, just like the first two times. I had my oxygen mask on, but I couldn't breathe, couldn't pump my lungs. I was terrified and tried to speak but was unable to move the right muscles, any muscles. I was frozen and breathless, but all they did was work around me, not realizing what was happening. I was awake, but the anesthetic was still in effect. My eyes were wide open, and all I thought was that I was going to die, right then and there.

But I gradually got my breathing up and going, and I could move my body again. As they started talking to me, I began to cry. I was so upset. I explained what had happened. They reassured me that I had the oxygen mask on, and I was always getting air with it. That my muscles were still numb, making it impossible for me to use them to get their attention. But the doctor acknowledged how frightening my experience had been and that next time it would be different with the anesthetic, it would be correct.

They got it right the fourth time, though I still woke up in the treatment room. At least I wasn't frozen. However, when I finally got upstairs and dressed and was fed, the evidence was really clear to me: I was "normal" again. I felt very good.

Not tipped over into mania good, but good.

Normal.

Later that day, when I talked with Dr. A., I told her I was feeling great, and I could stop my treatments and go home. She was a bit surprised but obviously pleased. And she was a bit concerned that with my happiness now, another treatment might go too far and bring on a high. The next day there was a conference with my mum, and I was cleared for departure the following day. It all happened so quickly, but I guess that is what I pushed for.

And I did push. Did I exaggerate a little bit about my "wellness" to my doc, to my family? As I had come to despise ECT so much, I might have put on a show and said anything to get out. But I don't think so. I was genuinely better, and I was relieved not to have further treatments.

The last day of a hospitalization, with everything packed and ready to go, is always a hard one. I had already checked myself out mentally. It was now a wait for the nurses and doctors, final reports and prescriptions for me to be totally free to leave. The doors to and from the ward were controlled carefully, so there was no slipping quietly out.

Once out of the psych ward, things levelled off, with the exception of anxiety. I had taken many combinations of Haldol and Ativan to calm myself during my stay. The hospital was a safe place. Out in the real world, things were different. I couldn't pace the floors, just go up to a window, ask for a hit, flop down on my bed. No, I had to take my happier self, the one with only a little depression, and move on out.

The world was wide open to me, and, despite my anxiety, I was ready to take it on.

Chapter 32

I had made it through my last hospitalization by early July. It felt like the final set in a concert, but with no encore—a neat wrap-up. I felt like I was finally leaving it all behind. No more stupid moves, no more hospitalizations, my mind feeling clear and strong. I got better just like I got sick in the first place. Quickly, definitively.

It would be interesting to know if, at that time, on that day in July when I left the hospital, my complete memory was intact. That I remembered all the way back to buying the car, overdosing, adopting a dog, booking all the travel, buying all the art, the Montfort—remembered all four hospitals I had stayed in. When did those memories transfer to a file marked "restricted access"? At discharge time? Or, gradually, over the months that followed? And why did it take my curiosity a year longer to uncover all that happened? I don't really know, but as I put all my missed memories together, I am shocked.

I had been warned that memory loss was a potential side effect of ECT. I was told that I might lose time on the day of treatment. But that hadn't been the case. I remembered everything during ECT: Jeff flying up from Brooklyn at the end of June, my meetings with Dr. A., the actual treatments themselves. I wasn't aware that there were weeks that had disappeared from that spring, that the ECT had in fact had a huge impact on my memory. I didn't think to question things until Jasmin stirred the pot.

And this one giant episode—I view everything from January to July 2019 as all part of the same episode—had disappeared from my mind. Particularly, events from February to early June. These events don't seem to have been stored in my brain, or at least a part of my brain that I have access to. They are blotted out in places completely and a little muddy in others.

ECT is an excellent treatment for pain and agony. It was worth it for me, it seemed to press restart in my brain somehow. But, I have paid a bit of a price: four months or so of lost time, murky pictures of memories that perhaps don't exist anymore. (And a creepy sensation whenever I see ECT depicted in a movie or television show.)

***

Once I was out of the hospital, though much was going well, the anxiety attacks returned. They were like spin-offs from a larger, more serious tornado, picking me up, twisting everything around. On one evening, I had to call my mother to ask her to leave her dinner companions to return home as I was shaking horribly. She came, her phone on speaker as she drove. I worked with my breathing as I had been taught and relied on medication: Haldol and clonazepam.

Despite this increase in panic attacks, I have to admit that since that summer, life has been kinder to me. I have not had the same intensity of illness, fewer episodes that are less serious. There was one point in the fall of 2019 when I did have a particularly strong depression, and Dr. G. and I spoke about me going back to the General for more ECT. But that never went anywhere, and I recovered. Sometimes, I am aware of a thin membrane that keeps depression away from me. So close, I can almost touch it, bubbly and damp. But I don't catch it. And though we haven't figured out how to stop the people listening in my brain and other minor psychotic stuff, I have only had two or three episodes of frank psychosis in the past months, which were easily treated. I am on much steadier ground.

The ECT definitely worked for a while, but I can't credit it for more recent successes. Or, maybe I can? Maybe it recalibrated my brain, changing neurons and synapses, whole structures, as the treatment went on. But, there is no scientific evidence for this, though much is unknown.

Part Four

Chapter 33

Quite often, I lie in bed at night, frightened. I worry that there will be a basement fire coming from the furnace room. My two cats and I would be trapped from the basement stairs; our fire route is my bedroom window, built to perform as such. I would know where to go, but the cats! The cats would run into cupboards or closets. They would never believe me when I urged them to go toward the window, never follow my voice. I could stuff them each in a pillowcase, I think, but I look at the scratches on my arms, freshly made as I struggled to get them each into a cat carrier, destination vet. I don't like to think about how they die in this scenario.

I worry a lot. I have a lot of anxiety, all sorts of anxiety. It is with me every day.

***

In the middle of grade 11, when I was 16, I ruined a short play by forgetting all my lines in front of hundreds of students. Several days later, an acquaintance commented that if it hadn't been for me, our little skit would have been the best part of the school assembly. I was so ashamed. And a profound phobia was born, fear of public speaking.

I was in history class, and the teacher said that we were to each read a paragraph aloud from our textbooks, starting at the front of the first row and snaking our way through the middle rows, all the way to the end row where I was seated. As each student read and my turn approached, I grew more and more anxious. Things started swimming, my breathing became fast and shallow, and my heart was doing funny flip-flops. When it came to my turn, all I could do was lay my head down on the book and not move. The teacher called my name, but I stayed like that, head cradled in my arms, frozen. I don't know what happened after that—after all the staring, the snickering and teasing. I somehow got up and out of the building, where I could breathe.

From that moment on, my fear of public speaking ruled my life. I was terrified to go into classrooms. Teachers might call on me for comments or answers or ask me to give a presentation. I couldn't risk that, so I spoke to teachers in advance. I would ask them not to single me out in any way at all. Usually, they would make allowances for me, but there were a few teachers who wanted me to continue, to tough it out. I skipped those classes every day until I basically dropped out completely.

Even though I never really finished high school, I did take a few courses at both universities in town when I was in my twenties. I attended one class on twentieth-century world history, one that I had really been looking forward to. The professor entered the room, and after he said his name, he stated that we should "watch out" and not snooze because he loved to pick a person to add a comment on the day's teachings. That was it for me. I closed my notebook, stuffed everything into my knapsack, and walked out of the room. Once outside, I burst into tears.

***

My dance with anxiety has been on and off throughout my life. I have had various symptoms over the years that could easily be filed in several different anxiety disorders—social anxiety, panic disorder, generalized anxiety disorder, and obsessive-compulsive disorder. I sometimes find extreme anxiety a lot harder to handle than serious depression. It can be all-encompassing and makes me feel physically out of control. I know that there are many people out there who experience one or more forms of anxiety, full-blown, and I know they have it worse than me. I don't know how they do it.

Today, my anxiety manifests in several ways. I still don't like large gatherings that require people to be interactive and speak out loud in any way. So that means absolutely no public speaking, on any level, for me. I avoid any situation that might put me in danger. An example that comes to mind was years ago, when I gave a pass to hearing a local author speak, as I knew there would be a Q&A afterward. I was convinced that I would be forced, with a spotlight on me, to ask a question, to speak. I realize this sounds completely irrational. But, I might do the same thing again, even today.

And still today, after the anxiety at the General Hospital, I have panic attacks. That has not gone away over the months since. There are things that have triggered panic attacks over the years. In my last apartment, before moving into my mum's place, I would look at the mess in the kitchen and simply hide on a chair that was tucked away in the corner. My heart pounding, I could feel the anxiety—it felt like it was coming from my stomach—swell up into my chest, where I couldn't rid myself of it. It would then truly overwhelm my brain. I would take a bit of clonazepam, lie down on my bed with Finny, and wait for the drug to swoosh in on my brain and help me. It took pretty much exactly one hour from panic to relaxation. And, of course, I used the relaxation techniques I had learned over the years during various bouts in the psych ward.

I recall a recent evening where I had a mini panic attack, something I think was brought on because I was in charge of cooking dinner. I found myself stirring a sauce when the familiar dread whooshed over me. I turned the stove off and sat in an armchair, doing some breathing exercises. They worked—I caught the attack early enough and did not have to take any medication for it. These panic attacks have increased over the years, to what they were when I was in hospital, and since. I am learning how to avoid them, yet I am still at times at their mercy.

***

"See you later" is one of the most repetitive phrases to come out of my mouth. Scared that I will not see the person again, I make sure that the phrase is the last thing I say to them. This includes cats. And it is not just the actual phrase, but also how that phrase is delivered. I have to repeat it in several ways that creates a pattern. I have to be looking at the person in a certain way and also not looking at them in a certain way. I only say "goodbye" if it is followed by that magical phrase. Turning out the light at night comes with a ritual of "See you laters" directed at my cats and my mum, who is sleeping upstairs. Once I've completed the pattern, I must not open my eyes. To do so means that I have to repeat everything I just got through.

That is an older anxiety that has carried on to present day. Other rituals come from my past as well, including stepping on cracks in the sidewalk in a symmetrical way. I think I look awfully funny to anyone watching me. I take tiny steps, then large ones. Another tiny one, and then a normal one, and so on, until I reach my destination. How about checking the stove in an obsessive pattern? I am sure many can relate! Or touching cold or hot surfaces with my hands in symmetry. (My brother Alan once said, when I was a teenager, that I was a "slave to symmetry.")

If I have an anxious thought (for example, fearing that I will die in the night and not see others ever again), it will only increase in strength until I carry out an action (in this case, chanting "see you later" in a ritualized way) that causes the anxiety to lift. This action neutralizes the anxious thought, and its repetition calms me, makes me feel better. It may seem kooky, but that is the essence of OCD. I do not have a serious case of it, my anxieties do not take an hour or more of my time every day. The thoughts and the rituals, with a little stammer to them, are an annoyance more than anything, for my part. I know how OCD can really rip a person up, and I am glad I do not have to live through that. There is that continuum again that Dr. G. loves to talk about, with me perched on it, lucky to not be up the line a bit in full OCD mode.

***

When my mother turned 70 a few years ago, I (tipsy) made a short toast to her at the party, my words coming out perfectly with strength and clarity, funny bits and all. Afterward, people around me slapped my shoulder, said "Nice speech, Joc." But, when I saw my mum, we grabbed each other's hands, both of us amazed at what I had just done.

"Did I just do that?" I said, squealing.

"I think you did!" my mum said. "That was just fabulous.

I sat there thinking, 'Who is this amazing woman?!' It was definitely you."

We both laughed.

Now, I don't think I will be giving TED talks in my future, but that speech was in fact a stellar accomplishment for me, even if fortified by a couple of glasses of sangria.

Public speaking is not something I have to deal with on a daily basis. I can pretty much eliminate it from my life. It is, instead, the more cloying panic attacks that can really disable me. I do not know where I am going with these, but I have to keep on top of them. I have come too far in battling schizoaffective disorder for these attacks to destabilize me all the way back to the beginning.

Chapter 34

The light has turned green. I enter the intersection surrounded by a bobble of people as they criss-cross in front of me. Men in suits on their way home, students, old ladies, kids on skateboards. And then me, a third of the way through the crosswalk, straining against the light, trying to make it across. Fat not completely hidden by a massive yellow T-shirt, sweat down my back, down my front, on my face, in my hair so it is damp and sticky. An old green bag decorated with ugly brown flowers hangs from my shoulder. Huge hiking boots that rub up against the bottom of my plus-size green Capris. I walk with my face turned down, watching for cracks and potholes, feeling exposed on the hot stage that is the intersection.

I have been so out of shape, ever since I was a kid. Out of shape and overweight. I remember my first trip out west at the age of 43, my first experience of the city of Vancouver, the West Coast. Our hotel was in the city centre, and we strolled down to the harbour to dine on fish and seafood from the nearby waters. And then a walk was suggested, and we made our way to Chinatown before turning around to head back to our hotel. *Thank God,* I thought. I had been slowing the walkers down, stopping to look in shop windows, pretending to be engrossed by the fancy displays they contained. Really, I was catching my breath. But, I wasn't pulling the wool over anybody.

Vancouver wasn't the first time I slowed others down, and it was certainly not the last. One time, my family went to Morocco for 10 days, after visiting Spain. I was 30 years old—this would have been in the spring of 2000, as my brother Jeffrey had just married Natasha, and before meeting up with us, they had been on their honeymoon in Catalonia. We travelled to the High Atlas Mountains in the Southeast of Morocco, rugged hills and desert scrub all around us. A two-day trek was planned, but everybody knew I was unable to do the walking. So, we hired a donkey. Yes, we had one donkey with a guide, me on top swaying each time the animal shifted its weight. I was relieved but also embarrassed and a little humiliated.

***

Ever since I was a teenager, I have struggled with my weight. I hovered around 160 pounds for years but would sometimes get a little slimmer, closer to the magic 140 pounds. That struggle became more intense as I went on psychotropic medication at the age of 25. On meds, I gained weight. I don't know if that is because these drugs would play around with my metabolism, or if they increased my appetite, or both, but starting with my first psychiatric medicine, I had a new enemy on my hands: my body. I had squared off with it before, beginning at age 13, but this was the real thing. I was in full battle gear.

With the extra pounds piling on over the years, my shaky self-esteem—shaky since my adolescence, or even before—took on a new wobbliness. I hated looking into mirrors, trying on new clothes, or trying to fit into old ones. This depressed me, and to deal with these unwanted feelings, I took to eating more. Carb-laden dishes like mac and cheese, pierogies, grilled cheese sandwiches, cream-sauced pastas. My comfort food.

***

Not a day in my life goes by when I don't think about my body, whether it is what I should eat on my diet or what I should wear to minimize my size. Not a week goes by without starting or stopping a particular diet. I haul around a lot of weight (at its height, my weight was 263 pounds), and I feel it every moment.

I have a scale that talks to my phone, an app that shows my weight and my BMI, and the trends up and down. I am religious about it. I had a recent phone call with my cousin, the only one to know about my eating and diet shambles, and she wondered if maybe that app was unhealthy for me, as it feeds into my obsession with my weight. I know she is right, but can I internalize that, what I know to be true? That I have an unhealthy relationship with my body? Can I capture that?

On all my recent diets, when I reached 200 pounds, for some reason, I would end it there. I was incapable of going any lower. It wasn't because I didn't know how to lose weight. I did. I had gotten that far. And, it was not a plateau, a common phenomenon if one is dieting to lose weight. Maybe it was my body fighting, fighting off my shamed mind, and its constant need to be slim. My mind saying, "200 pounds is just fine, and you're going to stay there, so be happy with it." My body keeping me where I actually am healthy, where it doesn't have to be starved. And, my mind accepting this, finally, my mind allowing me to be 200 pounds with confidence and peace. If I did accept it, my whole life would be better. I would not have to deal with so many anxieties about my weight. I could just be. Yes, being at peace with one's weight is wonderful. I can write about it here, but future paragraphs say a different story. I am not at peace, and I keep on searching.

***

There is an upcoming reunion with my mum's entire family coming from all across Canada, the US, and the UK. It will be about 50 people, including cousins and their offspring, all the aunts and uncles. I am struggling to be lighter by then. It is a goal, and if I miss it, I will feel like a big nothing, just a nuisance, there for a laugh.

It is so sad to say that this fits my pattern. There is nothing new. I am 51 years old, and I am nowhere different from at 18. I have no words of advice, no guidance or instructions, no body of evidence to show the world. Why am I even writing about this disastrous part of my life, a disaster that I continuously play into? Should I keep my own voice silent, let the space be filled by body-positive writers? Those voices should be heard by everyone; they comfort me, but for some reason their words just don't stick.

***

I lived through the past two decades with more of the same. My weight up, down, drugs tinkered with. I settled into it, I guess. I was very unhappy about it, but I guess I lost my fight.

But there was one day during the fall of 2008 that really hit me, the year I was living in Brooklyn. A very pregnant Natasha and I were working on pricing items to be displayed on the shelves of Whisk, getting them ready for

Christmas.

"Hello!" somebody called out. We looked up and saw a warmly dressed woman waving at us from the front door. "Are you guys open?" she called.

"Well, we aren't really open yet, but, sure, you can come in. It's pretty messy in here!" I was standing behind the cash area and could see that the woman was pushing a pram. She made her way over to us, gushing about the shelves with their beautifully coloured ceramic pieces and shiny pots and pans.

She said hi to both of us, and then focused on Natasha. "What's your due date?" she asked.

"A couple of weeks," said Natasha. "How old is your little one?" She got up and looked in the pram. "Oh, what a sweetie!"

"Almost two months," the woman said, turning to look at the cash area, her gaze resting on me. "And what is your due date?" she asked me. Out of the corner of my eye, I could see Natasha's body freeze, caught in the act of cleaning a kettle.

I didn't miss a beat. "Oh, not for a long, long time," I said. I was smiling, waving my hand at her dismissively. I turned away, got busy in the cupboard, waiting for her to leave.

Later that day, I would stuff shame in my mouth, two bagels and lox and extra-large cookies from the shop just up the street.

***

How many women go through this struggle! Societal expectations (at least in the Western world) to be of a certain body type, a skinny body type, hit almost every woman at some point in her life, even if she is already slender. Society wants more, more, faster still.

I have been fat-shamed for as long as I can remember. From comments on what I was wearing, about how much I had eaten, all the way to boys passing by hurling insults out there for all to see and hear. And of course, there is what I see at the movies, in advertisements, on social media, on TV, what others whisper about, yell about. Even today, as a middle-aged woman, people's remarks can sting me, make me feel ashamed of what I look like, what I weigh. And how dare I? How dare I walk around, looking like I do?

My mum and I shared diets while I was a teenager, starting with the brutal Scarsdale Diet, which had great results but no lasting power. And then how they would yo-yo, those pounds, different diets over the years. Growing up in the shadow of that, the messages passed on to me were clear. I had to weigh a normal weight, be slim and fit, to be totally acceptable. Of course, my mum never said this to me, but her actions and opinions of others spoke loudly.

All shapes and sizes of women's bodies are beautiful and should be celebrated as such. I wish I could embrace mine and just accept what I look like as who I am, with nothing needing changing, no parts of my body needing to be cut off. Sometimes I do feel beautiful, that my beauty is visible still, no matter my size.

Through the years, sometimes my weight would go way down, and I did fit into those clothes and feel okay with mirrors. I got attention from men, from Marcel and the assault, to just plain old "hey babies" and whistles. When I walked past a construction site, I felt like my legs weren't working properly, that as I walked past all those staring eyes, I looked physically out of control, wobbly and awkward. I bet so many women can relate to this.

I think I became uncomfortable with this kind of attention

from men and staying walled off by fat kept me mostly unseen, free from catcalls and whistles. I didn't say one day, "Become fat again, and you will not be whistled at, you will not be assaulted." (Not that fat people can't be assaulted. Of course, they can and are.) But underneath it all, somewhere deep in my brain, that is exactly what was said.

But occasionally I am seen. Occasionally I am targeted. It is when I am walking down a street, minding my own business, that it might happen. I hear, "Fat cow!" yelled out at me, yelled at the pounds, yelled at the body that carries them. Boys or young men are always the culprits. But this is the only attention my body draws lately, and even now, it seldom happens. To be a 51-year-old overweight woman is to be invisible. And I am not sure if that is a good thing or a bad.

Being even a bit overweight brings with it many stereotypes, most of them untrue. Lazy, weak, indolent beast who can't control what goes in her mouth, eating nothing but ice cream and sugar tarts, drinking litres of pop. Sitting on the sofa, scarfing it all back, not knowing when to stop, unable to stop. That is what many often think when they meet a fat woman, if they think anything at all.

***

During my first hospitalization in 1995, while the doctors were still getting to know me, the resident asked me if I thought I had an eating disorder. I smirked and replied, "Only if 95 percent of North American women do. It's a cultural disorder, not a mental disorder, isn't it?" Sometimes I will doubt the doctors, their diagnoses, their medications, but I have no doubt when it comes to disordered eating, a disordered way of looking at myself and my body and sense of self-worth. I have that! You can put my name in that column, that crowded, well-populated column. Even though I do not meet the requirements for any of the major eating disorders, I know I belong there. Me and the 95 percent.

Well, actually, I wonder if I do in fact meet some of those requirements. At least, in the past. This is the part I leave out when I make light of actual diagnoses, when I talk about a kinship with all the other basically normal women out there, the 95 percent. This I have left out of conversations with my doctor, friends, my mum—only telling my cousin and not another soul, until now, right here. You see, I have often kneeled down on a cold, tiled floor, using my left hand to hold my hair back, with my right fingers stretched down my throat, as far as they would go. I have kneeled down around the toilet, the seat up, making myself retch over and over again.

But, I failed even at this. I would have just finished stuffing myself with all my rich, creamy foods. There would have been a lot to come out, if I could make myself throw up properly. But, instead, it was just a retch, bringing up hardly anything at all, but sending my body into spasms. After a few minutes, I would sit up, flush whatever liquids had made it out, and splash cold water over my face.

I have done this at least a hundred times in my life. It never worked, and my weight would continue to bounce around. Did I have bulimia, in which bingeing and then purging food is a main feature? No, I don't think so. It wasn't normal, my behaviour, I know that. I am sure, like anxiety, mood, and psychotic disorders, there is a continuum of severity and disablement when it comes to disordered eating. I sit somewhere on that line, having cozied closely up to a full-blown eating disorder at times in my life. A secret of such shame, that I couldn't let other people in on it. Not even Dr.

G. Not even my mum. And the shame persists.

***

Over my first hospitalization, I was told that valproic acid was the drug to be on for bipolar disorder. It would be good for my mood swings and not put on the pounds. But seven months later, I was back in hospital, with the doctors saying I had to try lithium, that it was clear I needed to be on both lithium and valproic acid. They didn't talk about weight gain anymore. I think they had given up.

I haven't been on those drugs for ages. I was switched to a newer class of antipsychotics and mood stabilizers instead. On the first one, my weight climbed up again, much to my dismay, panicking and desperate to keep from being so big. We added a second, and then the biggest rush yet of pounds. Today, I am still on these two meds at high doses, and they are another part of my weight puzzle.

But that is just me and my metabolism and how the drugs work in my body. Many people try these drugs, stay on these drugs, and do not gain a single pound. For them, these drugs can work well, do what they are intended for: mood stability, diminishing psychosis. For me, though they piled on the pounds, they do work to keep me together, enough to be functioning, enough to carry on like a normal person, more than that, even. And I have to accept that trade-off. I don't really have any choice in the matter. The meds help keep me fat. But I have to keep on fighting my body anyway, a long, drawn-out, losing battle.

Chapter 35

I am now a convert. Well, maybe not a convert, necessarily. But, after many, many years of resistance, I have finally come around and am fully embracing exercise, especially as a tool to fight my anxiety and mood swings. It is not because I am only now learning about the many benefits of getting your heart revved up, your muscles worked out, and your head cleared out. I have known about those for years. It is just that that knowledge has finally stuck.

A while ago, my sister-in-law Matilda introduced me to podcasts, and I was intrigued. A whole bunch of neat ones, from NPR and the CBC, to esoteric, intriguing stories and talks. I was hooked. Through the warmth of spring to the beauty of autumn, I started walking again, but this time I had a podcast to get me going. I would strike out on walks as long as an hour, three or four kilometres in length. When I got back, I would have rosy cheeks and a new sense of well-being. I usually got overheated and would sit out on the screened-in porch with my cats until I was cooled down enough to carry on.

***

The first time I really exercised was when I was 12 or 13. I would accompany my mum on an hour's walk, measured by car at 5.6 kilometres, long before the obsession with step counting. Rosy cheeks. I did that off and on throughout my early teens. I stopped doing that in high school and didn't really pick up anything in its place.

Fast forward a decade, when I tried jogging after dark. It was 1995, and I was living with Ruby in the Glebe, and I had started seeing Dr. G. every Tuesday afternoon. He was supportive of my athletic endeavour but felt doing it at night was not the way to go since it would keep me revved up and delay sleep. But I was too embarrassed to do it during daylight, so I stopped altogether. I was a pathetic jogger.

When I was 35, I joined Curves, a low-key circuit training system meant for women only. I actually enjoyed that. Boredom didn't set in, since every two minutes or so you were changing the machine or exercise. I did this at a Curves in the neighbourhood I grew up in, one that was now trendy, and had many coffee shops. It was too hard to say no to a triple-shot latte and a baked good to keep it company, a desire that counteracted my workouts. Needless to say, after only two months, I dropped out of Curves.

I made a good stab at exercise at a local community centre. I went mid-afternoon when it was pretty quiet. I did weight machines for top and bottom muscle groups, as well as my core section, and followed this up with either stationary bike or treadmill. But it was getting too good. I figure—and everyone around me seems to agree—that once I am doing well at something, once I have found success, I drop out. That is a pattern that runs through all areas of my life, from scholastic achievements to maintaining a healthy weight to starting projects. I don't know why this pattern is so prevalent in my life, but I am trying to identify it and trap it down, understand it and implement change so I can do things like finish this book.

My time at a big-name gym was horrible, just horrible. The atmosphere was garish, big, and loud, filled with trim and super-fit people. I hated the exercises, and I hated using the treadmill in such a public setting. Quitting that was a no-brainer.

The last joint I tried was Planet Fitness. There is one about four kilometres from where I live, in a big strip mall, and I gave it a good few months. It has a great set up. Some overweight people work there, and some overweight people work out there. It is very inclusive, very body positive. I did the treadmill exclusively, no weight machines, even though they have a million of them. I know that weight training is just as important as aerobic exercise, but I was intimidated by the machines and didn't enjoy using them. After a while, I lost interest in going to the gym regularly, so I quit Planet Fitness.

***

The evidence is overwhelming. It is all over the place. Everywhere I turn, I read that exercise boosts brain health, heart health, sleep and, of course, helps with weight loss. And it can help you deal with your mood and anxiety. Mood and anxiety—I am really paying attention to that. Exercise seems to stimulate various chemicals in your brain that improve your emotions and focus, as well as memory, a bonus for me as I struggle with my memory in big ways and small.

I have had type 2 diabetes for a number of years now, most likely as part of the side effect profile of the novel antipsychotics I take and their propensity to cause metabolic syndromes. I am on medication to control the diabetes (more medication, damn it!), and that plus smart eating has brought down my numbers to the normal range. But my aim is to someday stop the drugs and lead my body on a health campaign that includes dealing with diabetes without them. What I eat is a huge part of that campaign. But I have also learned that exercise goes a long way in regulating blood glucose levels. I don't know how possible this will be for me, but I will try.

***

In 1979, after my dad's first major heart surgery, he was prescribed exercise to build up his heart health and strength. I don't know how much medical science understood back then about exercise and its effects on the brain. But not only did my dad get back in shape, he also helped his brain, unknowingly, get back in shape as well.

He started walking one kilometre a day. (My father, ever the stubborn New Englander, referred to these as "mini miles" for the entirety of his life.) Gradually, he built the distance up. Then he started jogging. I don't think I have ever seen such a slow runner in my life. His pace was slower than what his walking speed had been. He wore striped athletic pants and a T-shirt, and as usual, his comb-over would flop all over the place.

***

My mother reminded me recently that several times on walks together over the past 5 years or so, I would turn to her and say, "See, I love this exercise. I am going to get skinny and fit, just like that woman we just passed. I am going to be in awesome shape!" And oh, I believed it. But it just never stuck. Maybe this time it will. I have faith in myself. There seems to be a pattern in my life lately, this shift towards wellness in my mental illness, so having faith is not unrealistic. It's a circle for me, for us all. I need to feel good in order to exercise, but I need exercise in order to feel good. As my personal history attests, starting exercise and maintaining it can be a real struggle. If you are depressed on top of that or are really nervous and anxious out in public spaces, getting the motivation to go for a walk can be next to impossible.

It is the maintenance stage that is always my downfall. So, I walked over the past months successfully, feeling pretty good. But then came winter. I am a faller. I fall at least three times every icy season. So, I have gradually put down my phone, no longer obsessively tracking my steps.

It seems that no matter what kind of exercise I do, it always seems to be *the* one, the one that is best suited to my time, my money, my effort. I stick to it with a vengeance, talk up its virtues. And then the struggle. I don't know what it is—am I just lazy? It really is a struggle, and I have never quite figured out why.

But this time, I am maintaining quite well. Shut inside, I have started doing a variation of a walk with podcast. I have been running around the house, bouncing up and down, all the while listening to very loud music. At first, I could only manage 10 or 15 minutes. But now, my ridiculous-looking aerobic workouts last for 40 minutes at least. I even do stretches on an old yoga mat that had never met its potential. And this exercise, after a few months in, has shown no sign of letting up.

Come the New Year, I will definitely have wishes that circle around diet, health, and exercise. They will be new, and I will be very excited about them. I will have a new, positive outlook. But we will see just how far my new habits take me. I will walk again, once the ice has melted, I think that much is clear to me. With my indoor musical workouts to take me through to spring—will I keep at it, or will I sink back into the sofa? I am feeling pretty good about my chances. It really, really feels like this time it will stick. I hope that's not my pattern speaking up, because I think I finally got it.

Chapter 36

Many years ago, to help regulate my sleep during one of my highs, I was prescribed chlorpromazine, a drug known as Thorazine, as in "Doing the Thorazine Shuffle." The first time I tried it, I took 100 mg, anticipating a rough night. This was an experiment. Within minutes, I was flat out on my bed.

I woke up with my brain still dark, trying to think of where I was and what I was doing. I was in bed, it was a Saturday, and I was supposed to be at work. And I was late. But, when I put my feet on the floor, it was like I was moving my legs through thick sludge. What the fuck? As my head lolled around my right shoulder and I struggled to keep my eyes open, I remembered the Thorazine experiment. It had worked, and then some.

On the bus to work, I wondered how people could take hundreds of milligrams of this stuff. I was completely, drooling, drugged. Somehow, I made it to the kitchen store. I walked in around noon, and my not-very-happy manager greeted me. "It's a long story," I mumbled to her. "I am so sorry. I took the wrong medication last night, and it made me so sleepy that I only just woke up." I walked to the back of the store, to my space, and started straightening books over and over again. But, I kept nodding off, even while standing. I was so unbelievably tired.

"You know, sweetie, I think you should go home," my manager said, feeling softer as she saw me hold onto a shelf filled with copies of *Coyote Cafe*. "We'll be fine. You need to go sleep this off."

The bus took a detour to avoid a parade on Bank Street, and I struggled to get off near my stop. Once inside my apartment, I didn't even bother taking off my shoes; I just collapsed on the bed. Sleep was instantaneous.

A couple of hours later I woke up just a little bit, somehow my fuzzy brain telling me to go to the bathroom. Oh, God, I thought. I have to pee. But I can't move. I groaned. I'm just gonna do it. And I peed myself. Rather than waking up fully, all I could do was wet the bed.

Sleep came again, and when I finally woke up for good, it was 9:00 p.m. I vowed never to try that drug again.

Years later, 100 mg of Thorazine didn't even touch my insomnia. I needed more and more of it as time went by. Sometimes, I would take 800, 900 mg of it in a desperate move to get to sleep. I would often get out of bed as the hours ticked by, to take even a little more. This antipsychotic drug is one that I wrestle with up to the present day, taking it on nights where sleep proves elusive. It's a trade-off, though. Although I get to sleep, I have to walk around the next day with a foggy brain. Thorazine is a very tricky drug, rendering many on it to be slow-moving, drug-soaked, and out of it. Not nice.

***

The idea of taking meds and staying on meds brings up a lot of issues. There are concerns over side effects. Will you experience any, and will they be noticeable to others? And, what would people think if they knew you were taking pills?

Would they judge you, label you? Do these drugs tinker with who you are, at your core? Will they permanently change you? Will you ever see your unmedicated baseline again? How long will you need to be on them, and how will you know when to stop? What are the challenges, the side effects, of going off a med? And is all of it legit in the first place?

Some experts argue that psychiatric medications are not very effective, and can cause harm if used long-term. If they are going to be used at all, they should be used in acute care only. Some people state that mental illness does not exist. Others cite religious reasons for staying away from drugs. Still others believe going the medication route is a cop-out. Surely, you can pull those bootstraps up, find the inner strength to deal with your symptoms with no help from other people, let alone pills. And, of course, many people quit their meds as soon as they start to feel good, good usually being different from better.

***

My father took Xanax, a benzodiazepine (which are minor tranquilizers), on occasion to help him sleep. In my teens, I also had a lot of trouble sleeping, so I would raid his bathroom cabinet and grab a few pills to help me through the night. As is common with benzodiazepines, I gradually became more tolerant of the medicine's action. More would be needed to get the same effect.

I liked Xanax and other benzos like Valium a whole hell of a lot. I finally got my own prescription, so those nightly raids into my father's pill bottles were no longer necessary. Over the years, I turned to clonazepam, another very popular benzodiazepine. One of the good things about clonazepam is that it generally doesn't cause weight gain, a real bonus considering where I was at with my body. Actually, I don't have a clue as to what side effects clonazepam might throw at my body. Feeling sleepy? Isn't that why I am taking it? No, its side effects are lost in the pot of side effects brought on by the use of other drugs, like antipsychotics and antidepressants.

***

I was released from my first hospitalization in 1995 on one drug, valproic acid. And that was the beginning of it all. That one major drug, kicking it all off, all the medication, more than 45 over the years. I have come to be a seasoned pro.

There are many side effects of psych drugs, some of which are easier than others. I have, at times, had ones that are pretty common, such as headaches, dry mouth, and dizziness. Some of them sound scary, but I am told they are not harmful. I think there are several side effects in particular that steer people away from drugs, and I can understand why. A major one is hyposexuality—basically, low sex drive. Another, more troublesome one for me, is weight gain. And the third one, though I no longer experience it, is the sense of being drugged. Those three can really scare the hell out of people contemplating medication. I can't say I blame them.

My med pile-up began early on. I had started lithium during my second hospitalization in the fall of 1995. It gave me a serious tremor in my hands; forks and spoons would rattle against bowls as I attempted to lift them to my mouth, the food on them invariably falling on to the table or onto my shirt. I was on a drug for the tremors, but it only worked so well to smooth them out. I was on an antidepressant, now that I had the lithium to prevent me from getting high off it. The drugs were just beginning to add up to a lot.

Psychiatric disorders can be hard to treat, and finding the

right medicine, or combination of medicines, can be tricky. It is not an exact science. It's a very common experience for people to have their drugs switched around or added to on a regular basis. I am not alone in that.

I have an illness, just like people who have other kinds of illness. I have to remind myself of this when I dole out the pills into a little bowl and swallow them all before I go to bed, swallow all the side effects. Just like any illness.

***

I started taking Haldol as a permanent addition to my daily drug regimen in 2013, after using it intermittently for years to treat mania and psychosis. We started with 5 mg a day (that little round green pill, that special pill). I am currently at 20 mg, and that still doesn't work perfectly. I have break through psychosis every now and then, and when I do, we raise the dose to 25 mg for a while. The highest dose I have been on is 30 mg. It is a wonder I can walk, that I can do anything at all.

With Haldol (like other antipsychotics), I run the risk of developing a movement disorder called tardive dyskinesia (TD). My tongue might stick out uncontrollably, I might grimace a lot, turn my head to the side frequently, move my arm repeatedly in a funny way. Once it starts, it may never go away, not even after the offending antipsychotic has been discontinued.

I have tried other antipsychotics, ones that are less likely to cause TD. I've tried all the "novel" antipsychotics available in Canada, leaning toward the older ones in that class, the two that I currently take, as well as Clozapine. This drug is a tough one, but it has saved so many, erasing their hallucinations, easing their delusions. Given that I have a treatment-resistant disorder, Dr. S., on one of my hospitalizations, decided to try me on Clozapine. But it made my blood pressure drop so low that I was ordered to lie down in bed for the day. On another hospitalization, he decided to try it again, but the same issue came up. My blood pressure just got too low.

Even though Haldol makes me feel like there is a clamp on my brain, I will probably take it for the rest of my life.

***

It was early January 2018, and another of the few times that I stopped taking all my medication. I know I was upset and angry, and I know it was after my visit with a dermatologist about my bloodied, scratched arms.

After the break for Christmas, I started up with Dr. G. again. I was not in good shape. I had stopped taking my meds several days before, at the end of December. It had been a sudden decision, helped by the voices. My journey through getting my itchy arms properly diagnosed had been full of signs and signals, people doubting me, telling me I was crazy. "Well, fuck that!" I said, as did my voices. "I am not crazy!" And so, I put down my psych meds, as they were only for people who were, in fact, "crazy."

"It wasn't just her," I told Dr. G. "It was the first resident, the one who did the skin biopsy. He and his supervisor kept asking me what you thought of my arms, if you had said anything about the subject. They asked me if they could call you. I was so mad. They didn't trust me at all, and thought because I had a mental illness I was making it up, or scratching because I was depressed or psychotic or something. And I wasn't. I was perfectly fine."

"I don't think your itchy arms have anything to do with

your illness," Dr. G. said. "And, it doesn't look like a side effect of anything you are on. I am certain of this—it has nothing to do with your illness."

"Well, the dermatologist they sent me to thought it was. She asked me all these questions, she examined my arms, and then she told me the itchiness was a mental thing, and because I had a mental disorder, that was my explanation. Stupid bitch. Well, I'm sorry, but I don't need my meds anymore. If that's what all these doctors are saying, well, I have to go backward, back in time. To see if I really do have an illness. Because I'm not so sure anymore."

Dr. G. didn't seem at all surprised. "Okay. So, you've had a bumpy few weeks. Tell me, when did you stop your medicines?" he asked me.

"Four days ago. And look at me, I am fine. I'm not feeling up or down or crazy. I am just fine." I knew I sounded angry, but I didn't care. I was so certain about my decision.

But my thoughts over the following days were a swirl of darkness and anger. I didn't know it, but my mind was slipping. I thought I was saying a fuck you to all the drugs, to my diagnosis. But, instead, they were saying fuck you to me.

It took about eight days until I was floridly psychotic. The world became a frightening place, with people infiltrating my brain, pulling out information and chasing me down. Loved ones were dead, and somehow it was me who had killed them.

I arrived at Dr. G.'s the next week with a suspicion that he was in on the plot. He told me that we should consider the hospital, because I was very ill. I saw him the next day, and then again the following one. Three days in a row, him trying to convince me to start back on my meds. Finally, the following week, he brought up the idea of hospitalization again. There was no way that I would do that, go there. And, he couldn't force me this time. But, there was something I was feeling, something mirrored in the urgency of his voice. My voices were telling me that I was a psycho, that I truly was a psycho. And I was once again hurting people around me, and I needed it to stop. I needed it all to stop. I was exhausted. I finally agreed to take Haldol, and only Haldol. Like before.

During this episode, I went public. I had gone to a Shoppers Drug Mart to get some anesthetic cream for my arms, only to realize when I got home that the tube had already been opened. *What the fuck?* I set the tube down, certain that it contained poison meant for me.

The next day, I went back to the drugstore, to the back of it where the pharmacy is. "What the hell?" I yelled at the staff busily sorting and counting pills, while I waved the tube at them. I found the pharmacist that had served me the day before, focused on him, called him over.

"Why did you do this? Why did you give this to me, this specific one?" I demanded from him. I showed him the tube. "This is what you gave me yesterday." I was becoming agitated. "I was meant to be dead. Why? Why are they trying to kill me?"

The pharmacist was calm. He took the tube from me, examining it. "I am so sorry. We apparently gave you the tube that we keep open for. . ." He went on a little bit, stuff that I didn't understand.

He gave me a new box of cream, and I swirled around to leave, only to see people standing and watching. I looked at one woman and yelled at her, "What the fuck are you looking at?"

***

Medication taken for the long-term continues to save my life. Without meds, I would have grown so depressed that I would likely have committed suicide many years ago. I would have been so manic or psychotic that I would have required institutionalization. Or I would have been on the streets, dying out there.

Chapter 37

I have been very lucky to have Dr. G.—he has been a really good match for me. When I am well, as I have been for a good while now, our conversations can wander all over the place as we compare notes on books, food, and streaming ideas. But even with these enjoyable sessions, he is still evaluating how I am doing. He will watch for changes in my speech, my energy, my thinking, and he will work from there.

Not only does Dr. G. prescribe my meds, but he also uses a combination of talk therapies with me to help keep me going. We've had so many discussions, so many conversations and much work over the decades that I have seen him, and I know that is very much a part of what keeps me afloat.

That day in February 1995 when I first met him, I presented with severe depression. He immediately gave me samples for Zoloft, which I started that evening. Unfortunately, my brain had moved on, and I overdosed on a benzo, mixing it with a lot of alcohol and ending up in the psych ward. But Dr. G. realized that first day that we needed to clear my head out a bit with meds before we could get started on the work of psychotherapy. I was too far gone. With severe illness episodes, medication will be obvious.

What do I mean when I write about psychotherapy? First of all, on a really basic level, having the opportunity to share and vent one's inner thoughts and feelings with somebody else, somebody who is safe and trusted, and to receive validation from that person, must be the number one thing people get from psychotherapy. It is human to want safety, security, and complete acceptance of self. There are types of psychotherapy that have these ideas as a base—psychodynamic, interpersonal, cognitive behavioural therapy—and I am sure Dr. G. uses any one of these and more when he meets with me weekly and sees where I'm at. The fact that I am in psychotherapy is more important to me than the type of therapy that is used.

Sometimes, having psychological mindedness can be healing in itself. When I learned that my own life had patterns, when I identified them and began to work with them, the game began to change. For example, I saw how the lack of structure that plagued me in my teenage years came to affect me today. I found it difficult to concentrate and organize things as I aged and saw that this was a pattern based on how I functioned earlier in my life. As a result, I have worked on and sharpened my cognitive skills, and implemented more structure that has now allowed me to do things like cook and write.

As Dr. G. tells me, we have a high level of control over our behaviours, a poor level of control over our thoughts, and no direct control over our feelings and emotions. We cannot change our emotional reactions just by willing them to be different. But we can change our reactions by changing our behaviours, paying attention to them and to cognition, allowing them to hold influence.

A good example of this kind of process would be to imagine that I am allergic to chocolate ice cream, and it happens to be my favourite flavour. I can change how I handle the allergy, how I circumnavigate it, find another flavour that I enjoy almost as much, but I can never change the fact that I am allergic to chocolate ice cream. I can only change how I deal with it, which is where psychotherapy comes in.

Talk therapy on its own would not have been enough to treat my bipolar disorder, psychotic disorder, or anxiety. It would not have put an end to medication for me. But it really, really helped. And that remains the case. I require both psychotherapy and medication to keep my mental health in working order.

***

I used to assume that I lived within the medical model of mental illness, that is, that these illnesses are physiological and are treated with medicine. I shared some writing I had done about living within this model with my American cousin. She wrote back and gently suggested that I check out something called the Recovery Model, which was a big thing in the US. My cousin wondered if it was a good fit with what Dr. G. and I had been working towards.

After talking to my cousin, I started in on my research, and realized that she was right. The Recovery Model (I still believe much of mental illness has a physiological base, and often requires medication) is more of a holistic approach to mental health and is based on two simple premises. The first premise is that it is possible to recover from a mental health condition, recovery including improved health, increased wellness, and reaching your full potential, but not being "cured." The second premise says that the most effective recovery is patient-directed, i.e., individuals have control of decisions about their care.

The Recovery Model highlights having good social supports—people that one feels connected to and who do not judge in any way. I know from experience that these relationships help me cope better with symptoms and spillovers of my illness.

I realized, as I did more reading, that I had already incorporated much of the model in my life, but it was useful to have this framework to affirm that I was on the right path.

Psychotherapy, as I write about above, is essential to the management of my mental illness. But there are other actions that I consider on my quest to be as well as I possibly can. And, I have learned that this holistic view fits well into the Recovery Model.

Following a good diet can bring about improvement for people living with a mental illness. Eating well is important. My diet is very good, and I know that if I stray away from good nutrition, I will start to feel kind of crappy. I feel very clean and ordered after a day of healthy meals.

Exercise, I think, is integral to healing the mind of all sorts of problems. I really struggle with it, as I write earlier, but when I commit to it, even for just a week or two, the change in me is obvious. There is definitely a boost in most people's energy after exercising a few times a week. And it doesn't have to be pedal-to-the-metal workouts. A simple walk a few times a week can make a big difference.

Overcoming a panic attack is not only thanks to clonazepam. During my hospitalizations, I had learned breathing exercises and relaxation techniques that have proven valuable not only during an attack, but in overcoming simple anxiety. A big breath in, and slowly out. In, and slowly out. Concentrate on my right foot melting into the bed, then melt the left one. This all the way up my body until I am relaxed.

A really important one for me to watch is sleep hygiene. If I don't get at least six or seven hours a night, my mood can escalate into hypomania and mania, or my thoughts can get chewed up by psychosis. I try to get a good eight hours a night, but often I will develop insomnia. I use the relaxation techniques that I write about, yet still, I might need a couple of nights in a row with medicine to help me nod off.

I continue to have relationships where I am offered (and return) unconditional love, support, and honesty. Jasmin, my cousin, Ruby, and CS, a close friend who lives in the US, would be four that fit the bill. And that does not include various family members who provide similar supports or Dr. G. I am very lucky to have these people in my life.

Something that is unique for me is the focus on my writing. The self-discipline and structure that I write about earlier now comes from a very stable place. When I am unwell, I develop a form of writer's block, but usually, I am able to spend a good few hours in front of my computer every day. This has been huge for me, a person who never finished anything in her life, a total lack of follow-through. And sitting here writing and succeeding only lays the groundwork for more positives in my life, more things I can achieve. Kind of unbelievable to me, to be honest.

A few weeks ago, I took a couple of books out of the library on the topics of mindfulness and meditation. I was seduced by my research into them and believe if I can get into the practice of these techniques, I will be even further ahead. It seems that mindfulness can help you deal with all sorts of things, including stress, anxiety, and depression. It can even help with physical health, and overall, can improve well-being. I haven't gotten far in the books, but what I have read looks exciting and hopeful.

It seems that mindfulness is a constant journey, keeping oneself in the present, really living every moment. I am able to start flirting with it now as I have come so far in my recovery. I have the focus and am at a place where I am open to this kind of self-care (my peeks at yoga on YouTube would be another important step). I just have to make the jump.

My continuum of wellness seems to be an integration of meds, the therapy with Dr. G., and the structure I have in the Recovery Model, all mixed with this more existential chapter of my life, in learning about mindfulness and ways to use my thinking as a tool in staying well. Never in a thousand years did I think that I would arrive here.

Chapter 38

With the help of hindsight, it is now clear that not everything we considered a side effect of a med was in fact a side effect. As I continue to do well, it seems that a couple of behaviours were in fact part of my illness, and not as a result of the difficult medicines I was taking. These are behaviours I have to go back to now, to re-examine and reconsider. I continue to take these drugs, yet what I considered to be side effects are no longer present.

For years, my self-care and grooming skills were pretty poor. I was lucky if I showered once a week. Usually, it was more like once every 10 days. I didn't care very much about what I looked like, with the slightly greasy hair, in messy clothes, with my pale face and no makeup.

I had lived so long with a slight dulling, a slight dampening of the person I once was so many years ago, before illness struck. Memory and energy had both been down a notch or two. I looked a little odd in social situations, a bit off, and I no longer had a certain kind of brightness to my personality. It had disappeared long before.

Dr. G. and I had many conversations over the years about these problem areas. He felt strongly that they were as a result of the medication I was taking, that they were side effects. That the three antipsychotics I took restricted these areas from me, disabled me from engaging in them, a simple shower or a smile.

But all those problematic behaviours are gone now. Today, as has been the case for much of the past months, I am motivated, engaged, and enjoying some self-discipline. I shower every two days, look at the clothes I wear, consider my hairstyle. Along with some vitamins and supplements that I ordered yesterday, I even threw in a lipstick. That says it all.

Even though I still take the same harsh drugs today that I have for years—there really hasn't been a change in them—my behaviour has shifted dramatically. I don't blame my poor-quality self-care on the meds in my system anymore. I no longer think my lack of energy and motivation, my mental dulling, were side effects. I think, instead, there is something there that has more to do with symptoms of my illness, symptoms that have now largely cleared up.

I think perhaps my brain and body were functioning for so many years on some sort of lower tier, something that dragged me down into the mud for extended periods of time that had little to do with mood swings and bouts of psychosis. Again, like adolescent mood swings, it is often impossible to tear apart the issues to see what is really at stake. As Dr. G. said recently, it is hard on any given day to tell whether something is a little bit of depression, a side effect, or a negative symptom of a psychotic disorder. And for me, any of the three could have been possible. Negative symptoms are a feature of schizophrenia that describe normal aspects of a person's behaviour that they no longer have. These symptoms can include lethargy, apathy, social withdrawal, and impaired attention. On the occasions I saw Dr. S., he insisted that I had negative symptoms. Dr. G. disagreed. But, today, we wonder if that might have been the case.

We now know my behaviours were not collateral damage from my drug piles. But what they were, what form of the illness they stemmed from, we may never know. I am okay with the ambiguity.

To deal with the rogue episodes of illness that still do hit me, we now adjust the levels of various meds that I already take, depending on the situation. This is the first time in forever that I have been on a steady cocktail of drugs. We used to change it all the time, for so many years. Not anymore.

It has been months since the horrors of 2019, and some basics in my life are so much better. I am more experienced. I am more insightful and more composed. I am better able to express what is happening to me. I have realized the strength of psychotherapy and the efficacy of medication. And, I have learned the power in me.

Conclusion

These days, as I write, there is legitimate reason for a collective anxiety attack. A coronavirus—COVID-19—is running rampant around the world, settling for long periods of time in what are known as hotspots, changing our actions and habits drastically. We wear masks, afraid of the droplets that bear disease. We constantly wash our hands. We keep two metres apart, even from our friends and family. We know to spread out in a line, a queue to the liquor store looping through the parking lot. We are safe when we are back in our cars, the masks shed, and disinfectant gel clapped through our hands.

At first, we tuned into the prime minister, his daily address every morning at 11. He was reassuring, calm, with money promised to ease the burdens that everybody faced. After a while, though, we stopped watching, since there was nothing left to see. Instead, we listened to the medical experts, to the scary predictions. We stayed inside.

During the time of this plague, housebound people learned new skills, picked up new habits. At first, shelves in grocery stores were empty of flour, sugar, and yeast as many took to the art of baking bread. Zoom and FaceTime calls replaced meetings and family gatherings; grandparents talked to grandchildren who lived only a few kilometres away, blowing kisses at the screen. Everyone longed for contact, for a hug. Just a hug; surely, we can manage that.

Everyone has their own COVID story. I have been lucky in mine.

But I do not know when I will see my family again. The border is closed; an order that is renewed every month. Alan, Jeff, their families, are very far away, farther than they really were. I know they work at staying safe in their neighbourhoods, in their lives. I feel comforted in this knowledge.

I miss hanging out with Ruby Tuesday and her family, even though we didn't do that very often. We were to have Thanksgiving with them in October, that wish turned upside down by more regulations.

Financially, things are on the wire, definitely a universal experience. Like others, I am scared each month. Will I make ends meet? I get my disability cheque but no extra income from little jobs. So, once again, like she did in all my apartment years, my mother supplements my income. Right up to today. And I don't know what I would do without that. Her money brings me relief, yet pain and disappointment.

Those living with mental health issues are finding this time incredibly stressful. Symptoms take on a new meaning, flaring up in stifling ways. And those who have never experienced a mental health concern are finding themselves shocked by their own anxiety attacks, flattened in the night by their depressions, saddened in so much loneliness. Children are anxious too, longing to play with friends and to be with other people. Longing to be back to normal. Help is accessed over video or over the phone. Dial it in.

For so many people, the sense of security is missing. Fear, uncertainty, stress, isolation, powerlessness all get in the way, all contribute to this. If you are insecure, if you constantly live under the threat of getting sick, of your loved ones dying, of not knowing, you will never settle down, never get a good night's sleep.

I have been working on this book for almost 18 months now. My hair has grown out, and I no longer dye it red. There is a white skunk stripe down the middle that so many women covet. I had a birthday, 51, in late July. How lucky to have a birthday in the ripening of summer, when the bounty of vegetables is too much to hold, falling out of my arms, shiny in the sunlight.

But it is early winter now, there is no cornucopia at this time of the year. No matter! I will eat Brussel sprouts, broccoli, and carrots. I will feast on rutabaga and turnip. I will get up early, make some espresso, read the news. Then push the restart button on my espresso machine.

These days, I have long phone calls with friends, and long email exchanges. We talk about everything that has changed over the past year, the difficulties the virus has set up for us. And yet, we talk as if nothing has changed, the tales of our friendships and memories spoken about in closeness and intimacy.

The time of the virus has been a curious combination of much looking inward, as well as opening oneself widely, reaching out in this virtual world.

***

Ruby and I were talking on the phone last week. She was telling me about a friend of hers who arranges all her online purchases to be delivered by the same UPS guy.

"Yeah, and I think she does a lot of ordering," she said.

"I bet," I said. "You know, she's probably having an affair with him, with the UPS guy."

"Oh, absolutely! That's great," Ruby laughed.

"There's a story in there." I was laughing too. "I bet you could write something dark about her marriage, and something darker about the affair. A *Gone Girl* sort of thing. Those books are everywhere now."

Immediately, my brain started filling in the little cracks and crevices of story lines as they grew, populating my brain with many narratives, winding me up. There is indeed a story to tell. I had to get off the phone, dash down notes of ideas while I still could. That buzz you get when your creativity is juiced. Similar to hypomania, at once a pleasant feeling and yet an uncomfortable one too.

So, not only do I have a story for a book, but I also have a film script. And, once I had that story, I immediately had another one, better than the UPS affair. I see film scripts, but that is all fantasy. Although when I am done writing this, I will pick up one of those stories and try my hand at it.

***

Sitting here today, I am offering up evidence that I have made my way down the path, and that I'm still making my way. It is a path where my thoughts stay in my brain, where they do not slip-slide just out of reach. When my thoughts start on that slide, it is as if my arm is forever stuck under the driver's seat, patting the rough fabric full of crumbs and old gasoline receipts, searching for something I am sure is there. No thoughts here to be found! Surely, they must all be contained in the walls of bone that create my skull, home to a brain that does not always play by the rules. But I have been training my brain. I can't necessarily get it to jump through fiery hoops or swing like a trapeze artist, but I can get it to go through the basics—even more than just the basics. And that is good enough for me.

I have been absent for 25 years. Gone, off the face of this Earth, nowhere to be found. Others will tell me that this is not the case. They tell me that I have always been there, somewhere, if one was to look hard enough; my skin and bones and fluids holding steady, consistently betraying the traits that they claim make the true me—the essential recording, 1969. Traits and characteristics that hung tight, even as I fought to keep mouth and nose above water, desperate to keep from being swallowed whole in one endless burning gasp.

And now, 25 years later, am I back, am I still the same person, still that essential recording? The record, its seminal tracks laid down, has been worked on, new tracks being patterned over the originals, layers that grow with each addition. So, 2020 sounds very different from 1969. But, maybe now you can still hear it, somewhere, those first few tentative tracks laid when I was born to this world. Maybe that has never changed. Finally, I can hope.

Acknowledgements

My great thanks to Claudia Chowaniec, for showing me what could be done; Mary Hardwick. . .We're in this together!; Peggy Lister and Mary Frances Marshall, for always being interested, and always hopeful; Maureen Magee; Patricia Anderson; Allister Thompson; Amelia Gilliland and Jennifer Dinsmore, for their fantastic editing and advice; Matilda Luk, Jeff Patten, Natasha Amott, and Alan Patten; all my aunts and uncles, for being my greatest cheering squad; my cousins, Paula Lafferty and Sarah Davidson; and my friends Dagne Forrest, Jasmin Kay, Catherine Swanson, Helen Deachman, Edith Moore, and Audrey Starkes, for reading chapters and various revisions with love and patience; Jeff Moffet, at long last; Dr. Michael Gaudet, for making my life a better place to be; Aunt Cathy Aitken, for being wonderful when I was in the hospital and as I wrote this book; finally to my mum, Monica Patten, for being my best reader, for all her love and support, and for saving me.

About the Author

Jocelyn Patten calls Ottawa, Canada, home, where she lives with her mother and two cats. She is currently working on a novel featuring a heroine with bipolar disorder. *Love & Theft* is her first published book.

Manufactured by Amazon.ca
Bolton, ON